EXISTENTIAL FOUNDATIONS OF PSYCHOLOGY

With a New Foreword

Adrian van Kaam

UNIVERSITY
PRESS OF
AMERICA

LANHAM • NEW YORK • LONDON

Copyright © 1966 by

Duquesne University

University Press of America,™ Inc.

4720 Boston Way
Lanham, MD 20706

3 Henrietta Street
London WC2E 8LU England

ISBN (Perfect): 0-8191-3805-3

Co-published by arrangement with
the Institute of Formative Spirituality,
Duquesne University

TABLE OF CONTENTS

Behavior, p. 348; Skinner's Approach to Application of Animal Findings to Human Behavior, p. 348; Anthropological Psychology's Application of Animal Findings to Human Behavior, p. 351; Conclusion, p. 354.

FOREWORD

Existential Foundations of Psychology played an historical role in the emergence of the science of formation. To understand this role and therewith the critical dialogue with movements in psychology that this work represents, one should understand its genesis.

In 1954 the author was asked temporarily to restrict his concentration on his chosen field of graduate study in pedagogy, andragogy and spiritual formation so as to make himself available for some years for an assignment to study and teach psychology at Duquesne University.

At that time certain prescientific assumptions of an atheistic or agnostic behaviorism, humanism and existentialism shaped the terminology and the mind of a number of psychologists and psychiatrists.

Loyal to his appointment and to the terminology of his newly assigned field of teaching, he suspended during this period his use of the language of formation, as found in his Dutch publications, and adopted temporarily the terminology of psychology — but not without critically broadening and reforming its meaning in light of his former studies in formation.

His critical implicit dialogue with atheistic and agnostic opponents, some of whom called themselves existentialists, while using their own language, was published in various articles now contained with others in a recent (1983) publication by Dimension Books entitled *Foundations of Personality Study: An Adrian van Kaam Reader.*

Two books dealing with various aspects of this critical reformation of existential thought were *Existential Foundations of Psychology* and *Religion and Personality.* The latter was first published by Prentice-Hall, then as a paperback by Doubleday, and more recently in a new, expanded edition brought out by Dimension Books. Foreign publishers issued the French and Italian translations of this work.

Existential Foundations of Psychology was published by Duquesne University Press and later issued in paperback by Doubleday.

Religion and Personality represented a critique of the atheistic and agnostic assumptions of existentialism from the viewpoint of the philosophy and psychology of religion, using their own psychological terminology while reforming critically its meaning, partly in light of an implicit scholastic philosophy.

Existential Foundations was a frontal assault on the subjectivism itself inherent in the assumptions of certain existentialists. The book became a plea to widen existential psychology to a universal anthropological psychology, sufficiently foundational to integrate objectively on a scientific basis all validated findings and insights of the various "differential" psychologies, covering both the subjective experiential and the objective measurable aspects of human life.

This intentionality may explain why the author does not quote any of the existentialists. The abyss between their use of the same terms and that of the author was too deep to justify such references.

The attempt to integrate the different contributions of various schools of psychology in a universal frame of reference tentatively called *anthropological psychology* stimulated the ongoing development of a rigorous integrational-dialectical research methodology. This was one of the main fruits of the author's brief interlude in the field of psychology.

When he was allowed to resume his own field of study with its terminology, he broadened this research methodology into a refined tool for the scientific integration of formationally relevant findings and insights of different arts, sciences and formation traditions. The reader and the student or practitioner of formation science will gain a better insight into its methodology by tracing its sources in this book.

Readers who want more information on formation science are referred to the journal, *Studies in Formative Spirituality,* published by the Institute of Formative Spirituality at Duquesne University, and *Formative Spirituality, Volume I: Fundamental Formation,* published by Crossroad, New York, 1983.

Adrian van Kaam
Institute of Formative Spirituality
October, 1983

INTRODUCTION

The following study is a dialogue between the field of scientific psychology and the newly emerging awareness of the structure of man in relation to his world. All science evolves in the light of the implicit view of reality which imposes itself on man as an inevitable result of his evolution in knowledge and experience. The science of psychology, in order to keep in harmony with this evolution, must continually re-examine its foundations, investigating whether or not its structure of fundamental constructs has assimilated the new attitudes toward reality developed by humanity in evolution. Such an expansion and deepening of the fundamental structures at the basis of scientific psychology does not necessarily mean that the traditional theories, data, and methods of psychology will be eliminated or even changed. It means that they will be seen in a new perspective, that their position within the total structure of the science of psychology will undergo a re-evaluation.

Originally, man's awareness of himself and his world is pre-reflective, pre-philosophical, and pre-scientific. Sooner or later, however, scholars and scientists reflect on this pre-reflective insight in the light of their own fields of specialization, such as physics, physiology, philosophy, psychology, and psychiatry. The author of the present work believes that one central aspect of the new view of man is the radical perspectivity of his knowledge. This insight can be made explicit in a psychological, philosophical, sociological, anthropological or any other reflective elaboration. This book attempts to make explicit in terms of scientific theoretical psychology the meaning and implications of this insight.

It is the conviction of the writer that psychology will be forced to assimilate perspectivity and its implications into the fundamental structure of psychology. He does not believe that other developments of the science of psychology as a whole can survive because the awareness of man's perspectivistic or existential structure of knowledge is already too strongly alive in contemporary awareness to be either eradicated or dismissed. Two other possible directions of development are the one school (one method) approach or the totally disintegrated approach to psychology. The one school approach cannot be maintained, for perspectivity demonstrates only too clearly that a science can advance only by means of the development of an increasingly wide variety of perspectives. Therefore, the existential or perspectivistic view of psychology subscribes to the necessity for a continual multiplication of methods and viewpoints.

Concomitantly, the existential approach maintains that psychology can be made serviceable to man's practical interest only if the results of perspectivistic research are constantly integrated so as to contribute to the solution of the concrete problems which man faces in his concrete life situations. This integration is not a philosophical but a scientific theoretical integration in the light of practical problems confronting psychology and challenging it to shed light on man's life situation. Scientific theoretical integration demands, however, hypothetical constructs which can serve as a framework for this integration. Man's philosophical reflection on his implicit awareness of the perspectivity of his knowledge preceded, on a historical level, his scientific psychological reflection on this same awareness. Therefore, philosophers have been able to develop concepts that are useful for the integration of the results of perspectivistic psychological research in the light of the practical questions which the psychologist attempts to answer from the limited viewpoint of his specialization. Thus the psychologist sometimes finds it practical to borrow such philosophical concepts and to utilize them as quasi-hypothetical constructs.

Obviously, these constructs acquire a different meaning in the science of psychology than they have in the context of philosophy. The reader should be aware of this distinction while reading the following chapters. Even when certain terms used are similar to those found in existential philosophy, they do not always have the same meaning in the context of psychology. Because of the danger of misunderstanding, the author has felt obliged to refer as little as possible to existential philosophers who may have influenced his thought: they might rightly protest the alteration of the meaning of their concepts in the new context, as it were, of the scientific theoretical discourse of psychology. The following exposition is guided necessarily by the peculiar traditions, methods of exploration, experimentation, and theory construction proper to the science of psychology. Psychology incorporates man's emerging pre-reflective awareness of his perspectivity within the traditional dialogue of its own field of competence. Therefore psychology, when it has absorbed the implications of man's insight into its existential structure, must still be fundamentally separate from philosophy, physics, sociology, or physiology even when these disciplines have also assimilated the implications of the new awareness of perspectivity insofar as it is relevant to their special fields.

The expression "existential psychology" should not be misunderstood. It does not mean a new school or area of psychology comparable to other schools of psychology. Existential psychology is a temporary movement within the field of psychology as a whole that attempts to assimilate into the field of psychology the implicit awareness that man's knowledge is perspectivistic. As soon as the science of psychology has discovered and totally assimilated this newly emerging awareness, we shall no longer speak of existential psychology, for psychology as such will then be existential: it will be in harmony with the latest phase of the evolution of human insight. After this assimilation has been achieved, psychology will again await its further fundamental enrichment through assimilation of the next development of our view of man, which may emerge as a result of the next phase of the human evolution.

Existential psychology is thus an attempt to assimilate into the science of psychology the implications of the contemporary perspectivistic view of man insofar as it is directly relevant for the evolvement of empirical, clinical, and theoretical psychology. This movement toward reconstruction of psychological science by assimilation will become superfluous as soon as psychology has fundamentally restructured, deepened, and expanded itself through integration of the insight into man's radical perspectivity which has recently emerged in Western humanity as an inescapable result of its cultural and historical development. Because the present work is a first attempt to explicate this unavoidable task of assimilation, it cannot be the final word on the subject. The author will feel deeply rewarded if he is able to raise important questions and propose problems. Though he has attempted to answer some of them, he is aware that he must rely on the constructive criticism and help of all his colleagues concerned with the same basic problems that face us at this moment of crisis in psychology. Because his subject matter is so profound and complex, the author did not hesitate to be repetitious in the hope that repitition might keep clearly before his own eyes and those of his readers the course of his thought.

ADRIAN VAN KAAM

January 17, 1966

CHAPTER ONE

THE NATURE AND MEANING
OF SCIENCE

Man may seek the meaning of science by approaching it as a typically human endeavor and asking: What is it in human nature that leads to the emergence of the scientific attitude? In what sense is human existence itself a foundation of scientific interest? Once I have the answer to this question and understand how the scientific attitude is rooted in the very nature of man, I may begin to grasp what science really means. From that moment on, I may be able to trace back to man's existence all forms, aims, and methods of science and to demonstrate that they are manifestations of his nature.

Thus I may hope to arrive at an understanding of the nature and meaning of science by exploring how science is rooted in my own nature. In order to do so, I must first of all know my own nature. Is my nature different from the nature of the things around me? Many thinkers have attempted to find an answer to this question. I can hear three different voices of humanity explicating the nature of man: the positivist, the rationalist, and the existential voice.

THE POSITIVIST VIEW OF MAN

When I consider the positivist explanation of man's being, I discover that positivists do not distinguish fundamentally between man and the things that surround him. They state that

1

man and other things are basically the same, differing only in appearance, that both are outcomes of the same processes and forces which blindly play in the cosmos. According to this view, I am in the world as a complex piece of matter among numerous more or less similar pieces. It would be sheer arrogance for me to pretend that I differ basically from the things around me. I am a fragile fragment of nature, a trifle, an incident, a minute moment in the vast ocean of changing matter; I am in the world along with other things, such as a stone in the river, a weed in the garden, a speck of dust in expanding space.

This point of view as adopted by thoughtful people cannot be dismissed lightly, nor can I say that their perception is based on mere imagination. There must be something in human appearance that leads to the notion that I am like the things around me. Indeed, when I think about myself and others, I must admit that I am also in a certain sense a thing and that I also display the features of a process. This is so true that disciplines such as physiology, biology, biochemistry, and neurology are able to identify and describe a multitude of processes in my organism. While I recognize this fact, I am also aware, however, that only man develops sciences about his own mechanisms. I never saw a stone, cactus, or crystal reflect on its chemistry. As a human being, however, I can establish a science concerning my biophysical attributes because I can perceive them intelligently, because they really have meaning for me. My being has meaning for me, processes have meaning for me, and the things around me have meaning for me. But things and processes have no meaning either for themselves or for one another. If there were nothing else but things and processes, nothing would have any meaning; there would be nobody for whom they could mean processes or things.

When I consider the many processes that govern my organism, I feel that I am related to them differently than oil, wine, or vinegar, for example, are related to their chemical structures. Oil, wine, and vinegar are identified with their mechanisms; they cannot distance themselves from these mechanisms. I experience, however, that I depend on my organismic properties

2

in one way while I escape them in another; that I adapt to them faithfully and yet in a certain sense withstand them with facility; that I am absorbed by them and yet take a stand toward them. Even under the overpowering impact of a painful or exciting biophysical process, I am still able to experience that it is I who undergoes this event; I can still impose a variety of meanings on this physical performance of my organism; I can still experience that I accept or reject, like or dislike, adapt unhesitantly or withhold a wholehearted assent to my bodily conduct. When I take a stand in respect to the processes of my body, I already go beyond them, I transcend them, I experience that I am more than they are. No thing or process is able to spontaneously take a stand toward itself or toward other things or processes. Only man can take such initiative.

It is true that I may be able to build into a machine or robot the practical implications of original and spontaneous perspectives of reality. I may devise a computer, a teaching machine, or a robot which—within the range determined by me—may make technical "choices" among different possible courses of action. These selections, however, will be mechanical variations of the pragmatic implications of the fundamental choice originally made by me and embodied afterward in my technical creation. The robot, moreover, can never become really like me so long as it retains its machine-like qualities. It can never uncover spontaneously a total new meaning in people, nature, and things nor take a stand wholly in and by itself in a creative, unpredictable, or surprising human fashion. Imagine, for example, a mechanical hair stylist devised to care for women's hair and to adapt itself selectively to the inexhaustible variety of female heads and hairdo's. Such an amazing robot could never of itself change its perspective and—let us say—fall passionately in love with the attractive subject of its care!

I must even say that the meaningful "thing" or "process" is possible only with the emergence of man in the cosmos. Even the verb "to be" in the statement, "there are things and processes," is meaningful to me only when I recognize that other men and myself are present in the world as subjects who discover

3

such meaning. For whom would the verb "to be" exist if there were only things and processes? I may conclude that the process-like aspect is only one important aspect of my human nature. Positivism has splendidly explored and elaborated this essential feature of man's nature, while neglecting other fundamental aspects. It has carefully investigated the organismic participation of man in the world of things. The positivist rightly demonstrates how the human organism shares somehow in the multitude of processes and laws which are formulated by biology, biochemistry, physics, physiology, and other sciences. In consequence, positivism has stimulated the biophysiological sciences to explore diligently the degree to which human behavior remains subjected to the measurable impact of a universe of matter. This magnificent and massive exploration will continue, for science will never exhaust the richness, subtlety, and complexity of this particular profile of man's being.

THE RATIONALIST VIEW OF MAN

This one fundamental perspective alone, however, cannot provide for me a full account of my unique human situation as I experience it in my daily life. For my biochemical processes do not fully explain to me the fact that I know myself as existing for myself, while at the same time I spontaneously experience things and processes as having meaning for me. I experience this aspect of "meaning-giving" as a profile of my life which is at least as essential and original as my organismic participation in biochemical laws. My nature reveals to me that I am involved in the world not only in an organismic but also in a meaning-giving way.

I may even become so overwhelmingly aware of this meaning-giving aspect of my life that I forget about the organismic processes which also belong to my nature. When I describe the nature of man, I may then be tempted to ignore his bodily-organismic aspects. In this case, my description is again one-sided because I have stressed only one aspect and concealed another. To omit the contribution of positivist thought on man is just as

4

pernicious as the omission of the "meaning-giving" attribute of human existence.

It is the rationalist and idealist thinkers who fall into this biased view. They inflate unduly the subjectivity of man; they overemphasize his power of giving meaning to the world. Their slanted considerations regard his limited, embodied subjectivity as an absolute and sovereign subjectivity, restricted in no way by his biophysical conditions, by his sense information, and by his being bound to the world. It is true that without man's subjectivity, without his capacity to discover sense and meaning, nature would have no meaning; things and processes would simply not exist for him. Without man, who is the discoverer of meaning, the universe would be meaningless and empty. Even the meaning "universe" could not exist without someone for whom it means "universe". When I affirm things and processes, I affirm them in their being for me and for all other men; outside this affirmation, there is no human meaning in the cosmos.

A rationalist or idealist view of man, however, places extreme stress on this specific human aspect. Such exclusive preoccupation leads to a distorted view of my nature; it makes me—the thinking subject—the supreme source, the independent creator, the mysterious spring, the hidden well of all processes and things which I experience. All of them are considered as mere productions of my inventive thought. I do not even know whether things in nature correspond with them. In such a subjectivistic approach, the scientific designs which I, the subject, invent and project are considered to be more dependable and trustworthy than the things "out there" which they capture under some of their aspects. The real things out there, however, actually reveal more aspects, views, or profiles than any scientific design can cover. If I am a subjectivistic scientist, however, I may simply assert that those aspects do not exist at all, or that they are unreal, insignificant, and unimportant because the rational measurements invented by my thinking subjectivity cannot be applied to them. In short, that which does not fit my subjective, rational, mathematical creation should be disregarded. Faced with a choice, I shall enhance my inventive subjectivity at the expense of the richness and density of reality.

Such subjectivism, while most conspicuous in scientism, reaches its extremes in idealistic philosophy. Subjectivism, if pushed to the limit, leads to the conviction that all my experience is merely the reflection of my isolated, self-sufficient, inventive intellect; everything is nothing but a mirage of what I think, feel, wish, and imagine; the reality and density of the world evaporates into the mere contents of my consciousness. So-called "things" and "processes" are pure products of my thought without correlates in reality. My knowledge is nothing but the lonely presence of my thought to itself. Such a sterile subjectivity, imprisoned in itself and fully self-sufficient, is not a human kind of subjectivity; it contradicts my spontaneous perception in daily life. Therefore, I cannot really believe in it. Deep down, I am forced to admit that things are real and not merely my invention and imagination. Even if I loudly declare that nothing is real except my thought, I still manifest in my very behavior the fact that I do not really believe what I say. For in my daily actions I clearly take into account that the world in which I live, move, and labor is real and unescapable, is density and resistance. If I did not behave in accordance with the reality of the world, I would be the constant victim of serious accidents. If I really lived in my behavior what some idealistic thinkers believe in their isolated rationality, I would destroy myself.

THE EXISTENTIAL VIEW OF MAN

Neither the positivist nor the rationalist view fully represents man as I actually experience him in daily life, although each of these perspectives uncovers real insights into essential aspects of his nature.

When I observe man as I meet him in reality, I realize that he is neither a mere thing like other things in the universe nor self-sufficient subjectivity which maintains itself in splendid isolation from the world. He is not locked up within himself as mere thought and worldless self-presence. Instead he is always

6

already outside himself and in the world, he involves himself continuously in the density of reality in and around him: he *is* a dialogue with things and processes in his own organism and in his surroundings. At the same time, he remains a subject in the world and *lets the world be for him* by steadily uncovering its manifold meanings.

In short, I really experience myself as a being-in-the-world, an ex-sistence, a presence, an encounter, and an involvement. I am inconceivable without my human world. Conversely, the human world as I experience it is inconceivable, imperceptible, and unimaginable without me, without man. Man's world reveals itself as sky, mountains, valleys, forests, streams, and oceans. But without man there would not be the human meaning of sky, mountain, valley, forest, stream, and ocean. I cannot even imagine what they would be like without their specific meaning for man in a humanized universe.

To be man is thus fundamentally and essentially to exist, and to exist means to-be-in-the-world. The subject which is man simply does not happen without being involved in the world; it presents itself only in relation to the world. The subject "I", the self that I am, cannot occur other than as the source of activity which is in some way oriented to the world as it appears. The self cannot be conceived, affirmed, experienced, or imagined without the world or some aspect of the world to which the self is directed or in which it is involved. Expressions such as I think, I do, I feel, I imagine, I anticipate, I dream, and I own all imply a being-in-the-world, always presuppose something which is more than the isolated self alone.

The assertion that the subjectivity of man presents itself only in relation to the world cannot be precisely demonstrated, for it cannot be derived with certainty from another and more fundamental insight. If it could be derived from a more basic insight into man's nature, then the assertion that "being-man" is "being-in-the-world" would no longer be the most fundamental description of man. Since there is no formal proof for this assertion, its truth can be *indicated* only by demonstrating that no mode of being man can be conceived, perceived, or imagined which is not at the same time a mode of being-in-the-world. It is indeed impossible to fully describe any mode of being-man without implying some aspect of the world in the description. In our daily parlance, this aspect is usually only implicit in our statements. I may say that I walk, talk, imagine, or fear, but these declarations always imply that I walk somewhere in the world, that I talk to somebody or about something, that I imagine or fear something, no matter how vague and indefinite it may be.

In other words, human consciousness is always consciousness of something which is not consciousness itself. It is a being together with the world, an encounter with, an orientation to, a directedness, an intentionality. Consciousness is an orientation to what it is not; it is always consciousness *of*; a consciousness of nothing is not imaginable for it would no longer be consciousness. Consciousness is not a "thing" closed in upon itself; it is an act, an act of revealing, the act of man that reveals the world; it is a radical openness for all that may manifest itself to man.

This balanced view of man unites the two aspects of man's being which have been explored one-sidedly by positivism and rationalism, by objectivism and subjectivism, by naive realism and idealism. Centuries of intense thought, of fierce intellectual struggle were required of Western humanity before this precarious balance between the subjective and the objective was won.

The existential view thus sees me, man, as a being-in-the-world. I am not in the world, however, in the same way that chairs are in a room, cigarettes in a package, or candy in a box. These things are not affected meaningfully by other things which surround them, and they in turn do not affect other things meaningfully. I am influenced, however, by the world in which I dwell and I influence this world. I "dwell," "inhabit," "sojourn" in the world; I "cultivate," "transform," "humanize," "personalize" the world by my simple human presence. I am not in the world as a stone is in a wall, a broom in a closet, or a vegetable in a freezer; they are contained in the wall, the closet, the freezer in a spatial manner, side by side with other motionless things. But I am involved, engaged in my world; I am preoccupied with my world in many ways; I am concerned, I care as no stone, broom, or vegetables can care. I am acquainted, familiar with the world; I am at home in the world. I find myself irritated, annoyed, fascinated, depressed, bored, excited by the world. I find myself using, developing, organizing, accepting, rejecting, explaining, fostering, cultivating, questioning, searching, and discussing the world. The stone, the broom, the vegetable never find themselves in any of these attitudes or activities with regard to the things that surround them. They are merely "side by side" with other things in the same container. But I as man really encounter the world in these many attitudes and operations. The world reveals itself to me in its manifold lived concreteness when I am with the world in these many modes of daily "lived" encounter.

Science and the Existential Nature of Man

The original, spontaneous way of being-in-the-world is thus not the scientific mode; my concrete daily experience is not scientific. My first, natural experience is spontaneous, multi-dimensional, unorganized, somewhat vague and undetermined, while my later scientific experience may be planned, strictly defined, well designed, systematized, and logically formulated. I can easily observe this difference between my spontaneous and my scientific experience when I compare, for example, my spontaneous and my scientific experience of a rat in motion. As a child I may have seen a rat suddenly run away when my father switched on the light in the basement. This experience was quite different from my present experience as a scientist when I observe, in terms of operationally defined categories, the response of a carefully selected laboratory rat to a measured stimulus in a scientifically designed experimental situation. However, I should not therefore jump to the conclusion that the world of my spontaneous experiences is nothing more than a senseless chaos of incoherent impressions that tumble after one another without rhyme or reason. The world of spontaneous experience has its own design, its own language, its own "logic", its own coherent pattern of meaning, its own "Gestalt." Sigmund Freud, for example, already attempted to penetrate into the pre-logical language of infantile experience when he studied the world of meaning structured by the child's experience of his body.

All later language of science is derived from the typical language of primary experience which it presupposes as its point of departure. The world of my first experience shows spatial, temporal, intentional, and dynamic characteristics of its own which are quite distinct but not separated from the constructs of time, space, and dynamics in science. The abstract space spoken of by Newton, for example, presupposes the concrete space in which I live. The idea of an endless space, which is the container of everything situated within it, is an abstract idea, largely a product of subsequent thought. But I form this idea on the basis of my experience of concrete space as an endless container in which things are placed. In this space which I "live" in my spontaneous experience, things are far-away or close-by, high or low, right or left. This space is thus given to me as already oriented. The orientation of this space apparently does not exist independently of me. For in absolute space it would be meaningless to speak in such terms as far-away or close-by, high or low, which refer to space only as it exists for me, the subject. In my concrete existence, therefore, I am bound by spatial dimensions from which I cannot escape. Regardless of my thoughts, scientific constructs, and abstractions, the road on which I walk is low for me and the sky is high. In the production of instruments such as forks, spoons, knives, and rakes, I have to adapt myself to a spatiality that is simply given. Thus there is an oriented space of primary experience which imposes itself on me as an undeniable necessity. It is only on the basis of this primary experience that I can arrive, by a process of abstraction, at the scientific construct of space as an endless container without orientation.

It may be clear from this example that my world of primary experience, from which science emerges and on which it is nourished, is constituted by a different kind of fact and meaning than science itself. However, I can fully understand my scientific mode of existence only if I grasp first of all my primary mode-of-being-in-the-world. For the very possibility of the development of any science whatsoever is based on this natural primordial way of existence. Being a scientist presupposes being a man in daily life.

The above statement is more specifically true of the human sciences because of their specific subject matter. For human sciences will never present us with a full understanding of man so long as they are pure speculative knowledge or mere laboratory knowledge without reference to the real, lived world of man. In this case, they would be nothing more than splendid logical structures, experimentally validated but irrelevant to the actual "lived" human situation. Psychology would become merely a sophisticated exercise in systematic and statistical thought, magnificently illustrated by carefully selected, well-controlled experiments beautifully adjusted to an impressive system, related perhaps to some measurable features of behavior, but having little to do with the "lived" human reality. Human behavior as it really appears in its fullness would evaporate and finally disappear in the rarefied heights of technical, statistical, and experimental abstractions. Such a system would quantify certain relations between measurable aspects of behavior only to lose in the end the behaving man. Psychology would become a satire on the psychologist himself, for it would become an impressive feat of experimental, intellectual construction in which even the psychologist as a living person would find neither an explanation, a hearing, an understanding, nor a place. For there would be no relationship between the intellectual-experimental structure and the actual human life of the man who devised the structure.

The scientific psychologist is capable of devising relevant empirical research if he remains present to human behavior as it appears in real life situations. In other words, his scientific mode of existence should never lose contact with his spontaneous "lived" mode of life. Human science should never replace, erase, or distort human experience. The degree to which this happens

11

determines the degree of the irrelevancy of psychology to human life. Therefore the human scientist should not restrict himself to only objective and detached measurement and observation. To be sure, a necessary scientific detachment should dominate the second phase of his scientific research, a phase which succeeds and presupposes his immersion in the world of experienced behavior itself, where he has already discovered the relevant questions and problems. However, he should continually recover the immediate experiences of human behavior which preceded his experiments, his empirical research, and his scientific constructs. For the human scientist is not simply, nor first and foremost, a scientist but a human being. The foundations of the human sciences, therefore, cannot be reduced to a collection of objectifying, experimental, measuring, and theorizing manipulations.

This does not mean, to be sure, that the human sciences should be limited to the description and analysis of the spontaneous natural experience of human behavior. On the contrary, they should be strictly scientific about human behavior, but about human behavior as it really appears in the lived world of man. Human scientists should adapt their methods to behavior as it appears instead of arbitrarily adapting behavior under all its possible aspects to a few methods borrowed from physics or physiology. The task of the human scientist is to explore "lived" human behavior scientifically in its fundaments, conditions, and implications. He must penetrate particular, concrete human behavior with the light of scientific constructs of universal validity from which testable hypotheses can be derived.

The empirical and scientific attitudes of the human scientist do not at all exclude his attentive presence to human behavior as it appears in meaningful life situations. A distinction must be made here between empirical research which is relevant and that which is irrelevant to the understanding of behavior. Irrelevant empirical research is produced by the totally detached, abstract, and isolated investigation carried on by the neutral spectator of behavior who is indifferent to the relationship between his abstract game and the life situation of man. Relevant research is that which explores, describes, and empirically tests human behavior while preserving a "lived" relationship with it in the reality of life. Of course, all empirical research, relevant or irrelevant, necessarily presupposes a temporary detachment from actually lived behavior. Otherwise, no research would be possible. But relevant research *starts out* from an involvement in reality as it is lived, and it recovers this relationship after obtaining its scientific results.

Thus the human scientist must understand behavior as lived in the daily situation before his abstracting intellect can devise scientific constructs, empirical and experimental designs which are truly relevant to the understanding of this behavior. Indeed, scientific, abstract, empirical knowledge appears relatively late in man's experience. When it does appear, it already constitutes a thematization of particular kinds of immediate, spontaneous, "lived" experience. The immediate understanding of human behavior, on the other hand, occurs on a level of experience which exists in advance of any type of objectifying, whether rational or scientific. For this reason, the human scientist cannot express the results of his experiential, pre-empirical exploration of behavior in a manner which is rationally convincing or experimentally verifiable. The logically convincing and experimentally testable mode is necessary in science, but possible only in the second, empirical phase of scientific endeavor. So long as the human scientist works in the fundamental or experiential phase of human science, he can only elucidate his immediate perception of behavior by means of description.

Even in this fundamental phase of science, however, some type of intersubjective affirmation is possible. The scientist may invite his fellow scientists to interrogate their own perception to discover whether they find a topography of human behavior similar to his own. In this way, the pre-empirical elucidations of behavior which are originally personal may attain intersubjective affirmation. Such elucidations are the indispensable matrix of relevant scientific constructs and hypotheses, and of subsequent empirical and experimental research. Thus the experiential elucidation of the spontaneous perception of behavior is the missing link between the spontaneous and the scientific modes of existence of the human scientist.

A human scientist who has lost his roots and is no longer in touch with the spontaneous natural perception of behavior will easily ascribe a priority to scientific methodology. He will often conceal, because of his methodological preconceptions, relevant human behavior which is waiting for exploration. He may even lose himself in methodological analysis at the expense of never arriving at relevant human behavior itself. A continual preoccupation with scientific methodology leads to sterility. Moreover, a preconceived empirical, experimental, or statistical method may distort rather than disclose a given behavior through an imposition of restricted theoretical constructs on the full meaning and richness of human behavior. Such a situation becomes even more precarious when the human scientist blindly borrows scientific methods from the physical or physiological sciences. The methods of physics undoubtedly disclose certain measurable properties of human behavior, but beyond this they conceal more than they reveal. Unfortunately, the imperialism of the physical method may even cut human science off from relevant human behavior as it is revealed in the spontaneous, experiential mode of existence.

This caution against the premature introduction of scientific methodology does not in the least mean that the human scientist in the pre-empirical phase of his research should approach human behavior in a haphazard, random, aimless way. Although he does not give priority to methodological formulation in his pre-empirical elucidation of actual behavior, he does approach it in a certain mode, style, or manner. He seeks to maintain such unity between actual behavior and his psychological descriptions of it that the very meaning and structure of behavior itself is immediately revealed in his descriptions. This approach in the first, fundamental phase of psychological research is called phenomenological psychology.

Phenomenological psychology, in its broadest definition, is an attempt to return to the immediate meaning and structure of

The Nature and Meaning of Science

behavior as it actually presents itself. Phenomenology as a method in psychology thus seeks to disclose and elucidate the phenomena of behavior as they manifest themselves in their perceived immediacy. The human scientist, in this fundamental phase of his research, must thoughtfully penetrate his concrete lived perception of behavior and describe this behavior in its immediate disclosure. It is precisely the phenomenological method which allows him to penetrate to the structures of human behavior. At this pre-experimental and pre-theoretical level, the human scientist precludes all scientific constructs, methods, and theories. His immediate task is to make explicit, describe, and interpret the originally given behavior. The original datum of psychology is behavior itself, and the function of this fundamental phase of scientific exploration is to provide a conceptual clarification of behavior by making explicit its constitutive structures.

The phenomenological procedure in fundamental psychological research demands emancipation from all scientific-theoretical prejudgments, from all methodological and statistical limitations, which can only distort or conceal original behavior in its givenness. For the datum or phenomenon of behavior is always prior to any experiment, measurement, or theory *about* behavior. Therefore measurement, experiment, or scientific theory can never provide a sound point of departure in psychology. They are important and necessary modes of scientific exploration, but by their very nature they are always secondary, subsequent, and subordinate to phenomenological elucidation. Human scientists who preoccupy themselves exclusively with secondary scientific theory and subordinate laboratory experiments seldom arrive at a full understanding of relevant human behavior as it appears in daily life. For the road which they follow does not lead to actual, significant behavior. Having lost access to real human behavior, they may become preoccupied with an endless refinement, perfection, and sophistication of operational methods. But no refinement of method in the second phase of psychological research can make up for the lack of the phenomenological approach in the first, fundamental phase. What actually results is an increase in knowledge of the subtleties of operationalism and a decrease in knowledge of relevant human behavior. No method of the second phase of scientific research in psychology can of itself lead the psychologist to relevant behavior if he does not start from such behavior in its original appearance. The main purpose of the phenomenological phase in psychology, therefore, is to return to actual "lived" behavior as it manifests itself and in the manner in which it manifests itself: phenomenological psychology examines behavior as it is given.

MAN AS BEING IN THE WORLD IN AND THROUGH HIS BODY

If I desire to know how science is rooted in my nature, I must try to grasp not only that I am in the world as an "act-of-revealing," but also *how* I am in the world as an act of revealing. This knowledge may help me to understand what specific "mode-of-my-revealing-of-the-world" science is.

I am always in the world in and through my body: I am an embodied consciousness, an incarnated subjectivity. *All* my modes of existence are fundamentally modes of existence in and through my body. I am neither a disembodied self nor a mechanical organism, but a living unity, a body permeated by self. Because I am a bodily self, I experience myself in my behavior as an orientation to the world; I sense my outgoing self, my intentionality, at least implicitly and pre-reflectively. And this tending presence of my subjectivity to the world is always bodily presence. My body belongs to me, the tending, outgoing subject; I experience my body as that in, with, and through which I am present to the world; I "live" my body as that which grasps and seizes the world. My body is my spontaneous, unpremeditated entrance into the dense reality which permeates and surrounds me. I could not feel, grasp, assimilate, understand, perceive, elucidate anything in the world without this bridge which is my body, a bridge that is never absent but always present, a bridge which I truly am. My body makes the world available to me; it is in and through my body that the world becomes-for-me, becomes mine, my world. The total destruction or disintegration of my body is also the destruction or disintegration of my world. At the moment that I and my world are both ended, I shall no longer be ex-sistence, which is being-in-the-world. In daily life I know this fateful agent as the death of man.

My bodily presence to reality makes the world exist for me pre-reflectively before I think about it, probe it intellectually, reflect on it. The world is already there for me even before my reflection. For my body is my spontaneous lived presence to the world, obscure but real, vague but factual.

The fact that I am a bodily act of revealing the world has various implications. The first is that my actual presence to the world will always be necessarily a limited presence, and my actual revelation of reality a limited revelation. For my body not only makes the world available to my subjectivity, but also defines my limited position or situation in that world and consequently the limited availability of the world to me. My body makes my existence situated existence, my openness limited openness. The field of my bodily presence, of my senses and movements, is limited in time and space. I cannot see and touch at once everything that is visible and touchable in the world. How much of an object I can see depends on the actual position of my body. When I see something from the back, I cannot at the same time see its front. The reverse would be true if I were to find myself in front of the same object. Thus the various bodily positions which I assume give rise to various viewpoints or limited visions of reality.

When I, for example, study the behavior of a person who moves into my field of vision, I cannot escape the limitations of my bodily position. I may successively assume different bodily positions, shifting from one to another, but I can take only one position at a time. Every position which I assume will make available to me a different aspect of the moving person, such as his side view, his back, or his front. Every one of my positions will present me with a different perspective of his behavior. But ultimately I must make up my mind and select one of these many possible positions at any given moment of observation. My bodily position thus determines which view of the moving person will reveal itself to me within a confined field of perception, and my field of perception is always limited because of my being an *embodied* subjectivity.

This positional limitation of my perception is not the only one imposed on me by my body. My bodily existence differentiates the presence of my subjectivity in many modalities such as seeing, touching, hearing, smelling, and tasting. I cannot perceive a person or thing with all my sense modalities at the same time. At least, I cannot do so in a concentrated, intense way which will reveal to me all that can be revealed by each specific modality of presence alone. Each bodily modality of existence reveals a different aspect of the perceived world than other modalities. When I "look" at a person, I experience primarily other aspects than those perceived when I "touch" or embrace him. I say "primarily" for I am aware that by some kind of synesthesia the other aspects are at least implicitly present in my perception. For example, in looking at the fine texture of a silk shirt, I am implicitly aware of its soft tactile qualities. Or when my fingers feel the soft, smooth folds of this shirt in the darkness, I am implicitly aware that it will not appear to my eyes as heavy or rough. The basic quality of my perception, however, and therefore the basic revelation of what a silk shirt is like, depends on the specific bodily modality of existence in and through which my body relates to this object.

I may attempt to transcend both limitations of my embodied subjectivity, that of restricted bodily position and that of single modality. I may, for example, walk around a person who moves into my field of vision in order to see him from all sides, and I may even try to be present to him in all of my bodily modalities. I may touch, smell, see, hear, and even taste him. I may ask him how he himself feels about his movements, what makes him behave as he does, what he is attempting to communicate in his actions. In this way, I may try to build up a full understanding of his concrete behavior. However, even this knowledge will never be a complete *immediate* knowledge of this living person; even this comprehensive cognition cannot escape my bodily limitations. Because of my own shifting bodily positions in the world, I shall have obtained this knowledge primarily by a variety of shifting perspectives. The assemblage, montage, or aggregate of these perspectives will lead to a knowledge that will remain fundamentally fragmentary and retain the character of a collection of partial perceptions. It will not provide an immediate, integral understanding of the moving person, but a notion made up of numerous fragments of perceptions representing the results of my various bodily positions and modalities. Indeed, my bodily existence compels me to perceive the world always in limited ways. Consequently, my knowledge of the world is always originally fragmentary knowledge.

This limitation of knowledge by bodily position and modality seems evident enough in my perceptual mode of existence, which necessarily implies my assumption of a particular bodily position and my selection of one or the other sensuous modality in my presence to the world. But is my thought limited as my perception is? Is my thought about the moving person absolutely free from limitation? Or does my embodied existence limit not only my perceiving but also my thinking?

My thought is necessarily co-original with my perception. My thought about a moving person, for example, cannot be dreamed up arbitrarily; it necessarily originates with my perception of his behavior. All my ideas about this moving person, all my statements about him, are finally dependent on my bodily-perceptual presence to him in various bodily positions and modalities. Therefore my thinking approach to reality is also fundamentally fragmentary. My bodily being in the world makes it impossible for me ever to achieve a moment in which I can maintain all possible viewpoints in thought at the same time. The actual availability of the world to me is forever limited by the finiteness of my corporeal situation.

This human situation has far-reaching implications for the nature of the development of science: it explains first of all the differentiation of science into many sciences, and more specifically the differentiation of psychology into many differential psychologies, each one opening up its own perspective. This same insight provides the basis for the task of comprehensive psychology, which is an attempt to integrate the perspectives developed by the differential psychologies.

Finally, my body enables me to exist in a *social* world. I do not experience myself as an isolated discoverer of meaning. I do not perceive myself as the only man on earth, lonely and lost in an overwhelming multitude of blind processes and opaque lumps of matter, for which I do not exist as a meaningful other and which cannot discover meaning in me. I meet other men, other embodied subjectivities, who in and through their bodily presence to the world uncover meaning in the world as I do. I am even acutely aware of the fact that they judge me, that they are aware of me and impose meaning on me, that I belong to their field of meaning. I thus discover that I am not the only openness in the world, but that there are others like me who in and through their bodies are outgoing, meaning-giving subjectivities in the midst of people, animals, things, and processes.

The others communicate to me, in and through their bodies, their own uncovering of meaning in the world, and I respond to their communications. We may join one another in a community of men who decide to explore together, by means of certain methods, selected profiles of the world. This community of specialists in a specific area of discovery may stretch itself over cultures and generations. The social aspect of our embodiment, namely the bodily presence of our subjectivity to one another, is the condition for the possibility of science as an organized endeavor over generations of men.

BODY AS REVEALING BEHAVIOR

Behavior is the bodily presence in the world of the revealing, existing movement which I am. My bodily behavior reveals the world to me. My moving hands reveal to me a basketball as spherical, solid, and leathery; my throwing hands unveil to me its bouncing quality; my pressing hands discover its elasticity. The same behavior in others reveals to me how they too discover, in and through their behavior, the meaning, the sense of a basketball. Behavior as gestures, movements, and language is my being-in-the-world, my immediate presence to reality.

20

Thus behavior is not a mediatization or a symbolization of my intentionality or subjectivity, but rather my intentionality itself, my existing itself. In our consideration of the science of psychology as the study of behavior, we shall see how this fact enables psychology to declare itself the empirical science of behavior while at the same time the science of the *whole man* in so far as he appears in behavior.

I am in the world through my body, and as such I am a behaving subjectivity. The perceived world is relative to my behaving intentionality, for it is always a world for me as a behaving subjectivity. Behavior, therefore, cannot be studied by itself, for it is fundamentally a revealing act and can be understood only in terms of my world which I as behavior reveal around myself. The behaving body-which-I-am is the *original* locus for the appropriation of sense and meaning. Behavior is the original existential presence by which my body makes the world be for me.

Meaning is thus not ready-given in the world as a being-in-itself; sense and meaning are not "out there," clear-cut like a map or photograph. If such were the case, I would have only to take in passively a representation of the things out there. On the other hand, sense is not merely an arbitrary invention of my mind or my creative imagination; sense is born in and through my life, which is bodily being and behaving in the world. Sense emerges in and through the dialectic relation between me and my world. The notion of body-subject developed by Maurice Merleau-Ponty helps to clarify the statement that my body is revealing behavior.

I must strive, first of all, to understand something of the original, obscure field of my existence from which science emerges. Science itself operates with clear, well-defined constructs and concepts. But the emergence of science presupposes spontaneous experience, and the emergence of the scientist presupposes the spontaneously living human being. While I can be perfectly clear about a scientific system which I have developed, I cannot be so clear about my initial "lived" experience of the world which preceded my scientific development, and which is the original source of any scientific concept that I may elaborate in precise ways. Nevertheless, I am interested not only in the exact and logical development of scientific systems, but also in their initial origin in spontaneous human existence. My original, spontaneous interaction with the world before I approach it as a scientist is not a presence to things which are already sharply delineated and categorized; it is rather my being involved in a field of existence in which everything is interwoven with everything else, in which everything points to every other thing. It is a movable, fluid field, vastly different from my precisely organized collection of scientific constructs.

I should anticipate, therefore, that it will be impossible for me to view my original human field of lived experience in full precision and clarity. I cannot transcribe this region of prime experience into systematic constructs which together form a tight, theoretical, scientific system. For as soon as I begin to build a scientific system, I have already ceased to consider my primary field of spontaneous being in the world. In spite of these reservations and restrictions, I can still express coherently my growing insight into this pre-reflective, spontaneous realm of my existence. At the same time I remain aware that I do not and cannot know distinctly and exhaustively this obscure, original root of my scientific life. My understanding of the realm in which all science begins will always be blended with not-understanding; my perception of it will be permeated by blind spots. While it is crucial for me to devise precise constructs when I build a scientific system, it is also essential to recognize the obscurity of my primordial field of "lived" knowledge from which my scientific theory emerges and to which it points. Such a recognition will prevent me from making my theory of behavior inflexible, closed, and immutable; it will keep it open, hypothetical, and provisional.

This pre-conscious, pre-objective field of my original perception is thus so obscure that ordinary reflection cannot really penetrate it. My body, according to Merleau-Ponty, is a subject or, in other words, a meaning-giving existence, even if I am not yet conscious of its meaning-giving activity. My body has already invested my world with meaning before I think about this meaning. It is not the same as the imposition of meaning on the world by my consciousness. Certain things in the world, for example, already mean shelter, food, or obstacle for me as body-subject before I am consciously aware of it. I am thus already a meaning-giving existence on the pre-conscious and not-yet-free level of my bodily existence. Numerous examples demonstrate that my body exists as a giver of meanings. I see colors, I hear sounds, I feel with my fingers the roughness and smoothness of things, I smell odors, and I taste flavors. Sounds, odors, flavors, and colors do not exist as such completely in themselves "out there" in the world, independent of my bodily presence to the world. Without man, without me, there would be no sights, sounds, and flavors but only some unknown substratum that can appear as sounds, flavors, and colors as soon as I am present to it.

My experience tells me, on the other hand, that sounds, colors, flavors, and tactile qualities do not exist only in me and not in reality. I experience that the sunshine itself is warm, the grass green, and the rose fragrant. All these sensitive meanings are, as it were, the face which the world shows to me. I am in my bodily behavior a manifold question, and I make the world reply in many ways. The world itself is color and shape in reply to my seeing; it is a field of sound in answer to my hearing; it is savory in response to my tasting. But it is clearly not my conscious free ego which questions the world in this way. I do not willingly and consciously ask the world to reveal itself to me in color, sound, taste, touch, or smell. This interplay between the questioning me and the replying world takes place before I consciously think about it, or before I make a conscious, free decision to interrogate the world. This original dialogue between me and the world is preconscious; it takes place on the level of my bodily existence and is connected with the structure of my body. Here I do not "choose," but I "find" something that is already given before any choice.

I am thus already a meaning-giving existence on a level on which I am not yet conscious of myself, and on which I am not yet free. The sensitive meaning, therefore, of color, taste, smell, and sound is a result of a pre-conscious dialogue with the world. This dialogue takes place at such depth that I am unable to penetrate it through my reflective consciousness. Neither am I able to influence this dialogue by means of my free decisions. Below me, therefore, as conscious subject, is another subject that is pre-conscious and pre-personal. This subject is my body itself, for all forms of meaning which emerge on this level appear to be related to the structure of my body. Consequently, I should not identify my meaning-giving subjectivity with my conscious and free thought only. I should recognize that my body itself is already a subject.

At the same time, I should realize that meaning originates in a dialogue. In a real dialogue both partners are active. This implies that I, as a behaving body-subject, must be somehow active in my encounter with the world. My body is not passive in this dialogue. On the contrary, it assumes spontaneously and actively a position which makes this dialogue possible and facilitates it. For example, if my body wants to see something, it must assume the correct ocular position. The pupils of my eyes, for instance, must be dilated according to the darkness of the field of vision. In other words, my body has to situate itself if a certain sensitive meaning is to emerge. My freedom and consciousness are not involved in this spontaneous assumption of a position. I do not know at all what happens in and through my body while I am seeing.

In my scientific life I take up again and continue my preconscious existence, my pre-reflexive way of being in the world. As a scientist, I am able to devise well-defined scientific constructs and impressive experimental designs. On closer inspection, however, I realize that these designs and constructs pre-

24

suppose the meaning which originated in my pre-conscious bodily presence to the world. An experiment that measures, for example, to what degree a certain behavior of rats is reinforced by certain types of rewards, is steeped in preconscious bodily knowledge of the world. For I presuppose that rats react when properly stimulated, that their body is a possibility of movement, that there is an oriented space inseparably and naturally bound up with their possibility of limited bodily movements. I presume, moreover, that rats have built-in needs to respond to rewarding stimulations if exposed to them under the appropriate conditions. I spontaneously incorporate this assumed need into my experimental design. I never attempt to demonstrate these presuppositions experimentally. In any case, such a demonstration would be impossible. I cannot discover experimentally that a rat is a rat, for such an experiment would already presuppose what I am trying to prove. If I did not know rats at all in my daily experiential life, I could not initiate any experiment whatever concerning them. My scientific life never begins with zero; as a scientist, I always start from a meaning which I find already there. This meaning, however, originates within the dialogue of body and world. The conscious scientific mode of existence, then, always refers to the preconscious bodily mode of existence.

The scientific mode of existence is a conscious, free, planned, and selective "taking up" of meanings and relations already given in the preconscious dialogue of my behaving body. My body *gives* me the world through an interplay with the world, but in such a way that my bodily behavior organizes the world. The world's structure thus depends on the structures of my body. My body is a possibility of meaning-giving activity, and the so-called natural world is the whole of the meanings resulting from the dialogue between my body and the world. As a scientist I take up this world in a conscious, reflective, selective, abstractive way, but I do not constitute it, for it is already there for my taking. The "natural" world is the result of the dialogue between my body and the world: a dialogue which precedes existence-insofar-as-it-is-scientific and a world which ante-dates the abstract world of science. My body already dwells in the world before my scientific-dwelling-in-the-world can take up my pre-conscious bodily dwelling.

The pre-conscious behaving body is thus the ultimate source of my scientific designs, theories, and constructs.

The Behaving Body on the Conscious Level of Existence

Is my role as behaving body completed when I transpose my pre-scientific, spontaneous existence in a scientific, abstractive, experimenting existence? Every mode of my existence is embodied, for I *am* bodily behaving presence to reality. Therefore, the role of my behaving body is different but still paramount on the scientific level of existence. I must realize that my pre-conscious bodily dialogue with the world becomes gradually permeated by my consciousness, that I assume my bodily behaving more and more in a conscious manner, that my conscious self is increasingly present in my bodily behavior. This does not mean that I shall ever be able to penetrate the deepest original, spontaneous, pre-conscious dialogue between my body and the world. I shall never know in a clear and distinct way, for example, how this dialogue leads to the sight of color, the scent of a rose, and the taste of honey. But I am able gradually to organize, expand, foster, limit, and concentrate my bodily, behavioral presence to the world. I can do this in a fruitful fashion, however, only when I take into account the data presented to me in my pre-conscious dialogue with the world, which is the always present, unescapable basis of my life, my thought, and my science. Its total disappearance is the disappearance of me, is my death.

The increasing permeation of my behavior by my consciousness also leads to a fuller expression of my reflective and pre-reflective self in my bodily behavior. For "expression" is an indispensable and deeply influential mode of being in the world. My presence to the world in and through my behaving body can thus be more or less conscious, more or less concentrated, intense, full, and rich. My capacity for intense personal presence increases with my growth and maturation. In other words, my organism becomes more and more my personalized body during the course of my existence.

My movements as an infant, for example, were somewhat wild, jerky, and disorganized. My anger was expressed in a primitive way; my little body squirmed, kicked, and screamed; my face became purple and my breathing was impaired. As I grew older, however, I manifested in my behavior that I was more fully present in my bodily senses, postures, and movements than I was as an infant. This increasing emergence of consciousness enabled me, among other things, to express my anger more efficiently. And this effectual, socially acceptable, bodily expression of my anger made me adept in dealing with my neighbors and proficient in my conquest of reality.

I have sometimes seen, on the other hand, a drunken man who is enraged because he cannot fit his key in the keyhole. His fury, instead of leading him to experimental probing of the keyhole, erupts in unadapted movements directed against the house as a whole. I can observe comparable reactions in an adult who becomes panic-stricken or loses control in an emergency. People may say that such a person forgets him*self* or is beyond him*self*. The bodily behaviors of infants, drunkards, and panic-stricken people are thus similarly ill-adapted modes of involvement with reality.

The increasing presence of the conscious self in human behavior can be observed in many bodily expressions. The face of an infant is somewhat empty in expression. Painters prefer to depict the faces and figures of older people. In the mature personalized human body, the face, hands, movements, and posture radiate the presence of a self much more fully than in the immature body of the child. For this reason a clergyman, a musician, or a wrestler may sometimes be spotted by a sensitive observer of the human scene even if he has little information as a clue. Their professional modes of existence are inherent in all their behavior. Even the manner in which they move reveals them.

This progressive incarnation of the conscious self is observable even in the young child. When I compare carefully the movements of the hands of a child and those of the paws of a monkey, I note a striking fundamental difference. The functional and expressive quality of the paw of a monkey is basically limited by biological needs and stimulations, while the spontaneous functions and expressions of the hand of a child are of a virtually infinite variety and refinement. This is one possible explanation of why there are no painters or sculptors who dedicate their artistic lives to the recreation of the paws of animals. A great number of artists, however, have painted and sculptured over and over again the human hands. The visitor to the Museum Rodin in Paris is struck by the amazing variety of human hands in which Rodin expressed the profound and dramatic presence of the human self.

The human self permeates not only the functional and expressive movements, the mimics and postures of man, but also the physical and chemical surroundings in which he moves and lives. The whole man as embodied self leaves his mark wherever and whenever he emerges in nature and in culture. Man influences, masters, takes hold of, embodies his surroundings; he transforms them into his world through his bodily being in reality. This is true not only of the individual man but of mankind as a whole. The human race as a community of men develops by being present together to reality as it unveils itself in millennia of evolution and human history. It is in such creative, historical community that man constitutes the numerous cultural worlds of meaning which mark his erratic, frequently interrupted ascent and enlightenment.

The way in which we structure our hearths and homes today, for example, is the outgrowth of a long history of bodily perception and manipulation of the world. By the acts of seeing, touching, and using, we have uncovered in reality the meaning of stone, wood, glass, and tools, of protective walls and roofs against rain, snowfall, and burning sunshine. In this sense, our existence is fundamentally co-existence, vertically in history, horizontally in contemporary culture. Vertical co-existence means that we assimilate what others have unveiled before us, while horizontal co-existence implies that we are influenced by the insights and experiences of those who presently live with us. Not only our forebears but also our contemporaries unveil in bodily behaving, in sensing and moving, aspects of reality which are relevant, for example, to the construction of the place in which we live; and we profit from sharing in this movement of their existence. Even rebellion against the points of view of other men is elicited by the ideas against which our revolt is directed and cannot be understood without the view which it attempts to correct.

When I understand that my exploration of the world is fundamentally a bodily exploration, I realize at once that science is not only a mode of existence but also one of the central modes of human existence. For the scientific attitude is a way of concretizing in an effective and organized manner my bodily encounter with reality. This is eminently true of experimental science. For authentic experimentation implies an efficient and well-organized embodiment of my searching insight. This insight is embodied in my sense observation and in the manipulation of reality by means of my experimenting hands.

Technology also means the organized embodiment of my involvement in reality. This technical embodiment changes reality and subdues it, as it were, to my conscious human self. In other words, I embody not only my own organism, but also the world. My culture becomes my second body. Consequently, also, the world of science and technology is an unique expression of the emotional, intellectual, and spiritual presence of man. Suppose that a sole survivor of a shipwreck is stranded on an island and feels himself to be completely alone and forlorn. Suddenly he spies, at the other side of the island, a small house with a garden; a spiral of smoke rises from the chimney on the roof. He is overjoyed and deeply moved, for this home and garden are the very embodiment of a human presence. At this fateful moment, the island is changed for him totally; it becomes at once a human world.

Everywhere in human history we find traces of this embodiment of man. It enables us to reconstruct the psychology of a prehistoric tribe on the basis of the behavioral creations in which they embodied their human selves. Prehistoric grottoes covered with the wall paintings of our ancestors hold a peculiar fascination for us. For we realize that there we communicate with our co-existents who lived thousands of years ago. They are present to us in the rocks and stone in which they embodied their human selves. These human selves are not strange to us but deeply familiar.

Bodily presence to the world means primordially a presence by means of bodily senses and movements. When a man changes an acre of wild prairie into a lovely garden, he is present to the earth, the weeds, and the stones by means of his eyes, his sense of touch, and his ears, all of which are aware of the grit that grinds under his footsteps. He is also present to the earth by means of his measuring walk and his digging, weeding, planting hands. In such ways man and mankind are always embodied and embodying.. It is this continual event of incarnation which changes the world. The active embodiment of the conscious human self by the human race appears to men most strikingly in our own day. Science and technology as the incarnation of human skill and knowledge transform the world at a pace never dreamt of before in the course of our evolution.

To be sure, science is only one mode of existence. Art, for example, is another bodily mode of existence. A striking example is the dance. When I study the development of the dance in primitive tribes, I realize that these people expressively embodied their thoughts, feelings, and attitudes regarding religion, war, childbirth, weddings, rain, and agriculture in their bodily movements. They attempted, moreover, to influence in a magical way the course of events in their world by means of these bodily manifestations. Emotional, experiential uncovering of the world always prevails in the dance as it does in other artistic endeavors. For this reason, art loses its character when it becomes too intellectual, pragmatic, or technical.

As a scientist, however, I aim primordially not at an emotional-experiential uncovering of the world, but at the unveiling of my surroundings by means of a well-organized, planned, and controlled use of bodily senses and movements. When I reflect on this scientific uncovering of reality in the light of what I have already explicated, I realize at once that my empirical, scientific mode of existence is a most human way of being in the world. For it is now clear to me that scientific existence is rooted in the very structure of my nature and my primordial situation. First of all, I am a self-body unity. Therefore, my human way of learning is by means of bodily senses and movements. Even as an infant I tried out all things by tasting, chewing, touching, throwing, looking, hearing. I experimented all day long and mastered my world in the course of this process. I was an incipient scientist. Science is always a controlled, planned, and organized bodily participation in that which is bodily given. On the other hand, that which is in no way observable can be made an object of science only when it is made observable. Scientific knowledge, therefore, remains in principle dependent on externally observable data.

This necessity of bodily mediation moves the scientist to invent instruments which expand the power of his bodily senses and movements. Such expansion is the necessary condition for new discoveries and for new forms of cultivation and utilization of reality. The scientist invents microscopes to increase the power of his eyes so that he may knowingly embody himself in the microcosmos. He constructs telescopes as a prolongation of his seeing organism so that he may be present in space. He develops space craft to prolong his bodily movements so that he may dwell in thoughtful observation among the stars.

31

This tremendous development of observational power is inspired and maintained by the most fundamental drive in man, the drive to exist, to participate in being, to embody himself in reality. Embodiment, incarnation, bodily participation, is a very deep urge in mankind. All human activities and inventions are its expression.

THE SCIENTIFIC MODE OF EXISTENCE

If I wish to understand my scientific mode of being, I must first of all clarify the similarities and dissimilarities between my original and my scientific existence. Second, I must demonstrate precisely how I change from an original to a scientific attitude.

PRE-REFLECTIVE AND REFLECTIVE MODE OF LIVING

I am necessarily and spontaneously oriented toward the world. Through my presence to the world, the veils of reality are removed; in this sense, existence is unveiling and revealing. It is my essence, my very nature to be a revealer of reality. In my encounter with the world, reality is revealed and made meaningful to me. My every encounter with a person, a dog, a tree, a desk, or even a stick brings to light some aspect of reality. I call such revealing encounter experience. Experience is thus any revealing presence to any reality whatsoever. The expressions, "I experienced cold and hunger," "It was a great experience," and "I experienced the dullness of a rainy day," all imply perception of some reality, a presence to some manifestation of all that is. In this perception, meaning is unveiled: experience is my revealing presence to the world.

This primary awareness, this meaning-giving experience, is pre-reflective. Pre-reflective means that I am familiar with a person or thing as a part of my lived world, as something that belongs to my spontaneous experience. I have not yet thought about what this person or thing that I am meeting *is*. If I do think about it, my pre-reflective knowledge becomes reflective.

32

Reflective knowledge arises from a consideration of, or bending-back upon, my experience. For example, during a single day I may move my car out of the garage, shovel snow, say "Hello" to a neighbor, and feel shocked by news of the stock market. Each of these incidents leads to meaningful behavior on my part. I know each one of these situations because they belong to my world and I respond to them spontaneously. But it is only in reflection on the experience of these situations that I know them fully and clearly and that I am able to communicate this knowledge verbally.

In my reflection on experience I "thematize" it. That is, I direct my conscious *attention* toward a particular experience. In this reflection I become more fully present to the meaning of the reality which is revealed to me in my experience. Only now I am able to express to *myself* and to others the meaning which I unveiled in my meeting with reality.

INTERRELATIONSHIPS OF THE PRE-REFLECTIVE AND
REFLECTIVE MODES OF BEING

My pre-reflective and reflective modes of being in the world are interconnected. For I can reflect only on what I have experienced. This is also true of my scientific knowledge, which is a special mode of reflective existence. Science necessarily presupposes experience and is always concerned with some aspect of it. In scientific reflection I place myself at a distance from that particular aspect of the world about which I am thinking. But I am at the same time the person who first discovered this aspect by being in the world and with this aspect of it. Moreover, when I am no longer involved in scientific reflection, I fall back into this original mode of being in reality; I continue to live in my everyday world as I did before my scientific study. As a scientist, I objectify, I thematize certain aspects of my experience; but in living my daily life, I am involved in the world and my life merges with it. For example, as a medical diagnostician I thematize and objectify that aspect of my perception of the hand of a patient that reveals it as a vulnerable structure of bones, nerves, joints, and muscles. I do so by using a system of abstract physiological categories. After my scientific work is finished, however, I fall back into my original daily mode of existence. While I tenderly caress the hand of my wife or sweetheart, I do not reflect on its muscular composition and its innervation by blood vessels and nerves.

Let us cite another example. In my everyday life I participate in my family situation and engage spontaneously in behavior which will motivate my boisterous offspring to go to bed at the proper hour. My personal participation in the situation teaches me how to handle it adroitly. As a psychologist, however, when I begin to think about effective relationships between parents and children, I may turn into an object of scientific reflection the spontaneous manner in which I persuade my children to sleep. Such scientific psychology is not given with my experience of life; it is the analysis, the unfolding, the objectification of a certain aspect of my experience of life. Psychology, like the other sciences, is ultimately rooted in my situated experience, which is related to my being a behaving body.

Therefore, I can devise scientific psychological constructs and theories only by virtue of an analogy with, or opposition to, the pre-reflective psychological relationships in which I have lived. Even when I do so, I remain rooted in my original mode of being in the world. My scientific view, therefore, always remains a view taken from a particular situation. I who make scientific statements about the world am the same person who lives perceptively and experimentally in the world. I seek light in both ways. My scientific constructs, judgments, and theories cannot substitute for the experience which emerges in my original presence in the world. Consequently, it is not so-called "bare facts" which are the starting point of science, but my pre-scientific experience. Thus there should exist a unity of reciprocal implication between my scientific and pre-scientific modes of being. When my scientific statements are totally divorced from my primary perception, they no longer make sense. For all scientific reflection is a reflection on my experience and my world. As a scientist I attempt within certain limits to understand something of the world in which I live, and I form scientific concepts which throw light on this world. Therefore, science can be made intelligible only from the standpoint of my original field of experience. For all my scintific and reflective knowledge is rooted in the dialogue between reality and me, and therefore presupposes the fundamental fact of my existence as a giver of meaning. This original field of awareness is the origin and purpose of all science.

For example, structures of behavior are available to me as a scientific psychologist because I myself, as a bodily behaving subject, am involved in intentional behavior in daily life. Therefore, the way in which I behave intentionally in the world cannot be irrelevant to the way in which I pursue psychology. My attitude toward behavior arises somehow from my pre-reflective existence. I experience behavior in myself and in others in a certain way; it reveals itself to me under certain aspects. All this is still prior to my explicit psychological judgments. However, these judgments have roots only when they are related to my original experience. I can be a scientific psychologist only from the standpoint of my particular situation. A psychologist today may consider the same behavior as the psychologist of fifty years ago, but he does so in a different historical and cultural situation. Consequently, the intentional behavior itself in its concrete form and appearance becomes different. For example, since Western humanity has learned much about unconscious influences on behavior from psychoanalysis, intentional behavior itself appears different to man than it did before the historical emphasis on unconscious drives.

Theory: Pre-Reflective and Reflective

The shift from original to scientific existence is not a change from "pure" unstructured experience to structure or theory. Primary experience itself already implies pre-reflective, spontaneous theorizing. In my daily dealings with reality I am guided by certain spontaneous considerations; in pre-reflective life I am not only a doer but also a planner. When I am forced to park my car in a small area, I move smoothly and carefully. As an experienced driver I do not sit down and reflect on the exact distance between the cars, on the measurements of my car, on the speed of my wheels. I am immediately present to the situation: I plan my practical movements pre-reflectively. This designing, projecting, and maneuvering is implicit in my practical behavior and characterizes my daily dealing with life situations. My immediate view of the parking situation transforms itself into a pre-reflective design or theory. Guided by a spontaneous scanning of the mutual relationships between such elements as the number of cars, the size of the parking area, the traffic situation, and the manipulation of the steering wheel, I know how to move in without scratching paint or fenders. The scheme according to which my pre-scientific theorizing develops may be characterized by the conditional relation: if . . . then . . . *If* I want to park between these two cars, *then* I must turn my wheel thus in this direction. Through such pre-scientific planning, I become clearly aware of my situation. Thus, the intention of my pre-theoretical planning is not to know the characteristics of cars, parking areas, and steering wheels as such, but rather to know them as they are practically relevant to my efficient orientation. Pre-reflective theory is thus praxis-oriented. Such practical theorizing involves my past experience. I have parked my car before, I have observed other people parking cars, and I have heard about the parking of cars. This past experience is made available to me in my pre-reflective theorizing.

Such implicit, pre-reflective surveying of daily life situations is also characteristic of pre-reflective psychology. When I need to obtain some immediate service from a moody person, I do not make a reflective analysis of his temperament and the possible factors in his past which led up to his disagreeable disposition. My practical need for immediate service mobilizes not only my present perception of the situation but also my *past* experience with moody fellowmen and my *future* possibility of obtaining the service required within the next moment. Before I know it reflectively, I find myself already engaged in behavior that placates the moody person and stimulates his willingness to be of service. My practical lived psychology is thus functional and praxis-oriented rather than speculative and insight-oriented. The difference between the two is striking when an emergency situation suddenly compels me to shift back from a scientific-theoretical to a pre-reflective, practical-theoretical attitude.

Suppose, for example, I am studying scientifically the nature and number of hallucinations in hospitalized patients. When a disturbed patient unexpectedly attacks me with a knife, I shift suddenly from theoretical reflection on hallucinations to a rapid pre-reflective scanning of the situation. This spontaneous survey guides my immediate, efficient handling of the emergency. In this case the reflective, scientific approach could mean the end of both me and the situation! While the ineffectiveness of reflective theory in this situation is too obvious to be stated, it should be noted that it is basically impractical because it takes me partly out of the situation, because I am not totally involved in it. Instead, I confine myself to observation of only certain aspects of it, such as the scientific nature and number of hallucinations. I see the situation only from a specific viewpoint, in this case that of the categories of psychopathology. This attitude in psychological research reveals to me only one area of reality and leaves out all other aspects. In a practical life situation, however, I can plan efficiently only when I spontaneously take into account all aspects which are relevant to my practical purpose, which in the case above is the immediate escape from a dangerous threat.

I have made a distinction in the example given between an efficient presence to the situation as a whole in the light of a practical purpose, and my presence to certain aspects detached from the situation in the light of abstract scientific categories. When I am engaged in scientific, psychopathological research which aims at the identification of certain categories, I abstract from the person as a whole and from his life situation. I am not concerned with his worries, hopes, dreams, his appearance, or his dislike of the situation. I detach from this whole human situation only those aspects which are relevant to my psycho-pathological study of the scientific nature and frequency of hallucinatory symptoms in a certain group of patients. All other aspects are left out of consideration. In daily life, however, when I interact with my friend, my wife, or my child I am spontaneously open to many other aspects, and it is almost impossible for me to abstract from them. This is one of the reasons why medical doctors and psychotherapists do not usually treat the members of their own families. It is almost impossible for them to shift from their daily involved attitude to the detached scientific one in regard to the same persons.

In the reflective-theoretical as well as in the scientific attitude, I adopt an entirely new standpoint with regard to people, whereby I acquire a totally new viewpoint about their behavior. This viewpoint in turn produces a completely new type of comprehension by which certain types of behavior are seen simply and solely as given incidences of psychopathological categories which may be computed statistically. This shift in comprehension consists in the act of detaching these aspects of behavior from their natural context by no longer conceiving them in their relation to the whole of the particular life situation of the unique, individual person.

When I enumerate incidences of hallucinatory behavior in a statistical survey, I disregard not only any possible application of these incidences to the behavior of the person and of the people related to him in everyday life, but also the relative position which this behavior might have within the psychological make-up of the person as a whole. For my research, the life situation as a whole does not matter. The aspect of behavior which I am studying is for me no longer within the life situation; it has become a statistical moment, an incident which is in no way distinguished from similar incidents recorded in books in my library. In this way behavior is stripped of its concrete situational determinations. I no longer consider a particular aspect of behavior in the perspective of an application based on a given life situation. The advantage of this attitude is that I am able to describe and determine with precision the structural moments of simply-and-solely given psychopathological behavior.

Let us take another example. I am learning the Greek alphabet. I can express this experience of learning in two ways which are fundamentally different. I may say, "It is fascinating to learn that intriguing alphabet from that encouraging teacher whom I like so much." So speaking, I experience my learning as my lived relationship to a meaningful situation with many elements which appeal to me. On the other hand, I may say, "Learning is a function of reinforcement." In this case I no longer consider my personal learning as a lived role within a full life situation brimming with a variety of meanings. I see it rather as a psychological construct which is subject to psychological laws and which fits into a neatly defined theoretical-psychological system. Compared to the first statement, the second one represents a shift in standpoint: my learning has been detached from the whole of a life situation within which it emerged; now it is considered as nothing but a psychological event which is simply-and-solely given, independent of any individual life situation.

In this latter perspective it no longer makes sense to state that learning is fascinating and that a teacher is encouraging. The only meaningful statement which can now be made is a statistical expression of the degree of reinforcement needed for a certain degree of increase in retention. This shift of standpoint is neither the outcome of the fact that I have actually ceased to learn the Greek alphabet, nor of the fact that I have abstracted from such possible practical learning. The only possible explanation is that I have assumed an entirely new standpoint with regard to my learning, whereby I acquire a totally new viewpoint toward it. This viewpoint in turn leads to a completely new type of comprehension by which learning is seen as a quantifiable process of behavior, as simply-and-solely given. This shift in my comprehension is the act of detaching the behavior of learning from the lived learning situation by no longer conceiving it in its concrete relationship to the whole situation.

When I express in statistics or graphs that a certain degree of retention is correlated with a certain degree of reinforcement, I disregard not only the possible application of this fact to personal situations like learning the Greek alphabet from an encouraging teacher, but also the position which learning might have within my particular life situation. In my scientific research, the possible application and concrete position of learning behavior have no significance, for behavior is no longer perceived within the world of everyday life. I may also reverse this statement and say that the position of learning behavior has become a theoretical construct within a theory of learning related to other theoretical constructs. It is no longer posited in a real lived world, but in an ideal, intellectual, abstract world, a man-made universe of discourse. The reflective theoretical mode of existence thus differs greatly from the pre-reflective theoretical one. The reflective-theoretical mode is no longer an implicit, spontaneous guide to practical behavior in a life situation as pre-reflective theory was.

Reflective theory implies an explicit, systematic attention to a selected aspect of a situation. It thus presupposes a shift of attitude, a second look. In behavioral science this means that I take behavior out of its natural lived context, out of the frame of my original world, and that I separate it from its life situation. From that moment on, this behavior appears as no longer related to the individual living person. I can now manipulate it experimentally, empirically, and statistically within the artificial situation of a theoretical system or experimental design. I establish as it were a new abstract context, a world of constructs, an artificial space for this incident of behavior that I have lifted out of its situation. I can now relate it to other similar incidences of behavior which have been isolated in the same way.

My scientific-theoretical approach always implies a certain viewpoint. As a scientist I see people, animals, plants, and minerals differently than I do as a spontaneous, unreflective participant in daily life. The reality encountered in my original mode of existence is brimming with meaning, but as a scientist I select only certain meanings of reality as the focus of my investigations. These objective meanings of reality which I can select as matter for study are manifold. Thus I can develop a wide range of scientific concerns, each of which is related to a different objective meaning of reality. Each one leads, therefore, to a specific well-organized system of thought and perception. As a scientist I thus restrict my perception of reality by asking only certain well-defined questions. The possible replies of "what-is" to these specific questions are correspondingly limited by the specificity of the questions asked. Consequently, the answers of reality will reveal only certain of its manifold aspects. Finally, all these specific answers together will be gradually integrated within a specific system of meaning, a comprehensive theory, a body of scientific truth, a science.

In other words, a specific science does not reveal "all-that-is" but only one realm of objectivity. This area of being is defined by the fundamental concern of the science in question. Therefore, every science constitutes its own objective world which is different from that of all other sciences. The differences between the sciences are thus based on the differences between the questions asked and the correspondingly isolated profiles of reality. Therefore, a complete conformity in aim, method, or results of the various sciences is in principle and in fact impossible. Fundamentally different questions lead to fundamentally different answers or systems of meaning. And fundamentally different systems of meaning cannot be added together, just as we cannot add cows, cobwebs, rivers, and rockets together with any meaning. For the same reason, it is unthinkable and even impossible to reduce one system of meaning to another

41

system of meaning; for example, psychology to physiology, or biology to physics. Such a reduction would be as impossible as the transformation of tulips to dresses, or vegetables to glass. If the reduction of one science to another is successful, it proves only that the science which is reduced either has not yet found itself as a particular quest for reality or has abandoned its own quest. In such a case, it is not yet a differential science in its own right with its own system of meaning, with its own inalienable methods which are the subtle elaborations of the unique questions asked by the representatives of the science in question.

I may conclude that the characteristic property of my theoretical-scientific existence is that I confine myself to an observation of the world without thereby being totally involved in the world. This reflective theoretical observation always implies that I take a specific attitude toward reality. Correspondingly, reality that is encountered in this way is always seen from a specific viewpoint. Which of its aspects reality will reveal to me as a reflective theoretical observer depends on my attitude with regard to reality. If I select a certain aspect or profile as the object of critical and methodical investigation, I lay the foundations of a specific science. By my attitude towards reality, I as a scientist begin to delimit an area of reality as the domain of my research. The precise differentiation of such a well-defined area from every other domain of investigation is my first step in scientific research.

The objective of every science thus represents a separated and well delineated domain that in turn is differentiated in sub-domains. These differentiations of a science are constituted by various perspectives which are taken in regard to the common objective of the science; they thus imply a differentiation of the common perspective. For example, the objective of psychology as a whole is intentional-functional behavior, while differential psychologies such as learning theory, psychoanalysis, and introspectionism approach this common objective from various viewpoints which are still possible within the common perspective.

Every new phenomenon which emerges in a science is examined to the degree that it conforms to the normative object-coherence of the specific science. For example, the phenomenon of religion is examined in psychology to the degree of its relevance for the understanding of intentional-functional behavior; beyond this, the study of religion is left to theology and other disciplines. Similarly, the phenomenon of brain waves is studied in psychology only insofar as it reveals intentional-functional behavior; beyond this, it is the domain of neurophysiology, biochemistry, and related sciences.

CRITERION OF SELECTION

As a scientist, I restrict myself necessarily to one of many possible viewpoints which emerge in my encounter with reality. Through my selection of a specific viewpoint, I limit that which was originally given in my experience. My objects in science are not objects which are given to me as such in primary perception; they are the results of my specific selective orientation toward reality. My original perception does not know about the objects of science, about H_2O, atoms, molecules, reinforcement, and Oedipal constellations; it does know about rivers, houses, trees, birds, flowers, love, hate, jealousy, and anxiety.

When I decide to consider certain realities from specific scientific viewpoints, I limit my perception of them by my scientific frame of reference. They are no longer what they were. So-called exact data are rather scientific interpretations of my primary experience. Scientific thinking foregoes primary experience instead of penetrating it. The scientific view of man and the world is thus the result of a certain modification of the human attitude. Science modifies my primary perception fundamentally. This selection of a certain viewpoint in my encounter with reality is dependent on me and on the community of scientists. I am not forced by reality to change my original mode of being into a scientific concentration on only this or that aspect of reality. It is I who decide to prefer one objective aspect of reality to other aspects as the focus of my methodical investigation. There are many factors involved in the selection of a scientific viewpoint, such as an implicit or explicit philosophy, the "Zeit Geist", the practical needs of society, the temperament and disposition of the scientist concerned, social pressures, and the cultural language with its built-in preference for certain phenomena, values, and goals.

This selection of a specific objective moment of man's perception as a focus of intellectual attention is not yet a science, but only the possible beginning of a science. The delineation of the field of inquiry, however, is of the utmost importance and must be repeated many times during the development of the science in question. For it is not always clear in the beginning what the exact aims and proper methods of a specific science are. A science is fully established in its own right when its scientists have discovered which objective and which corresponding methodology make their science fundamentally different from all other actual and possible sciences. As long as this delineation is not yet achieved by a science, there is always the danger that its scientists may exceed the limits of their proper interest and competence. If a science does not clearly comprehend its own proper mode of questioning reality, it will be unaware of its own limits. Consequently, it may become involved in questions which do not pertain to its primary interest and which transcend its competence. This happened, for example, when theologians attempted to tell scientists that the earth was the center of the universe. It happened again when Sigmund Freud insisted that religion was only a neurosis.

Every science, then, should discover and make explicit the object of its fundamental interest. In this way, it will avoid intruding upon other special modes of grasping reality. Outside the boundaries of its own special interest, a science is not able to speak with authority. It may happen that, as the representative of a new science, I am not yet clear about the special interest, method, and area of investigation of my science. As a result, I and my fellow scientists may be attracted by the concerns, aims, and methods of another successful science which reveals a quite different profile of reality. I do not refer merely to being enlightened by the methods of another science or attempting to adapt them to my own domain of exploration. This is commendable and fruitful. Nor do I refer to the obvious fact that my research benefits from information obtained by other sciences. I have in mind the situation in which I, as the insecure representative of a young science, am absorbed by the objectives and methodology of an established older science to such a degree that I lose sight of the objectivated profile of my own scientific endeavor. Early physicists, for example, were at times philosophers of nature; alchemists became mythologists; and psychologists sometimes slipped into physiology or biology.

There is nothing blameworthy about shifting from one area of scientific investigation to another so long as the scientists are aware that they are leaving their former field of concentration. They should then make it explicit to themselves and to others that they are no longer speaking as, say, physicists or psychologists. However, they may mistakenly believe that they are still speaking as physicists or psychologists while they are in fact revealing philosophical, mythological, physiological, or biological aspects of reality. To be sure, what they reveal in this way may be extremely valuable for humanity and for the development of philosophy, mythology, physiology, and biology.

However, when psychologists who shift to another science stubbornly insist that in doing so they are revealing the psychological or behavioral aspect of human reality, they may considerably delay the development of psychology itself. This insistence is especially harmful when their methods are valid and impressive, when their findings foster scientific understanding of non-psychological aspects of man, when their communication of methods and results is lucid, convincing, and clear. The measure of their achievement may be the measure of postponement of the day on which psychology will discover itself as a science in its own right, with its own unambiguous fundamental interest which will render it irreducibly different from any other science of man. Many psychologists may give up the arduous endeavor of establishing the identity of their own science. They may lose the courage to bear the ambiguities, uncertainties, and awkward beginnings which are unavoidable when humanity embarks on a new science, a new adventure of exploration.

It is in a formal definition that a science explicitly states its own unique perception of reality, the object of its fundamental interest, and its proper mode of questioning the world. By discovering its own limits, a science not only avoids trespassing on the proper concern of another science, but also uncovers the specific area in which it should concentrate its effort. A clear awareness of their fundamental interest prevents scientists from dissipating their talents and energies in areas which do not pertain to their field.

Further Conditions of Scientific Development

A science is formed originally by a specific attitude of man toward a particular aspect of reality, but this attitude alone does not constitute a science. For it is quite possible for man to question an aspect of reality in a specific way without doing so in a scientific way. For example, a child acts in a naïve and primitive manner when he explores the mechanism of his father's watch, but no one would say that his efforts constitute a science.

At least four conditions must be fulfilled before I can dignify a specific mode of questioning reality with the name of science. In order that a way of knowing be considered scientific, it must be methodical, critical, communal, and integrational. A fifth condition must be added for the empirical sciences, namely observation and experience. Only when these conditions are present does a science exist in the proper sense of the term. Let us consider these five conditions briefly.

The Nature and Meaning of Science

My scientific concentration on a profile or aspect of reality differs from my casual, haphazard, or incidental attention in that it is planned, systematic, orderly, and coherent. It develops methods, tools, and techniques with which I can handle systematically the special profile of my scientific attention. My every-day knowledge is frequently naïve, inexact, and influenced by myth, folklore, and superstition. In daily life I have neither the time nor the ability to subject all my knowledge to critical evaluation. As a scientist, however, I critically evaluate every step in the process which leads to the uncovering of the aspect of reality I have selected.

As a scientist, moreover, I am not engaged in an isolated effort. I share in the fruits of the efforts of countless dedicated men of the past and the present. This communal aspect of science also makes possible the necessary inter-subjective check on my scientific work. I need this possibility of control and correction in order to prevent or to rectify the influence of my personal bias. My scientific endeavor also has an integrational aspect. I strive by nature for a coherent and orderly comprehension of the manifold discoveries of the community of scientists. The ultimate objective of every science is understanding and explanation. This is possible only on the basis of an explicit discovery and formulation of the unifying factors and universal characteristics which bind the disconnected facts related to the science into an ordered and comprehensive system. In every science, it is theory which performs this task of unification.

Psychology, for example, reveals two types of scientific theory, namely differential and comprehensive theories. A differential theory aims to bind together the data and insights which are discovered in a differential psychology such as psychoanalysis, behaviorism, or introspectionism. Comprehensive theory, in turn, integrates the theories and discoveries of the various differential psychologies. Every science is thus a methodical, critical, communal, and integrational investigation of certain well-defined moments of experience.

47

For the empirical sciences we must add the specific condition that the moment of perception selected as a focus of attention must always be observable by the senses. An empirical science may become predominantly theoretical, abstract, and quantifying, as in the case of quantum physics or learning theory in psychology. Yet it always starts from some original sense perception of my world or of my body as I find them in everyday life. There is no other basis from which science can arise. All that I know "scientifically" about the physical world is inferred from certain selected phenomena in the perceived world. This world remains my ultimate and only basis for statements about physical facts. My only way of exploring quantifiable, physical aspects of reality is that of observing objective perceptions and inferring from them the proper conclusions. This is true not only of physics but of all empirical sciences. My knowledge of physiology, for instance, depends upon my observations of what I call a body in direct perceptual experience. All my scientific constructs and observations are somehow contained in or derived from direct perception, and all scientific terms which I use in agreement with my fellow scientists ultimately refer to the same source. Immediate perception is the raw material of all sciences.

We may conclude that science is developed by methodical investigation of selected observable moments of perception; by critical evaluation of every one of its scientific procedures and discoveries; by the subjection of its results to the test of intersubjective agreement in the community of scientists; and finally by the integration of its insights and discoveries in differential and comprehensive theories.

CHAPTER TWO

THE SCIENCE OF PSYCHOLOGY

To discover what the science of psychology is, we must uncover the specific human interest which distinguishes it. Inseparably linked with this interest is the field of investigation which it constitutes. A precise view of this field will prevent the confusion of the specific object pole of psychology with that of any other science.

Our search for what psychology fundamentally is, however, can lead only to provisional conclusions. We can discover only what psychology is at the present stage of its historical development. No scientist knows *a priori* precisely how new discoveries may change our conception of psychology. A premature fixation concerning what this science should be would paralyze its spontaneous growth. In fact, any fixation at any time is premature insofar as the human existent can reach a relative but never a full and final maturity. This general statement is true of psychology as well as all modes of human existence.

The seemingly obvious method of discovering how psychology reveals itself today is observation of the activities of psychologists followed by explication of the specific common interest implicit in their scientific endeavors. It is really not surprising that the theoretical delineation of psychology as a specific mode of interest has been so long delayed by psychologists. It is not necessary for the work of the individual psychologist that he perceive clearly the viewpoint which he takes when he investigates behavior. His specific interest may remain almost totally implicit, absorbed as he is in his experiments or in the diagnosis and treatment of patients. His concrete empirical task itself may leave no time for reflection on what constitutes the essential direction of psychology as a whole.

The same observations may be made of any empirical science. Only when it is well established does it develop an explicit, general, theoretical branch which reflects on its foundations and integrates the activities and data of its scientists in the light of this reflection. The appearance of this unifying, theoretical reflection implies that a science has attained relative autonomy and become aware of itself. Only such a self-conscious science can clarify the confusing interests which obscured its identity during the earlier phases of its hesitant emergence. Many physicists of the past, for example, confused their science with a philosophy of nature which could not be proved or disproved by empirical methods. The coming of age of physics in theoretical physics has lessened this confusion.

Thus it is important for scientific psychology to make explicit the common viewpoint which is implicit in the endeavors of its scientists and which constitutes the science of psychology in the present phase of its evolution. When we observe psychologists in laboratories, clinics, and consulting rooms we become easily aware that they investigate the behavior of animal and man in various situations. Every empirical science requires an externally observable datum as its primary object pole of investigation; behavior is undoubtedly such a datum. When we analyze certain definitions of behavior critically, however, we perceive a contradiction between what psychologists do, or their "lived" psychology, and what some scientific theorists say that psychologists are doing.

Some theoretical scientists, for example, define behavior so comprehensively that any series of externally observable changes in any patricular object falls under their definition. In this case, one may speak indiscriminately of the behavior of molecules, snow, tulip bulbs, or children, a procedure which makes it difficult to distinguish psychology from any other science. A few scientific theorists, such as Harry Hollingworth and Rudolf Carnap, have been aware of this inference and consequently have defined many or even all sciences as sciences of behavior. Evidently, such a definition confuses psychology with other sciences; it does not describe the actual involvements of psychologists today. When we carefully observe the manifold activities of psychologists, we become aware that they almost invariabily study the behavior of animal or man in their laboratories and consulting rooms. No psychologist or psychiatrist up to the present has studied the "behavior" of stars or trees. However, even the restriction of the object of psychology to the behavior of animal and man is not sufficiently exact to prevent the possibility of a confusion of the object pole of psychology with that of other sciences; nor does it make explicit in a precise way the specific interest implicit in the activities of contemporary psychologists.

Behavior, to be sure, is an object of interest for persons as diverse as the beautician, the athletic trainer, the moralist, the philosopher, and the physiologist, as well as the psychologist. They all observe behavior, but their ways of perceiving it are indeed different. The beautician may observe that a certain manner of walking enhances the charm of a lady, while the athletic trainer may note that similar movements facilitate the development of certain muscles. The physiologist may focus his attention on the processes he observes in nerves, muscles, and organs, while the student of ethics may be interested in the moral intentions possibly implied in certain ways of walking. The philosopher, on the other hand, will establish what the behavior of walking is as behavior. The psychologist, finally, will concentrate his interest on that aspect of the activity of walking which we shall later clarify as intentional-functional-behavioral.

The example just given illustrates that our spontaneous, prereflective experience of any behavior implies the awareness of a variety of aspects of this behavior. Each of these aspects can be made explicit by a process of reflection and abstraction. Thus we can set a certain aspect of behavior apart, as it were, from the others in our experience. A scientist can select one of those aspects which he has abstracted from his experience of behavior and make it a specific object of study. Each aspect of behavior selected in this way points potentially to a new science of behavior. Every new science of behavior is thus necessarily different from every other science because it concentrates on a totally different feature. Moreover, it is determined in the development of its language, method, and frame of reference by the specific interest which constitutes this unique feature.

The various sciences of behavior are therefore so distinct that it is impossible for them to oppose one another so long as they remain within their own domains. It is obvious that observers can disagree with one another only when they speak about the same object of observation. When one observer is interested in rockets and another in rivers, there is no possibility of their contradicting each other so long as one reports on rockets and the other on rivers. These two observers move in different phenomenological worlds, in different universes of thought where they will never meet and therefore never confute each other. The same may be said of any two scientists pursuing different sciences of behavior.

Because these diverse perceptions of behavior are based on different points of view, they necessarily create different phenomenological worlds or systems of meaning. Every new manner of perception makes for a new world of meaning which remains inseparably linked to this perception and to the fundamental interest which underlies it. The beautician *as beautician,* therefore, can never affirm something which the athletic trainer denies; nor can the physiologist, so long as he remains within the limits of his special field, pronounce a judgment which the student of ethics, the philosopher, or the psychologist can refute from his respective point of view. Such a contradiction is in principle unthinkable. It is possible only when one of these experts, because of lack of clarity regarding his fundamental object of study, goes beyond the limits of his specialty, confusing two entirely different worlds of meaning. A psychologist who *as psychologist* makes physiological or philosophical statements about behavior can and should be refuted by physiological or philosophical experts. Similarly, a philosopher of behavior who ventures unwittingly into psychological explications of behavior may find himself in disagreement with the psychologist. Contradiction, however, remains impossible in principle so long as each expert moves only in his own field of scientific perception.

THE OBJECT POLE OF PSYCHOLOGY: INTENTIONAL-FUNCTIONAL BEHAVIOR

Our spontaneous experience of the behavior of animal and man implies an inexhaustible variety of aspects. Which of these aspects constitutes the object pole of psychology? When we make explicit the various interests of psychologists today in order to uncover those aspects of behavior toward which they implicitly direct themselves, the common object we discover is intentional-functional behavior.

The expression intentional-functional behavior represents *one Gestalt* abstracted from our spontaneous experience of the behavior of animal and man; it constitutes one unified object of investigation for the empirical psychologist. Therefore the intentional, functional, and behavioral aspects should never be perceived as if they were isolated entities. On the contrary, they are interdependent features of the one undivided object pole of psychology. These essential aspects of the object pole influence one another mutually and constantly. They represent an internal differentiation or articulation—not a separation—of one and the same object pole of psychology.

Even though there is no separation of these aspects of behavior, distinction among them is a necessary intellectual operation. Because of the limited, abstract nature of man's intellect, he can obtain a thorough scientific understanding of these aspects only by concentrating his research on one of them at a time. Therefore, the distinction among these aspects is due more to the limitation of man's intellect than to the object pole of his study.

This same innate limitation of the approach to scientific knowledge accounts for the fact that an individual psychologist or a certain group of psychologists may be predominantly interested in the intentional, or the functional, or the behavioral aspects of human and animal behavior as a specialized object of study. Every empirical psychologist studies intentional-functional behavior in at least one of these perspectives.

Some psychologists, however, such as the comprehensive-theoretical and the practicing psychologists, are concerned with all three aspects of the object of psychology in their concrete living unity. Comprehensive theoretical psychology strives for an integrating, over-all view of behavior. Therefore, it is concerned precisely with the unity of and the relations among the intentional, functional, and behavioral aspects. It presents the unity of human behavior. The theoretical psychologist develops scientific constructs in a constant dialogue with the data provided by phenomenological, functional, and behavioral psychology.

It is clear that behavior as a field of study for the contemporary psychologist requires more precise definition in order to distinguish it from behavior as an object of study for other scientists. We have proposed, therefore, to define the specific object of study for the psychologist as intentional-functional behavior of animal and man. We have suggested that this qualified object pole of study corresponds with that in which the majority of recognized psychologists are daily engaged. The behavioral aspect of psychology may be defined as *an essential aspect of the object pole of psychology, consisting of the whole of objectively observable modes of animal and of human response to situations, which manifests the intentionality and functionality of the subject.* The meaning of this definition will be clarified in the following discussion of the terms "intentionality" and "functionality".

INTENTIONALITY

The first part of our definition of the behavioral aspect of the object pole of psychology describes behavior as the whole of objectively observable modes of animal and of human response to a situation. Many psychologists would consider this part of our definition as the complete definition of psychology.

They would find it unnecessary and even undesirable to add that observable responses should in some way manifest intentionality and functionality. This addition, however, we maintain to be crucial for the validity of the definition of behavior as the specific field of study for the psychologist. Spasmodic vomiting, for example, when *merely* a consequence and a symptom of food poisoning, would be an objectively observable mode of animal or of human response to a situation. Yet such a response is of interest to the physiologist or medical expert, but not to the psychologist. In other words, not all kinds of observable responses lend themselves to psychological investigation. Only that kind of behavior can be the object pole of scientific psychology which is open to study not only by means of biological, physiological, physical, or philosophical methods, but also by means of typical psychological methods. Precisely what kind of behavior would this be?

Let us cite a simple case. A monkey attempts to reach a banana near its cage. After trial and error, it obtains the banana by the manipulation of an iron rod which has been placed in its cage by an experimenter. This behavior of the monkey affects us immediately as being different in kind from the spasmodic vomiting behavior of an animal after food poisoning. One of the characteristics which we perceive in the food-getting behavior of the monkey is that the whole animal, the animal as tending subject, is involved in this behavior. Another feature is that the animal as subject is tending toward something that is not yet itself, something that promises to fulfill certain needs and therefore acquires the character of a goal of behavior. An attitude of food-directedness is embodied and manifested in the behavior of grasping for food.

We may change this experimental situation by placing the iron rod under an electric charge. The monkey suffers shock when touching the rod and now manifests avoidance behavior in regard to it. A new mode of behavior has been evoked as a response to this threatening situation. This behavior, however, is again characterized by a directedness or orientation. In this case, it is a tending away from the object concerned.

In neither case does the orientation of the monkey reveal itself to our immediate experience as blind, automatic, mechanical, relatively static, or built-in directedness as in the case of the vomiting responses of a food-poisoned animal. The orientation represented by the experiments with the monkey is highly variable; it changes with the varying experience of the striving animal. In other words, some kind of "lived" experience appears in the changing modes of directedness which are exteriorized in the tending behavior. Whether this experience is conscious or only "lived", the experiential quality is present.

We may conclude that the typical behavior which forms the field of study for the psychologist always implies a directing experience of the subject toward some reality, or its engagement in some reality that is not itself. We shall call this quality of directing experience or involvement *intentionality,* and the behavior that demonstrates this quality *intentional behavior.*

This intentionality seems to be present in animal behavior in a different way than it is present in man. The animal behaves *as if* it has recognized certain realities as such in an explicit way. But the animal cannot recognize these realities in an explicit human way. The tending experience of the animal is only toward biologically meaningful Gestalts of stimuli which are given in its biological world and which evoke certain responses based on aroused instinctual needs. Therefore, intentionality in animal and in man is not similar but analogous. Man is intentional in the most proper and the deepest sense. The intentionality of the animal seems to be a shadow or an image of man's intentionality.

INTENTIONALITY AND THE NATURE OF MAN

Intentionality in man seems to be so bound up with his very essence that a deep phenomenological insight into his nature is necessary to clarify the character and scope of his intentionality. Therefore, we shall discuss intentionality as a fundamental feature of human existence. As we shall demonstrate later, no science is developed without a basis of axiomatic assumptions which can be neither proved nor disproved by the empirical methods of the science itself. These assumptions are usually built-in, as it were, in the methodology of the science, which always implies a certain axiomatic view of nature and of knowledge. A comparatively new science, such as psychology, must make explicit its implicit assumptions in order to expose them to critical evaluation.

One of the implicit assumptions of psychology is that man is born with a potential openness or perceptivity for reality as it manifests itself in him and his surroundings. This natural dynamic perceptivity enables man to discover a variety of meanings in the manifold life situations within which he encounters reality under its many aspects. These meanings are dynamic, that is, they tend to initiate psychological functioning and behaving. A man who perceives a situation as threatening, for example, will feel and act differently from one who understands a situation as pleasant or amusing. Therefore, the study of perception of reality, of meanings and intentions, is of central importance for the understanding of behavior. The fact that man tends to discover varied aspects and concrete meanings in reality is due to his very nature: man *is* always and necessarily intentional; he *is* orientation, directedness to the world; he *is* potential openness for all-that-is.

The very possibility of hallucinations, illusions, and delusions confirms this basic fact of human existence. It is so essential for man to "intend" a reality, a world, that he is forced to create some kind of delusional universe if the surrounding world becomes too threatening for him because of his emotional problems. This reality-directed involvement which man *is*, is not necessarily an *explicit* awareness of his "lived" reality. For man usually experiences reality initially in a pre-reflective or pre-conscious way. In other words, the actualized intentionality of man is first of all "lived" experience. Man may express this primary "lived" experience in judgments. When he does so, he makes expressly conscious that which was at first implicit awareness. We may call this experience reflective intentionality. Thus man is always basically intentional, either implicitly or explicitly.

This fundamental intentionality of man actualizes itself, however, in many and varied involvements in his encounter with the world. For reality itself manifests innumerable aspects giving rise to a potentially infinite number of meanings. No man, therefore, can perceive all the aspects of reality or exhaust all its possible meanings. Actually, man is always limited in his presence to reality. He is restricted in his modes of perception by the structure of his body and his senses. He is also circumscribed by time and space because he belongs to a specific culture, which is in a certain phase of its development, and which has embodied its traditional intentionalities in a specific language. He is constricted, moreover, in his locations and surroundings. In addition, he himself limits his actual perception by the individual *interests* which he chooses and develops in his personal history. His actual intentionality is further restricted by his practical commitment to a world of work or a profession. Finally, man is limited by reflective or pre-reflective needs, desires, drives, and conflicts and by the particular phase of psycho-physiological development which he has reached at any given moment.

In short, man *is* a radical or fundamental intentionality directed toward all reality. His actual intentions, however, are always limited though amazing in variety. It is the business of the philosopher to dwell on the characteristic openness of man for being. The psychologist, however, studies the forms and contents of actual intentions as they appear in the functioning and behavior of man.

We are now ready to define precisely the term *intentional* as it is used within the context of our definition of psychology. *Intentional refers to those reflective and pre-reflective modes of experiential involvement in any reality whatsoever which are somehow manifest in behavior.* The latter part of our definition, which states that the modes of intentionality which the psychologist studies should be in some way "manifest in behavior" requires a brief clarification.

We have already seen in our discussion of science that an empirical science is concerned with data which are given in sense perception. Therefore, intentionality can be an object of empirical psychology only if it is present in some way in patterns of behavior which can be observed by the senses; or in observable products of this behavior such as language, literature, art, social institutions, and cultural customs. These latter bear within themselves the *sediments* of past intentional behavior. Psychology as an empirical science aims at the understanding of all sense-perceived behavior by the investigation of its determinants. The chief determinant of behavior is intentionality; for behavior without intentionality is not behavior but a mechanical process. Consequently, the specific object of the empirical science of psychology is not intentionality as such, but intentional behavior whether manifest in patterns of behavior or in their observable products.

Intentionality as such is an object of study for the philosopher. The theorist in psychology is naturally interested, however, in the ideas of the philosopher who explores the essence of human intentionality in the light of his study of being. The theoretical psychologist considers the relevance of these philosophical concepts for his own theoretical constructs, which he develops in a dialogue with the data of empirical psychology. At times, he may even borrow some of the concepts of the philosopher if these are in conspicuous harmony with the data and laws discovered by the empiricist. But these philosophical views remain for him only assumptions or borrowed hypothetical constructs, which he *as a psychologist* can neither prove nor disprove by means of his own empirical methods. Similarly, he is interested in the studies of the physiologist, which throw light on other conditions of intentional behavior which lie outside the proper domain of psychology. Here, too, he may borrow some of the findings of the physiologist, which likewise remain for him only assumptions which he can neither prove nor disprove through his own science of psychology.

Certain psychologists specialize in the study of the intentional aspect of behavior. They become experts in the methodical and critical explication of the experiences which appear in behavior, and they attempt to establish their intersubjective validity. This special field of psychology is called *phenomenological psychology*.

FUNCTIONALITY

The second essential aspect of the object pole of psychology is functionality which, together with the intentional and behavioral aspects, co-constitutes concrete animal and human behavior. The fact that functionality is a fundamental element in the actual areas of interest of psychologists may be illustrated by the experiment with the monkey cited above. The food-getting behavior of the animal implies an intentionality, an experiential involvement in securing a certain kind of food. The psychologist, however, is interested in much more than this intentionality. He may ask himself many other questions: "How is the intentional behavior of this animal related to outside stimulation, physio-psychological conditions, past behavior, instinctual-biological makeup, and spatial and temporal conditions? By means of what processes and functional structures does this intentionality become observable behavior? How is this intentionality related to other intentionalities? How does behavior reinforce the intentionality? How does intentionality realize itself by changing the environment of the animal? How does this environment, while changing under the impact of intentional behavior, in turn influence further behavior?" These are only a few of a potentially endless series of *how* problems evoked in the student of intentional behavior.

This wide breadth of interest of the empirical psychologist is even more evident in his study of man. The psychologist is better acquainted with the intentional and functional behavior of man because it is his own behavior. When a psychologist studies the intentionality of human love, for example, he first observes its presence in certain perceived or recorded patterns of behavior with which love is identified. His explication of the love which is implicitly present in the behavior of people may presuppose a verbal or even written description of his own love experience. Through such an account, the psychologist transforms his own experience of love into an observable behavioral product which can be compared methodically and critically with exteriorizations of similar intentionalities of love in other people. But the empirical psychologist will not stop here. He will ask himself how the intentionality of love came about. How does it develop under certain conditions in the environment? What does it mean for the other intentionalities of the subject, such as his anxiety, hate, fear, shyness, happiness, sexuality, and emotionality? How does it affect his behavior in various situations in the family, school, office, and places of entertainment? In this case, also, there emerges a never finished series of *how* questions which the psychologist attempts to answer by means of experiments, questionnaires, tests, clinical observations, analyses—in short, by all observational and experimental methods which are available to him or which he himself develops, if necessary, for the research in question.

The search for intentional behavior is predominantly a *what* question. The search for the relationships between various intentional patterns of behavior; between intentional behavior and situations; between intentionality and the other two essential aspects of behavior; between intentionalities themselves; and between past, present, and future patterns of intentional behavior, situations, and intentionalities is not primarily a *what* question. It is predominantly a *how* question, a search for working relationships. In other words, the psychologist is interested not only in the *what* of intentional behavior, but also in its functional aspect.

Functionality, to be sure, is only one aspect of the object pole of psychology. Because it is merged inseparably with the intentional aspect of behavior, we use a hyphen between the terms "intentional" and "functional" to express their essential unity. This unity explains why psychological functioning is always dynamically present in its functional-behavioral realization in a situation. There is no real separation between the two, but only an intellectual distinction which is dependent on the presence of certain articulations in behavior.

Similarly, the psychological functional structures which enable man to realize his intentionality in behavior are essentially different from physical, physiological, and biological functional structures. Numerous philosophers and psychologists—Bergson, Husserl, Heidegger, Merleau-Ponty, Lavelle, Nogue, von Weiszäcker, Minkowski, Strasser, Buytendijk, Straus, Linschoten, Graumann, Plessner, James, Stern, Hönigswald, Pradines, Koffka, and Van der Horst—have demonstrated that the "lived" space and the "lived" time structures which enable the intentional subject to function psychologically are essentially different from geometrical space and mathematical time structures in the framework of which the objects of physics and technology function.

FUNCTIONALITY AND THE NATURE OF MAN

We have related the various intentionalities of man to one another and integrated them in one hypothetical basic construct, namely the fundamental intentionality which we assume to be identified with man's essence. An analogous statement may be made concerning man's psychological functionality. For when we attempt to discover just how this functionality is rooted in man's nature, we are no longer in the purely empirical stage of psychology. We are moving into the area of fundamental assumptions which are made explicit in that branch of comprehensive-theoretical psychology which we call theory of foundations.

Let us assume that man *is* intentional functionality. This hypothetical assumption provides us with a useful explanatory foundation for the unity of intentionality and functionality in his behavior. For man's intentionality is not devoid of dynamism. The hypothetical construct of intentionality means not only that man is "*in*-the-world" but also that he is "*at*-the-world." Man's intentionality is not a static quality but a dynamic tendency. Therefore, man's subjective experiential involvement in reality implies that he, as selfbody unity, tends toward reality in a behavioral way. His intentionality constantly spurs him on to realize himself by partaking in reality as it manifests itself, assimilating and appropriating it. On the other hand, the same dynamic intentionality drives him to express himself in his surrounding reality, to insert himself meaningfully in the world, to humanize the world.

According to this assumption, man's functionality is the essential dynamic aspect of his intentionality. And because of the fact that man *is* always a bodily subjectivity, both intentionality and functionality are inseparably present in behavior, which is a bodily mode of being in the world.

To be sure, psychology does not dwell on intentional functionality insofar as it is an essential feature of man's nature. Psychology is not philosophy. However, theoretical psychology may use the philosophical concept of "essential functionality" as one of its hypothetical explanatory principles. Such a concept may be useful for the theoretical integration of the concrete intentional-functional-behavioral relationships which the psychologist discovers in his empirical research. What the psychologist as empiricist is chiefly concerned with, however, is man's concrete intentional-behavioral functioning in family, school, business, church, and other life situations. He is interested in the concrete normal and abnormal developments of this functioning and in the development of psychological functional structures. He is also concerned with the organismic and environmental conditions of this development.

Experimental psychologists specialize in the study of these functional relationships. Some of them are interested predominantly in the functional relationships between stimulating situation and behavior. We may call them behavioral-experimental psychologists insofar as their interest emphasizes the behavioral aspect. Other experimental psychologists search primarily for the functional relationships between the intentional aspect of behavior and the situation, or between the intentional aspects of various kinds of behavior. We may identify this group as clinical, social, or humanistic experimental psychologists. The specialized interests and endeavors of both groups of functional psychologists are necessary for the progress of their science. The same may be said of the scientific endeavors of phenomenological psychologists. The essential limitation of man's scientific way of knowing—which is always knowledge by abstraction—makes it necessary for psychology to evolve by differentiating itself in specialties.

At times, the expert who is committed to one or the other abstract aspect of behavior may lose sight of the whole. But even the overestimation of the value of his own specialty may be advantageous for the development of psychology as a whole insofar as it stimulates his complete dedication to his own field of study. However, this one-sidedness will remain fruitful for the development of psychology only when it is balanced by a well-developed branch of comprehensive theoretical psychology. The latter specializes in the whole, and keeps the dialogue open between comprehensive theoretical constructs and assumptions on the one hand, and differential theories and data of phenomenological, experimental, and clinical psychologists on the other.

We are now prepared to define precisely the functional component of behavior. *The functional aspect of behavior is an essential aspect of the object pole of psychology which refers to an individual totality of changes elicited by a reflective or prereflective intentionality, and which co-constitutes with this intentionality certain objectively observable modes of behavior.*

APPLIED PSYCHOLOGY

The common denominator of basic interest implicitly present in the scientific endeavors of recognized empirical psychologists is incorporated in the statement that psychology is the science of intentional-functional behavior. The practice of applied psychology is specifically related to this definition.

We use the term *applied psychology* to refer to the work of psychiatrists and psychotherapists and of clinical, educational, and industrial psychologists. An efficient application of the science of psychology to the problems of daily life presupposes an understanding of the intentionality and functionality of the individuals concerned and of the embodiment of these characteristics in patterns of behavior. It is clear that the methods and findings of phenomenological, functional, and behavioral psychologies facilitate this kind of understanding. For example, the discoveries of these psychologies concerning the intentionality, functionality, and behavioral patterns of specific age and cultural groups can obviously enlighten the practicing psychologist in his observation of human beings.

The practicing psychologist, however, does not restrict himself to the application of the methods and findings of academic psychology. He frequently involves himself in a type of research which is more directly related to the understanding of particular individuals and groups. He may also dedicate himself to the development of instruments and techniques. Some of these psychological techniques aim at the exteriorization of inner experiences; others foster change in the behavior of animal and man. An example of the first is the evolvement of techniques for interviewing and testing; examples of the latter are the development of therapeutic techniques and of machines for programmed learning.

When we first consider the highly individualized type of research which aims at clarification of the behavior of patients and clients, it may seem that such individual understanding does not relate to the object pole of psychology as it has been defined. A large number of psychiatrists, as well as clinical and analytical psychologists, daily study the disturbed experiences of patients. It seems to the casual observer that these clinicians are interested in unperceivable experiences and not in the behavior which expresses these intentionalities. A closer observation, however, reveals that they too study the experience and functionality of man insofar as these are objectivated in the observable behavior or in behavioral products such as free associations, test protocols, narration of dreams, facial and postural expressions, play behavior, role playing, oral or written reports of experiencing, and other exteriorizations of intentional-functional involvement.

The other type of research in applied psychology, as stated above, is the development of instruments and techniques for the behavioral exteriorization of inner experiences, or for the promotion of change in the intentional-functional behavior of individuals and groups. It is our contention not only that this type of research is proper to psychology, but also that it contributes at least as much to the growth of the science as academic research does, although in a different fashion.

Academic research in its pure form discovers and makes explicit intentional-functional-behavioral relationships already implicit in animal and human behavior. Applied research, on the other hand, is concerned with the invention of instruments and techniques which will change behavior. Thus academic psychology and applied psychology appear as two distinct and complementary areas of one science. While academic research refers primarily to the uncovering of the innumerable features and implicit relationships of intentional-functional behavior, applied psychology as research aims at the discovery of methods of combining these features and relationships in such a way that new constellations may arise which will promote change in behavior.

For example, the development of an efficient psychological technique for animal conditioning in a zoo or circus implies the combination of certain elements already discovered in animal behavior, such as need for certain rewards, fear of certain punishments, and typical relationships to the person who feeds the animal. These characteristics of animal behavior may be combined in such a way that a new constellation arises which cannot be found as such in nature. Particular rewards and punishments administered by a certain trainer who daily feeds the animal are associated, for example, with specific performances of the animal. This new constellation promotes changes in the behavior of the animal, which can now learn to exhibit a certain behavior when the trainer uses a particular technique.

Again, the discovery of a new constellation may refer to the invention of a psychological *instrument* which cannot be found as such in intentional-functional behavior; for example, a teaching machine or a brain computer. It may also refer to a *process* or technique which promotes intentional-functional-behavioral changes more efficiently and rapidly than psychological forces as given in man's nature. An example might be a psychological technique of salesmanship or of efficient management which is a new constellation of human characteristics and their relationships. Such a technique may depend, for example, on the arousal of certain basic human needs which could not be achieved so quickly without the planned psychological stimulation.

The distinction between academic and applied research in psychology, however, is relative. For the progress of the science of psychology is promoted by the discovery not only of hitherto unknown features of intentional-functional behavior, but also of new aspects of those already known. The two are closely connected. The discovery of new phenomena in academic psychology is almost always the result of taking a fresh look at what is already known. For example, the new view that behavior *is* at the same time both intentionality and functionality gave rise to the discovery that phenomenological and experimental psychology should be integrated as mutually complementary sources of the understanding of behavior.

An original approach to behavior also lies at the basis of the discovery of new psychological instruments and techniques in applied psychology. The invention of the practicing psychologist consists in the discovery of previously unknown possibilities in the patterns of intentional-functional behavior in concrete problem situations. A case in point is that of the industrial psychologist who develops a system of personal rewards for dedicated workers which enhances their feeling of being personally appreciated and thereby improves their motivation for work, which in turn increases the quality and quantity of their output. The first industrial psychologist who conceived of this efficient system may have been a practicing scientist who utilized the well known law of intentional-functional behavior that man is motivated by personal appreciation of his performance. He saw the possibility of a "built-in" appreciation in the form of a system of typical rewards applied in the industrial setting.

67

He tested this hypothesis scientifically and discovered that it worked in a significant number of cases.

It may have happened, however, that this working system was discovered first as a result of trial and error; and that only later, as a consequence of this development, the functional relation between personal reward and enhanced performance was discovered. There are numerous examples of the latter process in the development of psychoanalysis and psychotherapy. For example, methods of changing pre-reflective experiences into verbalized, reflective ones were at first discovered during the practice of therapy; only later, as a consequence of these discoveries, were the functional relationships between repression and forgetting uncovered. Another example, which in this case refers to a psychological instrument rather than a technique, is the invention of the brain computer. The use of this instrument, and especially its feedback circuits, led indirectly to a new view on certain neural processes.

Discovery in academic research and invention in applied research, therefore, are closely connected, or rather, they compenetrate each other. The inventions of the applied psychologist require new modes of seeing intentional-functional behavior in certain life situations. The discoveries of the academic psychologist, in turn, demand the invention of technical psychological methods. These technical means required by the academic psychologist are not only those which have a material character, such as laboratory instruments. Discovery in psychology requires not only empirical instruments to make new observations possible and to test and analyze the functional relationships of behavior, but also conceptual instruments or constructs, models by which newly acquired knowledge of behavior can be properly represented.

Academic psychology is always directed to the understanding of the intentional-functional behavior of animal and man. Applied psychology, on the other hand, aims at organizing the data of this behavior in concrete situations, in such a way that they facilitate an effective control of the behavior with respect to the needs and desires of man. The preceding discussion demonstrates, however, that there is an essential interconnection and interdependence of academic and applied research in psychology.

We may conclude that applied psychology is in conformity with our definition of the science of psychology, not only because it adapts the methods and findings of psychology to the problems of life, but also because it contributes in an original way to the growth of this science.

THEORETICAL PSYCHOLOGY

The aim of this chapter has been to uncover and define the specific fundamental interest of man which constitutes the science of psychology. The criterion for the validity of our definition has been the explicit or implicit presence of this interest as the common denominator in the various recognized areas of psychology. As a result of our investigation, we have arrived at the conclusion that psychology, at least at the present stage of its historical development, is the science of intentional-functional behavior.

We are now ready to consider psychology from the genetic point of view, to ask ourselves precisely how such a science of behavior unfolds itself. What are its phases? The science of psychology is a mode of human existence; it is a special mode of a more general mode of existence which is the pursuit of abstract knowledge. Science as an abstract human mode of knowing necessarily implies a process of becoming, during which the scientific endeavor differentiates itself in phases. Starting from the experience of single data and their immediate interrelationships, science develops in theoretical complexity in its explication of the increasing multiplicity of relationships which it discovers in an underlying unity. This complex activity of science is unavoidable because the human mode of knowing reality is not one single, intuitive, and comprehensive act which grasps reality at once; it is a gradual, slow uncovering of reality by means of a process of repeated abstraction and synthesis of the knowledge obtained in abstraction. For psychology, this principle implies that the reality of intentional-functional behavior is revealed to the scientist only through a step by step process.

One of the first necessary steps to be taken in the science of psychology is the observation of behavior. But human observation itself is a complex act. It is not the pure sense activity which at first sight it seems to be. A minimum of rational thought or theory is always implied in observation as its core and guiding principle. This theory may be hidden from the reflective awareness of the observer. He may have absorbed his naïve theory pre-reflectively while he assimilated the cultural views permeating the language and the customs which he adopted from early childhood. Nevertheless, some theory is always present—no matter how implicit—guiding all his observations.

The original theoretical-empirical observation of intentional-functional behavior is only a first phase in the development of the science of psychology. This natural observation must be extended and perfected by the use of instruments which extend the power of human observation, and by the performance of experiments which open up new areas of controlled observation not directly given as such in the appearance of behavior in daily life. Another early step in the practice of psychology is the phenomenological explication of the experiences evoked during natural and controlled observation. Following this analysis, further theoretical reflection and observation lead to the establishment of psychological hypotheses which can be verified in controlled observation or experimentation.

At the same time, this vertical differentiation of psychology into many phases, each with its own methods of research, is accompanied by a horizontal differentiation into many single areas limited by special fields of concentration, such as animal psychology, physiological psychology, and developmental psychology. These single areas of psychology are differentiated in turn into special domains. Developmental psychology, for example, becomes child, adolescent, adult, and old age psychology.

Moreover, each of these single domains may differentiate further into new fields. Also, we may find in each of them a variety of specialized theories which direct observational and experimental research within the domain concerned.

Finally, the rich accumulation of observations, phenomenological explications, functional relationships, and differential theories, which are developed in the many areas of psychology and accepted by the significant majority of experts in these fields, must be integrated into a general, provisional theory of psychology.

Every one of the developmental phases of psychology has a necessary dynamic function in the evolution of this science. Moreover, none of the research activities pertaining to any one phase can be disregarded without distorting the science of psychology as a whole. None of the phases is ever completed, for man will never exhaust the reality of intentional-functional behavior. If there is any hierarchy among these phases of development, it is only one of natural priority by which one kind of research is necessarily presupposed by another, the results of which it utilizes. Direct or implicit phenomenological explication, for example, necessarily precedes a scientifically responsible formulation of hypotheses concerning the impact of social factors on the response of subjects to a specific stimulus presented to them in a certain social situation. The necessary function of each phase in the dynamic evolution of psychology defines the value of its careful study. Our purpose is not, however, a detailed study of the science of psychology in all its necessary phases of development, but the exposition of the nature, aim, meaning, and function of existential and of anthropological psychology. These belong primarily to only one developmental phase of empirical psychology, namely comprehensive theoretical psychology.

Consequently, following the discussion of science in general in our first chapter and of the science of psychology in particular in the present chapter, we shall next consider one specific phase of the science of intentional-functional behavior, that is, comprehensive theoretical psychology. Just as some grasp of the meaning of science and of scientific psychology is necessary in order to understand theoretical psychology, so a clear conception of theoretical psychology is necessary in order to comprehend the existential and anthropological developments of theoretical psychology. The understanding of these recent developments of theoretical psychology is the final aim of this book.

CHAPTER THREE

PSYCHOLOGY AND THEORY

To clarify the theoretical mode of existence in the science of psychology, we must first of all consider the role of theory in science in general. Science, as a universal human enterprise, must be rooted somehow in the possibilities of the existence of man the scientist. If there were no potentiality for science in man's existence, science could not emerge in his evolution. But precisely how is the scientific attitude rooted in the existence of man? An answer to this question may constitute a fundamental insight into the role that theory plays in all science.

Science falls among those activities of man which are called "cultural" as distinguished from "biological." The cultural modes of the life of man are rooted in his existence, that is, in his basic characteristic of standing out in reality as it reveals itself. Every cultural enterprise can be traced, therefore, to some interest inherent in man's existence. Such interests are activated when existence differentiates itself in various modes of involvement during man's many encounters, or dialogues, with concrete situations. To ex-ist or to stand out is to be in *interested* contact with the world. Thus, man's cultural activities are the development of various possibilities of *interested* involvement.

We may speak of such modalities of contact as perceiving, feeling, loving, striving, hearing, acting, contemplating, touching, thinking, experimenting, and expressing. Almost every integrated appearance of human behavior is a combination of various modalities of contact. Medical behavior, for example, integrates the modalities of observing the patient, touching him, considering his symptoms, asking relevant questions, recalling and applying medical knowledge and experience, and verbalizing meaningful advice. These modalities constitute the structural unity of medical behavior. In other words, various modalities of existence are incorporated in the medical mode. A common purpose organizes these modalities in such a way that they constitute one mode of existence. All modalities that make up the medical mode of existence, therefore, are directed by the common medical project of diagnosing and curing the patient. *A mode of existence is thus a special structure of the modalities of existence. The unifying character of this structure is determined by a specific interest developed by the existent in the course of his existing.*

In almost any society, one finds individuals who have developed similar modes of existence. These persons feel attracted to one another because of their common interests. They consider the possibility of pooling their potentialities and developing together the mode of existence which they have in common. Man's existence is coexistence. This implies, among other things, that man seeks fellowship with those in whom he discovers kindred interests. The evolution of human existence is accelerated by the fact that men thus discover one another in the cultivation of common concerns.

Science is a mode of contacting reality. A man may specialize his existence or his being in contact with the world in such a manner that the scientific way of contacting reality becomes a predominant mode of existence for him. Other men may join him in this specialization of existence in the scientific mode. At such a moment of human evolution, science is manifested as a cultural enterprise. This pooling of potentialities leads to an accelerated evolution of the scientific dimension of human existence.

Psychology and Theory

ATTITUDINAL CONSTITUENTS OF THE
SCIENTIFIC MODE OF EXISTENCE

Scientific knowledge depends on the perception of the phenomena which are given to the senses. This does not mean that naïve seeing, hearing, or touching is sufficient for the development of science, which presupposes *thoughtful* observation and manipulation. It is precisely thought or theory which changes naïve, spontaneous sensing into scientific attention. Thoughtless awareness can never be called science. Therefore, thought or theory is as essential to the scientific mode of existence as is bodily perception. Thought embodies itself in the searching hands and eyes of the scientist.

Thought or naïve theory is already present in the child in his quest for knowledge. The attempts of the child to stand out knowingly in the world gradually become organized and meaningful. His curiosity, his inner seeking, manifest themselves in the manner in which he handles his toys and other objects that come his way. His behavior reveals to the observer that he is developing a certain effective way of acting. We may even say that primitive, prescientific theories inform and direct the searching movement and observation of the curious child. These naïve bits of theory are based on his experiences. They are, as such, a far cry from the well-organized theories of contemporary science, which are continually put to the empirical test. But, despite the differences, the theoretical attitudes of the scientist and the child are basically identical. Scientific theory is nothing other than the critical development, organization, and specialization of the naïve theoretical attitude which we observe in the child—the attitude of bodily observation and manipulation of reality. The two attitudes are inseparable. Man *is* an experimenter by nature, and man *is* by nature a theorist.

We may add that the technical attitude, too, is a characteristic manifestation of man's being. Man's thoughtful standing-out into reality, his observation and manipulation of the world, enables him to perceive things as actual or potential tools. Observe, for example, the naïve technical attitude of the child who discovers with delight that he can use one toy to fashion another and who proudly applies his thoughtful observation. He changes his little world intelligently while embodying his insight in a technical operation.

We may conclude that thoughtful observation, empirical manipulation, and technical application are rooted in the fundamental structure of man, which is his existence, or his being involved with others bodily in the world. It is for this reason that we find manifestations of these fundamental attitudes in men of all times and in cultures at all stages of development.

I have stated that man stands out in the world together with all other men who coexist with him. Man's natural coexistence explains the heights reached by science and technology in our day. Generations of men have cooperated in the gradual development and the critical refinement of the scientific attitude—a growing mastery of the world of mankind. Science and technology today embody the impressive acquisitions of the evolution of the human race.

It is not impossible that mankind may stand today at the threshold of a golden age. A prerequisite for such a unique period of harmonious progress would be the reintegration of the scientific attitude as a whole. With all its potentiality for integration, the scientific attitude is still split into one-sided components.

REINTEGRATION OF ATTITUDINAL CONSTITUENTS

The scientific attitude consists of various constituents, such as the theoretical, observational, manipulative, and effectuating attitudes. We may call these necessary and sufficient constituents. When one of them is totally lacking, we do not have the scientific attitude in its fullness. In this sense, every attitudinal constituent is *necessary*. On the other hand, these constituents are *sufficient* for the makeup of the fundamental scientific mode of existence. To be sure, other special attitudes may be adopted for certain kinds of science, for example, the mathematical attitude for physics. The mathematical attitude, however, is not a necessary constituent of the scientific mode of existence as such.

The scientific attitude necessarily contains various attitudinal constituents. This does not imply, however, that all these constituents are at all times equally and fully present. Ordinarily, one of the attitudinal constituents is dominant, while other constituents remain implicit. The attitude of scientific application, for example, is explicit in the engineer who constructs a bridge. At the same time, however, theoretical and empirical attitudes are implicit in his engineering insofar as the engineer draws on the theoretical and empirical findings of physics.

The history of science in Western culture is the history of the changing prevalence of the various attitudinal constituents of the scientific mode of existence. In the course of this history, every attitudinal constituent of the scientific mode of existence has had an opportunity to differentiate itself during its prevalence in the culture.

The irregular development of each constituent of the scientific mode of existence is due in part to the primordial situation of man. Even a casual view of the historical evolution of science reveals that the development of one constituent has always presupposed the development of another. Technical appliances for airplanes, for example, were elaborated only after a period of one-sided development of theoretical-empirical physics. The latter, in turn, developed only after a long process of one-sided philosophical theorizing on the nature of knowledge and matter.

A more basic reason for this irregular, though lawful, development of the scientific mode of existence, however, is the typical primordial structure of man himself. Man's existence is a bodily one. He is necessarily limited in space and time. He is limited in his energy, his insight, and his historical situation, which forces him to specialized preoccupations. A primitive tribe which must survive in the jungle has neither time nor energy for philosophical theorizing; a differentiated civilization which must develop complicated techniques to ensure its survival is also limited in philosophical theorizing. Man's bodily limitations allow historical situations to play an important role in the evolution of science. Therefore, the demands of historical situations have initiated, accelerated, or retarded developments in the scientific mode of existence.

This historical influence does not, however, explain a certain lawfulness observable in the development of science. We note, for example, that accelerated development of efficient observation and manipulative intervention is regularly preceded by the development of scientific theorizing. Such lawfulness in the characteristic evolution of science is due to the inner structure of the scientific mode of existence. The latter, in turn, is dependent on the primordial structure of man. There is only one order in which empirical science can be pursued: philosophical and scientific theorizing; sense observation; and concrete, manipulative intervention. These three together form the characteristic mode of man's scientific standing-out in the world. There exists, moreover, a hierarchical order within this triad insofar as a considerable development of the second or third phase presupposes a certain development of the first or second.

We may conclude that the evolution of the scientific mode of existence necessarily requires a temporary distinction of its attitudinal constituents. This distinction leads to the specialized and concentrated evolution of each constituent. Several stages must be passed before the attitudinal constituents of the scientific mode of existence can be reunited. In the naïve scientific mode of existence the three phases of theory, sense observation, and concrete manipulation developed together as a natural unity. But, in the course of history, these attitudinal constituents had to develop separately before they could again be reunited.

78

Psychology and Theory

A deeper insight into the prescientific view of prehistoric man may help us to understand more clearly the meaning and development of science. We need to be precisely aware of the differences between our daily postscientific perception of reality and the prescientific views which dominated primitive existence, for our seemingly "spontaneous" perception is indeed pervaded by unconsciously assimilated scientific views which are embodied in our culture.

When we inquire how primitive man looked at reality, we are impressed by the fact that his view of "what is" lacked the kind of critical objectivity which prevails in our scientific and postscientific perceptions. The absence of this kind of scientific objectivity does not, however, imply the absence of all objectivity, for even primitive man thought and talked about nature in abstract concepts and categories. Every abstraction presupposes some objectification. Without abstraction, primitive man would have been overwhelmed by a rushing stream of consciousness in which he would not have been able to isolate any point of orientation. Consequently, he could not have said anything about experience; he could not have construed a language, as he actually did.

The objectification of primitive man is, however, not the critical kind which is typical of modern man. Therefore, we characterize the prescientific stage of existence as naïve, uncritical, or prereflective. Our forebears did not reflect critically on the spontaneous notions which emerged when faced with reality, nor did they test those notions in experimental ways.

When we consider the subject matter of their spontaneous, untested views of reality, we discover that their vision of life was mythological. They did not develop a critical philosophy, physics, or theology. The vision of primitive man was bound to the legends and traditions of his clan. It was influenced by his spontaneous, immediate impressions of nature as it

79

appeared in his peculiar local situation. His view of reality was also linked to the symbols perpetuated by his tribe. These influences were, to be sure, outside agents. The fact that prehistoric man was bound to these external manifestations of reality demonstrates again that his world was not merely a subjective creation of his own. He based his vision of reality on customs, traditions, and manifestations of nature which revealed themselves to him as "objective" necessities imposed on his subjectivity.

On the other hand, the objectivity of the primitive view differs greatly from the objectivity of our scientific and postscientific vision. First of all, each prescientific, mythical view of reality was shared by only a relatively small, isolated group. The clan or tribe perpetuated a traditional mythological vision among its members. This view was related to a limited number of life situations typical for a specific tribe; with a peculiar tradition; living in special surroundings; and surviving by means of specific kinds of hunting, fishing, farming, searches for shelter, and preparation of food. Our own scientific or postscientific view, on the contrary, tends toward universality. In other words, we strive consciously for a vision which may prove true for all people everywhere. We approximate this aim by constant reflection on our impressions of reality. This reflection enables us to question these impressions and to devise experiments to test their validity. Testing purifies our primordial impressions.

Primitive, prescientific existence, on the other hand, was characterized by the absence of reflection. But it is precisely reflective knowledge which makes us aware that we are the source of our own thoughts and feelings. Such awareness leads us necessarily to the knowledge that we differ from the situation about which we think and feel. In other words, it makes us cognizant of our limited, but real, freedom. The same reflective knowledge enables us to question our spontaneous, uncritical notions of nature, people, things, and events. It also enables us to be critical of the ideas which we ourselves have introjected during our dialogue with our culture. Reflective knowledge is knowledge about our own knowledge.

The condition of a scientific view of the world is thus the emergence of critical reflection on one's spontaneous vision of the world. Such critical reflection implies, however, a negation, doubt, or suspension of the primitive view. As long as we experience our primitive view of reality as absolute, we cannot be critical about it. We cannot be convinced of the certitude of our view of reality and at the same time genuinely doubtful about it.

We may apply this rule of logic to the history of scientific and postscientific existence in the Western world. The reflective critical attitude could emerge in the West only on the basis of the dissolution of the primitive vision of reality. Stephan Strasser compares this historical disintegration of the primitive world to an explosion. Primitive man did not develop well-differentiated physical, metaphysical, or religious views of reality. His mythical perception took the place, as it were, of our physical, metaphysical, and theological comprehension. The dissolution of the primitive view of reality was, however, like an explosion of the mythical perception into its physical, metaphysical, and theological components. After this explosion, the primitive physical view of reality gradually developed into science. The primitive metaphysical view of the world, indistinguishably blended with the physical perception of prehistoric man, evolved by degrees into independent, systematic philosophy. The primitive religious view, which permeated physical and metaphysical perceptions, became theology in its own right.

DISSOLUTION OF THE PREHISTORIC VISIONS OF REALITY

An attempt at a universal view of reality succeeded the primitive views of the isolated societies which made up prehistoric humanity. The necessary condition of such a universal cognitive mode of existence was the disintegration of the primitive views of reality.

The occasion for this breakdown was the primitive societies' being thrown together in new empires. Such encounters familiarized the tribes with one another's mythological views. Each tribe discovered that other tribes also experienced their own mythologies as the only possible explanation of all that manifests itself in nature. Until this fateful moment of ideological collusion, each isolated society was convinced that its own was necessarily *the* view of reality. The close interaction with members of other tribes, however, led each society to the discovery that the others' myths and traditions differed. Their modes of existence, their existential positions, or their ways of standing-out into reality revealed themselves as strange and different, yet effective. The tribe with the different mode of existence also survived and maintained itself as an organized unity which coped successfully with untamed nature and with interpersonal problems among its members.

Such observation made it impossible for each society to experience the mythical existential position of its own tribe as the only possible one. Doubt, criticism, skepticism, and nihilism took the place of naïve certainty. Doubt forced the members of each tribe to reflect on their spontaneous impressions and notions of nature. As a consequence, reflective knowledge developed rapidly. Critical reflection led finally to an attempt to reconstruct the original, isolated views of the various societies into a philosophical-theoretical vision that would be universally valid.

The universal-theoretical view in turn led people to question reality to discover whether it was in all conditions in correspondence with the new theoretical vision. At this moment, science was born. The questions of society were translated into the empirical, operational idiom. Nature answered these empirical questions positively or negatively. The answers led to the elaboration or transformation of the theoretical position.

In early Western culture, we find philosophical reflection first of all in the writings of such men as Heraclitus and Parmenides. They were among the first to escape the limited mythological vision. They uncovered general validities in the appearance of nature. They studied the possibilities of human knowledge and the structure of nature and of man. Plato, Socrates, and Aristotle advanced this early philosophy. The Greek philosophical vision of reality became the basis of Western science. The philosophical-theoretical view of the Greek thinkers was, in fact, the necessary condition of the emergence of science. Therefore, we do not find science in early cultures other than the Greek, for the emergence of experimental science is dependent on scientific theory. Scientific theory of man and nature can arise only on the basis of a more general theory of reality.

Aristotle, for example, reflected on the species-individual structure. He discovered that man can say about the individual members of a species or class that which he can say about the species. This discovery awakened the insights that one may study a sampling of the individual members of one class of objects. The qualities which are discovered to be common among the members of this sampling of objects may then be predicated of the whole class of objects. For example, when one discovers that a hundred identical pieces of iron melt in fire, he may suppose that all identical pieces of iron will melt when exposed to fire of the same intensity. Such a conclusion leads to a scientific law. A mythological view of reality would not have opened man's mind to such a discovery.

EASTERN AND WESTERN DEVELOPMENTS AFTER THE BREAKDOWN OF MYTHOLOGICAL EXISTENCE

We have said that the emergence of empires in the Western world threw isolated tribes together. The collision of isolated tribes demolished their mythologies. As a result, a more universal view of reality emerged. But what about such Eastern empires as the Indian and Chinese? They did not develop natural sciences as did the West. But this does not imply that they did not attempt to establish universally valid views transcending the particular mythologies of their tribes. They did hold universal views, though they did not take the form of categorical views of nature. On the contrary, the Eastern universal view is embedded in the wisdom of living.

Eastern thinkers transcended mythology by establishing universal rules of wise conduct, such as we find in Hebrew writings, in Taoism, and in Buddhism. While the Greeks concentrated on external nature, Eastern thinkers concentrated on the subject and on the relations of the subject to his fellow man, his home, and his life task. We do not suggest that Eastern thinkers showed no interest in nature nor that Western philosophers gave no attention to the subject, man. But, in terms of emphasis, objectified nature prevails in the thought of the later Greeks, whereas the development and growth of the subject is the dominant theme in the Eastern theory of existence.

One cannot express a universally valid thought about reality without the use of categories. Such accepted categories, then, have a determining influence within a culture on all subsequent appreciation of the nature of reality. The later Greek thinkers adopted their basic categories—such as substance, accident, quality, and quantity—from the observation of external nature. Man is a substance, but he is a substance in a different way than a stone, a rock, or a ship is. The early Greek thinkers were well aware of this difference. The "objectivist" origin of the category subsequently proved poisonous, however, to the thought of Western man. In the course of the centuries, he developed an objectivist attitude in his understanding of the human condition. The Judeo-Christian heritage of the West temporarily balanced the objectivist slant of Greek speculation. This truce between the Judeo-Christian and the Greek vision of man promised a harmonious blend of civilization and culture. The decline of the Judeo-Christian influence, however, gave free play to the objectivist tendencies in Western humanity. Before the Western world realized this clearly, it was caught up in an objectivism which expanded until it forced even the subject into categories. As a result, Western thinkers often attempt to deal with man as though he were merely a measurable substance to be organized into objective units.

Such objectivism makes for an advance in civilization and a decline in culture. "Civilization" in this sense is the objectivist organization of matter in such a way that it enables man to function more effectively. Civilization produces bridges, air conditioners, refrigerators, mills, labor unions, and functional university buildings. Culture, on the other hand, is the development and expression of the personal qualities of the human subject. Culture promotes music, paintings, poetry, novels, creative science, a beautiful and harmonious manner of living, and imaginative intellectual encounters within the universities. When civilization and culture are wedded harmoniously, a well-integrated society is born. But when one of the two prevails, society suffers.

Certain contemporary Western societies reveal a rapid advance in civilization among the mass of the population while the same majority is not developing so intensively in personal culture. We can observe efforts to balance this dominant objectivism by a new humanism and even by the introduction of Eastern wisdom. These isolated attempts do not, however, appear to be greatly successful thus far.

To be sure, the scientific mode of existence of the West remained predominantly theoretical-philosophical up to the Renaissance. Even mythological motives did not disappear all at once. They permeated and sometimes colored philosophical theory. Medieval alchemy, for example, was a curious blend of philosophical and scientific theorizing permeated by mythological motives.

The late Middle Ages and the Renaissance saw the gradual split of the Western cognitive mode of existence into philosophical-theoretical, empirical-theoretical, observational, experimental, and applied modes of knowledge. Such distinctions were a methodological necessity. It would have been impossible for these modes of knowledge to develop in their own right had it not been for these actual distinctions. In reality, of course, these modes of knowledge cannot be separated absolutely. They always influence one another. But their temporary methodological distinction was a necessary condition for the growth of the scientific mode of existence. Such distinctions promoted a necessary division of labor. Various experts could now concentrate exclusively on certain aspects of the scientific way of life. A full differentiation of the various attitudinal constituents of the scientific mode was now possible.

One danger was inherent in this split. The expert in one of the differentiated attitudes of the scientific mode of existence might be carried away by his specialty. He might then be inclined to forget his dependency on other aspects of the scientific way of life developed by other experts. He might claim that his own approach to reality was "the" scientific one. And this is precisely what did happen. The tremendous growth of science, however, compelled the scientist to realize that his problems were closely linked with theoretical-empirical thought and even with philosophical theorizing. Moreover, the tremendous differentiation in the scientific realm itself offered a challenge for integration. Added to this challenge, as we have already seen, was the demand in Western thought for a recognition of the unique place of the *subject.*

Briefly, the differentiation of the scientific mode of existence has now reached a point where reintegration seems to be an inescapable task. We may conclude that this reintegration comprehends three aspects:

1. Reintegration of the constituent attitudes of the scientific modes of existence.

2. Reintegration within each field of scientific endeavor of the various differential theories and correlated data. This reintegration would lead to a comprehensive theory of the science itself.

3. Reintegration, especially in the human sciences, of the subjective and the objective realms of reality.

It is impossible for one person to be a complete expert in every phase of the scientific mode of existence. This impossibility implies that the integrative task will lead to a new branch of science in every field, namely, that of the comprehensive theorist. This phase of the evolution of science is most clear in physics. Theoretical physics as a specialty actually does exist. The same development must necessarily take place in psychology, for the development of comprehensive theory is not a question of choice or interest, but the necessary result of the inner structure of the scientific mode of existence. This structure, in turn, follows necessarily from the existential structure of man, the scientist, for there is only one way in which the scientific mode of existence can be developed: theoretical thinking, sensitive experiencing, and concrete manipulative intervention. Every new step in the development of a science necessarily requires renewed theoretical reflection on what has already been learned by sense observation and experimentation.

The Relationship Between Observation and Theory in the Scientific Mode of Existence

The aim of this chapter is to clarify the role of the theoretical attitude in the scientific mode of existence. As already indicated, the theoretical attitude is essentially human. If this is true, theorizing should manifest itself even on the level of prescientific observation. A close consideration of the essential relationship between observation and theory will demonstrate that they imply each other mutually.

Man is basically existence. His involvement in the world can be viewed under various perspectives or dimensions. One of these is the observational mode of existence, which implies the sensuous standing-out of a subject into the observable reality which reveals itself to him. The subject's taking a stand manifests itself, among other ways, in his theoretical attitude, for to theorize is to adopt a certain way of looking at something. The objective aspect reveals itself in that which is observed.

Observation is thus really preceiving what is "out there." But observation is also perceiving according to a theory of an observing subject. Therefore, existence as observation is necessarily theoretical and empirical at the same time.

We may illustrate this conclusion with an example from daily life. As I walk down the street, I see a child playing, and I make the observation to myself or to my companion that this child moves rather slowly. When I reflect, however, on my observation and my expression of this "fact," I realize that they are one-sided and selective, for this child is an inexhaustible source of meanings. To enumerate only a few: the traffic around the playing child is moving rapidly; the weather is hot and humid; he has blond hair; he looks weak and tired; he seems to be about eight years old; two men next to him are arguing about politics; the high, dark wall of a house narrows his horizon. We could go on and list an indefinite number of circumstances surrounding this child and his play.

As the observing subject, however, I select only a single characteristic, namely, the slow movement of the child. In reality, however, all these circumstances are in some way related and create the situation in its realistic totality. I have no right to say that circumstances other than the child's movement are irrelevant. Maybe the child is afraid of the other children; maybe he is awed by the somber wall of the high building; maybe he is confused by the men who shout mysterious phrases about politics in incomprehensible agitation; maybe the child's fatigue is far more relevant than his being slow. But I, the observing subject, abstract from all these other appearances of the child and his situation. I select only one phenomenon, namely, his slowness.

How do I abstract this one phenomenon from the whole phenomenological situation? I do so by placing the reality of the child-in-his-situation in a specific context. In this case, the context is that of speed of movement. I look through this frame, as it were, and, while doing so, I do not consider blue eyes, blond hair, the age of the child, or his being awed by the wall, but only the phenomenon of his slowness. Against the background of the meanings of "fast," "slow," and "movement," he appears to be moving slowly. I could have chosen another world of meaning, for example, the meaning of age. Then I should have observed, not his slowness, but his probable age, based on a system of meaning developed in my culture regarding age levels and their appearances.

But where do I obtain these theoretical frames of reference through which I may observe the child? Like every other theoretical frame, they are composed of many elements. One fundamental theoretical component is the language which I inherited through my culture. I am, in fact, inserted in my language. Language embodies a certain view of the world. It represents the modes of existence of the generations which lived before me in my country. Every language is a theoretical frame of reference which helps man to uncover various aspects of reality in and around himself. The same is true of such artificial languages as statistics, mathematics, psychoanalysis, learning theory, and physics.

Therefore, when I say that this child moves slowly, I express a fact, but I express it in a selective, abstract, or theoretical way. My experiences, my specialized interests, and my language are influential in my choice of a definite system of meanings. The "fact" of slowness is, therefore, the product of two main factors. One building block of this "fact" is an event that happens; the other is my theoretical frame of reference. The two are inseparably blended in what I call my observation. If I used no frame of reference, that is, if I took no stand, I should not ex-ist, I should not stand out in any way, and I should experience nothing. Therefore, whenever I observe, I always do so within at least a naïve theoretical frame of reference.

Every mode of existence corresponds with a world of meanings. My culture has embodied these modes of perception with their corresponding worlds in the natural or scientific language which I use. Only by this existential or selective expression is a fact a fact. Only in this way can facts be incorporated in human existence, find their place in it, renew, reinforce, and enrich it.

Sense observation can take place only when one or more of my senses are stimulated. Sense stimulation alone, however, is not yet observation of a fact. We experience that we are observing only when sense stimulation becomes meaningful in some theoretical frame of reference. A nontheoretical expression of a stimulation of our external senses would indeed be unthinkable and even impossible.

On the other hand, the term "existence" always implies two poles—the existent or the subject and that reality toward which he exists. Therefore, the observational mode of existence also implies a subject pole and an object pole. The object pole of my observation reveals itself to me as an experience of "being-found-there," of "being-not-me." I call this the experience of objectivity. As soon as I take some stand toward the stimulation of my senses, then sense data impose themselves on me within my theoretical frame as reality, that is, as object pole. At the same time, I, the observing subject, the existent, am in some way present in that which is given in my mode of existing. It is precisely the human light of my knowing which translates the sense stimulations into something intelligible and meaningful. The specific kind of intelligibility and meaningfulness is again codetermined by the theoretical frame of reference of me, the subject.

Meanwhile, the experience that the data are given, that they are object pole, that they are not me, never disappears totally. This remains true even when I leave behind prescientific, naïve theories and begin to develop complex, scientific—theoretical frames of reference. The theory which guides prescientific observation is usually so simple that the presence of the observational data is quite clear and convincing. As soon as observation becomes scientific, however, the theoretical frame of reference (for example, the theory of relativity or the stimulus-response theory) is so subtle and ingenious that the object pole seems to disappear. Of course, this is never really the case.

Even such a highly abstract theory as the stimulus-response theory refers in some way to some given reality. Indeed, the whole scientific mode of existence is built on the inseparable relatedness of subject pole and object pole within every so-called datum of science.

To clarify the role of the theoretical attitude within the scientific way of life, we have considered, first of all, the nature and development of the various existential attitudes which constitute this scientific mode. One of these is the theoretical attitude. We have also investigated the relationship between observation and theory in the scientific mode of existence. Beginning with a consideration of the mutual implications of prescientific observation and prescientific theory in human existence, we have sought the root of the relationship between scientific observation and theory in the nature of man himself.

We have concluded that, even on the prescientific level of existence, a moment of meaningfulness and intelligibility occurs in every observation. This implies, as we have seen, a moment of theory in every observation, for sense stimulation as such cannot explain the variety of meanings which emerge even when the same sense is stimulated by the same stimuli. We speak of people, for example, as nasty, kind, stupid, clever, polite, awkward, strong, or weak. Then we make statements concerning properties related to these behaviors, such as the statement that a stupid man should not be a professor. In other words, when we observe behavior, we are implicitly aware that there are different theoretical, abstract categories. We know this without studying scientific psychology. Thus there is a theoretically organized way of existence even on the prescientific level of human life.

The essence of human life *is* existence. It excludes the possibility of a purely sensuous givenness, of purely being-a-fact. Every so-called fact is embedded in some kind of theoretical context. It is always and necessarily embedded in some world. This world is constituted by some mode of existence, of taking a stand. Human ex-istence is never terminated. Even on the prescientific level, it is a constant attempt to assimilate reality; it is always a theoretical endeavor to make reality transparent. It is a theorizing existence insofar as it perceives concrete realities in intelligible contexts of phenomenological worlds or systems of meaning.

IMPLICATIONS OF OBSERVATION AND THEORY IN THE SCIENTIFIC MODE OF EXISTENCE

The mutual implications of observation and theory manifest themselves in the scientific, as well as in the prescientific, mode of existence. The empirical, scientific mode is a methodical, critical, organized mode of standing-out into a selected area of reality which is given to the senses. In science, the theoretical context and its embodiment in terminology are more refined, complex, and exact. The area of reality in which a specific mode of scientific existence stands out is more strictly delineated. Furthermore, the observations which result from this involvement in a specific area are more coherently organized in an open scientific system. Nevertheless, there is no fundamental difference between the prescientific and the scientific modes of cognitive existence. We may demonstrate this by applying the same theoretical process to the scientific mode of existence as we did to the prescientific mode.

One scientific mode of life—the psychological—will serve our purpose. The theoretical frames and the terminologies of psychology are, to be sure, more subtle and complex than the naïve, prescientific frames of reference. The specific area of this mode of existence is also more sharply delineated. We have already investigated this delineation in Chapter Two, in which we concluded that psychology's area of reality is intentional-functional behavior. Certain experiences or observations resulting from involvement in the reality of this behavior are organized in differentiated, internally consistent, theoretical systems. The organization of all these differential theories and their corresponding data within a comprehensive theory, however, has not yet been attempted on as large a scale in psychology as in physics.

We may apply to scientific psychology all the essential characteristics of the prescientific relationship between behavior and observation. Therefore, when a psychologist speaks of data of intentional-functional behavior, his statement should never be considered a mirror or a picture of that behavior. Every behavioral fact is only a fact within one or the other system of meaning, within one or the other theoretical context used by the psychologist. This framework may be, for example, learning theory, psychoanalytic theory, *Gestalt* theory, or any other psychological system of ideas. The psychological fact, like every other scientific fact, can never be a pure fact or merely a fact. Facts exist only in a theoretical frame of reference. Consequently, when a scientific psychologist uses the word "fact" or "datum," we should be aware that the terms always refer to a factual-theoretical aspect of the whole of intentional-functional behavior.

THE INCREASINGLY THEORETICAL CHARACTER OF SCIENCE AND ITS CONTINUAL RELATIONSHIP TO OBSERVATION

The development of psychology implies that it acquires an increasingly scientific, theoretical character. Thus it is distinguished from prescientific, everyday psychology, in which the theoretical aspect is less developed. Science in general may be aptly described as that mode of cognitive existence which implies a continually developing theoretical explanation of phenomena. The same phenomena were once less accurately defined in original, prescientific theoretical explanations. This increasingly theoretical development is most striking in contemporary physics. But it becomes more and more evident in psychology.

In spite of the inescapable evolution of science toward an expanding system of theoretical constructs, however, it must remain thoroughly empirical. This implies that the science of behavior, in spite of the primacy of the theoretical, must remain bound to behavior that is given to the observing senses. As we have seen in the earlier part of this chapter, the scientifically theorizing subject reaches out to perceptible reality in and through his senses and bodily movement.

If the primary theoretical aspect of a science were to lose all implicit reference to the data which are given to the senses, then it would no longer be science, but philosophy. The philosopher begins with immediate, empirical experience, about which he speculates. His abstract speculation removes him further and further from the immediate data. Finally, he arrives at statements, which are of such a nature that they cannot be verified by empirical operations directly or indirectly. Empirical operations are those which are basically bound to bodily sensing and moving.

Statements of comprehensive scientific theory, however, must be verifiable, at least indirectly, by empirical operations. The theory of relativity, for example, cannot be verified directly by such operations. But the scientist can deduce postulates from the theory of relativity which can be verified by empirical operations. The ontological truth that man is existence, however, cannot be proven *as ontological truth* by empirical sense operations. For this reason, psychology cannot borrow this ontological statement *as ontological statement* in scientific theory. The theoretical psychologist, however, may borrow the concept and change it to a hypothetical theoretical construct. The scientific theorist neither affirms nor denies the ontological truth of the statement. But he gives it the same status in psychological science as the constructs of the theory of relativity are given in physics. He cannot prove directly that the broad theoretical construct that man is existence is ontologically true; but he can deduce verifiable postulates from this theoretical statement.

For example, the theoretical psychologist may hypothesize that man on the proper level of his being always "ex-ists," or uncovers some meaningful world. Then he may suggest to "differential psychologists" that they deduce operational postulates from this statement. If the comprehensive theoretical statement is valid, one postulate might be, for example, that a man who is exposed to sensory deprivation will invent some imaginary kind of world. The differential operational psychologist can test this postulate by empirical operations. Experiments in sensory deprivation have indeed affirmed this postulate and, therefore, indirectly affirmed this hypothetical construct.

Why is it that every science becomes increasingly theoretical? We have seen that scientific existence is an observant existence. It is a standing-out boldly into reality that is given to the senses of the scientist. The psychologist stands out in this way into a specific area of reality, namely, the area of behavior. Doing so, he observes a tremendous number of behavioral phenomena. He observes people learning, playing, arguing, working, writing, and so on. Observation of any one of these behavioral phenomena on the prescientific level of existence already presupposes a prescientific theoretical frame of reference. Therefore, we might imagine that the psychologist could make it his task to simply investigate a great number of prescientific theories in which he discovers numerous phenomena. He could thus reduce psychology to a description of every behavioral phenomenon caught in every prescientific theory. Such a purpose, however, would involve the psychologist in an extremely complicated and, in the end, impossible enterprise, for he would inevitably bog down in the multiplicity of singular phenomena which he would uncover in the behavior of animals and people.

In other words, psychology, to be effective and manageable, cannot be concerned only with the observation and description of phenomena. It is theory which enables the psychologist to reduce to a few fundamental properties the many which have appeared to his sense observation. The theoretical psychologist develops a structure of ideas through which he attempts to express behavioral relationships. This texture of ideas helps him to structure behavioral phenomena. These phenomena then become intelligible in their interrelationships.

Therefore, the psychologist does not observe and describe phenomena of behavior merely for the sake of inventory. He assembles behavioral phenomena to construct theories which reveal something about the structure of behavior. One differential theory of behavior, for example, structures a group of behavioral phenomena by the construct of reinforcement. This is, of course, only a theory and, therefore, hypothetical. But this theory makes intelligible to a degree a certain number of behavioral phenomena which are observable. It does so by theorizing about behavioral phenomena which manifest themselves in numerous experiments in learning.

The structures which bind phenomena together, to be sure, are not immediately observable by the senses. Therefore, the psychologist can only devise hypothetical theories which approximate the nature, properties, and relationships of these structures. He can experimentally demonstrate only that his theoretical model is coherent with the observable behavioral phenomena. In other words, he can only test whether this theoretical structure is a model that points to what actually appears in the observable phenomena. Thus, all science remains bound to observable appearances.

Science, therefore, fosters the careful study of observable sense appearances which are directly available for observation or empirically evoked to test postulates deduced from scientific theory. The sense observation affirms or negates the intellectual structure which has been devised by scientific theory. In the beginning of the development of a science, one and the same scientist may possess the required knowledge, time, and energy to commit himself to observation, theorizing, and experimentation. When a science develops further, however, it becomes so complex that specialists are needed for each of these phases.

This development is especially manifest at the crucial moment when differential theory requires the supplement of comprehensive theory. Differential theory devises a conceptual structure which explains a particular group of phenomena studied by specialists in a given area of behavior. Comprehensive theory develops a structure of ideas which explains the variety of phenomena which are described in the various differential theories, for science necessarily leads to the attempt to understand the many phenomena and differential theories in their unity.

The scientific mode of existence by its very nature seeks unity in multiplicity. Both elements are necessary. The comprehensive-theoretical approach emphasizes the unity of science whereas the differential-theoretical approach guards the openness of science. If the comprehensive-theoretical psychologist were not to accept the findings of the differential psychologists, he would create a unity at the expense of the multiplicity of phenomena. His theory would lose contact with reality. On the other hand, if there were no comprehensive theory, psychology would be lost in the multiplicity of recorded phenomena and differential theories. The dialogue between observation and theory commands respect for behavioral appearances. The theoretical psychologist, for example, should never discard an exception in behavioral appearances which does not conform to his hypothetical theory. It is exactly this exceptional behavior which may become the starting point for crucial corrections or developments in psychological theory. The openness to behavior which does not fit the hypothesis is the guarantee of the multiplicity which must be integrated into a unity without being distorted in the process.

The preference of the psychologist for the scientific mode of existence is not for the behavioral phenomena as many, but for the many as integrated into a unity. The psychologist is interested in behavioral appearances in their endless plurality and multiformity. Whatever behavior appears he wishes to make his own by investigating it and adding it to the phenomena he has observed. The psychologist, however, is not interested only in bringing together the many behavioral phenomena. He also wishes to *com*prehend the many from a single

97

or from several points of view. These integrating, comprehensive, theoretical viewpoints are attempts to approximate the basic structure that appears in the phenomena.

Although this preference of the scientific psychologist is understandable, it should not cause him to lose sight of the absolute necessity for the experimental and clinical search for the many behavioral appearances. Otherwise, the desire for integration may lead to an inauthentic simplification and distortion of the given plurality. For this reason, the aspect of the scientific mode of existence which impels the scientist to explore as many behavioral appearances as possible is indispensable for the growth of the science. Equally indispensable, however, is the theoretical aspect of standing-out toward the fundamental structure which integrates and explains these phenomena as a unity.

THE THEORETICAL-OBSERVATIONAL STRUCTURE OF SCIENCE IS ROOTED IN MAN'S EXISTENCE

The theoretical-observational structure of science is not a result of arbitrary choice. It is rooted in the scientific mode of existence. The latter, in turn, is rooted in the primordial structure and situation of man. Therefore, there is no other possible way for the development of science. According to his primordial structure, man experiences himself as an unlimited dynamic intentionality. He experiences his subjectivity as an urge to stand out toward all that is. On the other hand, his subjectivity is an embodied subjectivity. Therefore, he has to stand out toward all that is in and through his bodily senses and movements. Furthermore, his embodiment restricts him to a certain place and a temporary phase in the historical development of mankind. Consequently, his actual, concrete standing-out is limited.

This necessity of standing-out bodily in a limited way compels the psychologist to develop differential-operational and experimental psychology first of all. This is the only road to behavior available to him as a bodily existent. His awareness of his unlimited dynamic intentionality, however, leads to his theoretical quest for a unifying structure of ideas which will enable him to *com*prehend behavior as an intelligible unity. Therefore, the constant tension, or dialogue, between theory and observation is unavoidable in human science and will never be resolved. It is rooted in the very structure of man. This tension is, however, at the same time the dynamic, propelling force which keeps science alive and growing.

THE THEORETICAL AND EXPERIMENTAL CONSTITUENTS OF THE SCIENTIFIC MODE OF EXISTENCE

Most important in the development of psychology is the experimental constituent of the scientific psychological mode of existence. As we have already seen, the experimental mode of being is a proper mode of being man, for it pertains to man's nature to ex-ist bodily in the world and to unveil this world. The theoretical psychologist cannot perform his comprehensive task without the experiments of the empirical psychologist. This is especially true when he wishes to develop a system of ideas which will help him to comprehend behavior as it manifests itself in behavioral phenomena. Therefore, the extension of the experimental mode of being to as many realms of psychology as possible is a definite necessity for the development of theoretical psychology.

Unfortunately, not every area of psychological interest is as manageable by the experimental psychologist as every other area. The study of the intentional component of behavior, for example, often seems to require methods other than the experimental. Even here, however, the differential psychologist should use the experimental method as far as possible. Thus he will be able to provide the comprehensive theoretical psychologist with more reliable data and more adequately tested differential theories.

Another problem with regard to the unlimited use of the experimental method is the ethical principle that the fundamental human rights of the individual should not be jeopardized even to obtain valuable psychological knowledge. For example, it would be interesting and worthwhile from the viewpoint of psychological knowledge to expose human subjects to clearly defined injuries of the brain. Psychologists could then study the impact of these injuries on behavior. The study of the results of brain injury in war casualties has already been undertaken. But a well-planned gradation of brain injuries inflicted on a large sampling of, say, a prison population, would provide a more exact design and a better control of the variables. It seems certain that valuable information regarding behavior would be gained. This would be especially true if brain surgery were performed on hundreds of confined subjects who could be observed over a long period. The subjects would suffer lasting impairment, but mankind as a whole might profit from the experimentation. So would the development of theoretical psychology. Despite the value of this procedure from the viewpoint of theoretical and clinical psychology, however, it could not be carried out because of ethical principles regarding the human rights of the individual.

Despite limitations, the theoretical psychologist is optimistic about the development of his field because of the advance of the experimental method in an increasing number of areas of animal and human psychology.

The Existential Character of Scientific Theory

We have investigated the scientific mode of existence, its attitudinal constituents, and their relationships. These observations enable us to perceive more clearly the existential view of scientific theory, which differs from the positivist and rationalist ones. I have emphasized that the scientific mode of existence implies a unity between the subject pole, or the scientific psychologist, and his object pole, behavior. The theoretical constituent of the scientific mode is predominantly subjective, but not only subjective. It is true that this theoretical constituent steadily increases in importance with the development of the science. The object pole of the psychological mode of existence, however, will never be totally absent.

100

Psychology and Theory

Psychology in its advanced state is a flexible, open structure of an ever-changing number of ideas which enable us to comprehend the phenomena of behavior. These theoretical structures thus refer in principle to the phenomenal appearances given to our senses. The theoretical ideas that make up the science of psychology are, therefore, not merely arbitrary, imaginative configurations. These structures always point to the phenomena. They are in some way imposed on the psychologist by his perception of behavior. Therefore, the object pole to which psychological theory refers always remains in some way present in the theory itself. At the same time, the theory represents, however, more than the phenomena which the psychologist perceives when he looks at behavior from differing perspectives.

This existential conception of science and, more especially, of scientific theory differs from the two chief pre-existential views of scientific theory—the positivist and the rationalist. Each of these isolates one of the constituents of scientific theory which are in the existential view inseparable. Positivism places everything, as it were, at the object pole, whereas rationalism considers only the subject pole.

The initial conception of positivism in psychology is that theory exactly mirrors the structure of behavior and that the observed behavioral phenomena are the effects of this underlying real structure. According to this view, such concepts as libido, id, ego, and superego mirror a hidden reality which underlies certain groups of behavioral phenomena. The phenomena are the effects of this dynamic structure. They stand in a causal relationship to the concrete reality of libido, id, ego, and superego. Similarly, the concept of stimulus in an original, positivist learning theory mirrors a reality that causes certain behavior in animals and men. This was the initial view of positivism. The unavoidable evolution in Western thought, however, quite naturally affected the positivist position in psychology. Therefore, new concepts and formulations have emerged in positivist psychology itself which manifest a new conception of science approximating the existential position.

Rationalism, on the other hand, fosters a view of scientific theory which is the opposite of the objectivist conception that dominated positivism. For the rationalist or the idealist, theory is nothing but a logical system of classifications. The psychologist developed this categorical structure as a tool for summarizing information about behavior. In the idealistic view, this system is merely subjective, and we cannot know whether the thing "out there" corresponds to our conception of it. The concepts of libido, id, ego, superego, stimulus, and reinforcement are merely subjective. They are only in the mind. We do not know whether they represent actual behavior. Here, again, we must add that the existential evolution of Western thought has finally led many rationalists and idealists to concepts and formulations which reveal the impact of the new cultural development.

Finally, the existential view of scientific theory unites the positivist and rationalist views in a flexible synthesis. According to this concept, theory is a subjective-objective creation of the scientist. Theory is subjective insofar as it is a creation of the scientific thinker. It is objective insofar as it represents *in principle* structural properties and relationships among the behavioral phenomena. Theory is thus a subjective frame of reference created by the scientific thinker to represent structural properties and relationships which he observes in the appearances of behavior.

CHAPTER FOUR

DIFFERENTIAL THEORETICAL MODES
OF EXISTENCE IN PSYCHOLOGY

DIFFERENTIAL THEORIES

All theories and possibilities of theory in science can be reduced to two main groups, comprehensive and differential. A theory in one single field of physics concerned with the properties of electricity, for example, differs from the comprehensive theory of relativity or of quantum physics. This distinction is evident to one who compares the uses, methods, developments, and scope of both kinds of theories. We shall later discuss some of the divergent characteristics of comprehensive and differential theories notable in psychology. But before doing so, we should like to point out how this self-evident distinction is rooted in the very existence of man.

Is there some differentiation in the primordial structure of existence itself which explains why all scientific theory is either comprehensive or differential? We cannot find the answer to this question by means of the empirical methods of psychology. Empirical observation teaches us that the distinction exists, but it does not tell why. The only method open to us is to make explicit our assumptions regarding man's nature. As we have already seen, psychology borrows such assumptions from contemporary philosophy, but deals with them as hypothetical constructs.

According to our hypothetical assumption, then, man finds himself as an existent subjectivity in the world. He is vaguely aware of the totality of all that is. His dynamic intentionality urges him to comprehend all being. But reality does not reveal itself to him immediately as a clearly structured whole, but as a vague aggregate of singular phenomena. Every new manifestation of knowledge regarding a particular phenomenon teaches man something about the whole of reality. Therefore, when man grasps, appropriates, and understands one single, particular, phenomenal appearance, he grows at the same time in the knowledge of the whole insofar as it manifests itself in this particular phenomenon. Man thus strives for a knowledge of the whole by seeking a knowledge of singular concrete appearances. Briefly, the primordial structure of man seems to be such that he tends at the same time toward a knowledge of both the whole of reality and of particular phenomena.

Why is it that the restless intentionality of man toward the comprehension of the whole must make a detour, as it were, through individual phenomena? The most fundamental reason seems to be that man's subjectivity is bodily. This means that man's actual concrete existence is always limited in time and space. Therefore he must encounter the whole of reality in its separate, material, palpable manifestations which present themselves to his senses. Only by growth in the clear knowledge of particular appearances can man grow in the knowledge of the whole.

As a result, the knowledge of man is dialectical. We use the term "dialectical" in the present context to indicate the polar relationship between the knowledge of particular phenomena and that of the whole. Man's knowledge shifts continuously, as it were, from an accurate, observational-experimental-theoretical knowledge of a specific phenomenon to a deeper, universal, theoretical knowledge of the whole group of phenomena to which it belongs. Then, from his new theoretical knowledge of the whole, man shifts back again to a renewed, deeper investigation of the singular phenomenon with the aid of his newly learned hypotheses. This dialectical nature of man's knowledge explains the constant tension between the comprehensive theories and the differential theories which are immediately bound to empirical observation of particular groups of phenomena. To be sure, there is no essential opposition between a comprehensive theory and the various differential theories with their experimental-observational components. The two approaches to knowledge necessarily compenetrate, sustain, and stimulate each other. For they are two essential experiences of one and the same bodily existence. The vague knowledge of the whole is primary. Then, differentiation takes place when man concentrates his attention on particular phenomena. This differentiated knowledge leads back to a deeper, more structured knowledge of the whole.

The primordial structure of the cognitive activity of man thus urges him in two directions. These two theoretical modes of knowing interact not only on the scientific but also on the pre-scientific level of his existence. When we observe people in the act of understanding their experience, we note their natural, spontaneous tendency to unite their individual experiences into wholes which are meaningful to them. They shift continually from a special attention to the phenomena of their daily lives to an interest in comprehensive naïve theory which gives meaning to this variety of otherwise isolated appearances. As we have already seen, their observation of particular phenomena already implies a theoretical movement. We may call this theoretical movement inherent in every observation a naïve differential theory.

A mother, for example, accepts implicitly the differential theory that her child should eat a sufficient amount of food. This theory enables her to be perceptive of the phenomena of refusal of food by her child. She may also have developed another naïve differential theory regarding her relationship to the child, which may be formulated as: "When I am disturbed, my child is less cooperative." This pre-scientific theory enables her to observe in the child various phenomena of refusal to cooperate. Her tendency to understand the possible relatedness of the variety of phenomena may lead her to combine her two differential theories. She may theorize that the refusal of food by her child is a sign of refusal of cooperation because she herself is upset. In the meantime, and in the same manner, she may have developed a variety of other pre-scientific theories concerned with other phenomena. All of these may lead to a whole network of observations which reinforce her naïve theories. Finally, when she has a sufficient number of differential theories and their corresponding phenomena at her disposal, her restless striving for total knowledge about her child may urge her to construct a comprehensive theory. She has observed, let us say, that she is upset when the child does not live up to her expectations. She has discovered in other situations that these expectations are due to criteria prevalent in her social circle. Ultimately, she formulates the comprehensive theory that parental preoccupation with social demands leads to bad eating habits in children. Of course, this whole process it at least partly unconscious, pre-scientific, and uncontrolled. Therefore, this particular comprehensive theory may be faulty. But it demonstrates that all the essential constituents of the scientific theoretical process are already present in the pre-scientific theoretical mode of man's existence.

The process of psychotherapy provides another example of a situation which enables man to become aware of spontaneous new differential theories. The patient ordinarily becomes conscious of phenomena in his life which he has previously been unable to observe. Moreover, the therapeutic process enables him to formulate a variety of possible comprehensive theories which may integrate his new differential theories and the phenomena he observes by means of them. Therapy thus facilitates the emergence of a spontaneous dialogue between pre-scientific comprehensive and differential theories. This process may enable the patient to create a world of meaning which is more congruent with his actual everyday experience.

Human existence, moreover, is essentially co-existence. Therefore, the task of uncovering reality is shared by many. One of the innumerable manifestations of this cooperation of persons who want to know is the development of science. Every science is an organized attempt of many individuals to understand a particular area of reality. The methods used to increase knowledge in every science necessarily conform to the existential structure of man as scientist. As we have seen, man involves himself in the whole of reality by taking a stand toward the particulars that make up this whole. Therefore, we find in every science the development of differential theories immediately related to observation of and experimentation with a limited number of phenomena. We also find in every science the development of comprehensive theories just as soon as a number of isolated differential theories sufficient to demand integration have been developed. Man's co-existence implies specialization in various sciences. Efficient co-existence also leads to specialization within each science. When each phase of a science has its own specialists, a more rapid and efficient development of this science as a whole becomes possible. When a science becomes complex, it is impossible for one man to be excellent in all of its phases. For this reason, the various sciences produce both specialized differential theorists and specialized comprehensive theorists. Such a development is now taking place in the science of psychology.

MUTUALLY EXCLUSIVE QUALITY OF DIFFERENTIAL THEORETICAL CONSTRUCTS

We have already discussed the fragmentary approach to the object pole of psychology. We have pointed out that it may be explained by the bodily character of man's existence. And we have concluded that this fragmentary approach cannot result in a total construct or model of behavior even if we combine the outcomes of all our observations. The rationale for our conclusion is the fact that we can never achieve a moment in which all possible viewpoints can be maintained simultaneously.

However, this is not the only reason why it is impossible to obtain a total construct through the multiplication of differential theories. Another reason is that the partial constructs, or aggregates of ideas, of these theories have meanings which are mutually exclusive. Even when the same terms are used, these constructs do not have the same meanings within the various differential theories. Therefore, we cannot combine them to form a homogeneous unity.

To understand this concretely, we may consider a psychologist who specializes in a differential theory, for example, the physiological psychologist. He has developed a solid theoretical, empirical, and experimental knowledge of physiology. Let us say that he is observing a moving hand from a specific theoretical frame of reference of interconnected physiological constructs. This texture of physiological ideas leads him to perceive certain appearances while not perceiving others at the same time. Certain phenomena of the moving hand reveal themselves to him; others do not. The theoretical stand which he takes determines what kind of phenomena reveal themselves to his perception. He does not perceive in the moving hand the phenomena, let us say, of reaching out for an object, of external behavioral characteristics, or of cultural expression. He is aware only of the phenomena which are revealed in the light of an aggregate of physiological ideas.

There are, however, other specialists in psychology who perceive quite different phenomena because they use different theoretical approaches. These psychologists might observe one and the same moving hand in many different ways. The theoretical constructs which are developed and applied by these various experts are also necessarily different. For the physiological psychologist, the moving hand is a manifestation of phenomena which are in harmony or disharmony with ideas proposed by physiological thinkers. For the social psychologist, the appearance of the moving hand expresses certain cultural influences whch may or may not correspond with ideas developed by theorists in his field. For the psychologist of learning, the movement of the hand reflects processes of conditioning and reinforcement. He discovers phenomena which are related to the elaborate system of ideas which is called learning theory.

The psychoanalytically oriented psychologist sees in the moving hand an expression of feelings and tendencies determined by a genetic process in the early history of the subject. He questions whether the phenomena observed correspond to a refined texture of psychoanalytic ideas spun out in years of intensive theorizing.

In other words, all behavioral phenomena can be inserted, as it were, into various differential theories of psychology. Every single differential theory is a frame of reference in which behavior is approached and known in one of its manifold aspects. Every single area in psychology is constituted by a specific fundamental interest of the observing psychologist. Each interest reveals one perspective of the total object pole of psychology which is intentional-functional behavior. These specific interests constitute the single fields of psychology. We may say that they are the differentiations of the over-all psychological mode of existence. The latter is in turn a differentiation of total human existence or involvement in the world.

We may conclude that every differential theory in psychology is essentially limited: only certain constructs belong to its frame of reference while others are necessarily excluded. Even when differential theories of psychology use the same constructs, they are integrated into different tissues of ideas. Such integration necessarily changes the original meaning of these constructs. For example, the idea of "energy" has different meanings when used in the differential theories of psychoanalysis and of physiological psychology. The same is true of the idea of "learning" when integrated within the differential theory of strict behaviorism and that of client-centered therapy.

From all we have said, it becomes more and more clear that science is fundamentally a well-organized aggregate of ideas, a theoretical structure, and that the scientist is basically a thinker, a theorist, and only secondarily an observer. All that precedes this state of theoretical organization of phenomena is pre-scientific.

Differential-Theoretical and
Experimental Modes of Existence

We have seen that the experimental mode of existence is a necessary constituent of the general scientific mode. How is this experimental component related to the differential-theoretical one which we have been analyzing?

The experimental is a proper mode of existence for man. It is man's nature to be involved bodily in the world and to unveil the world gradually by bodily observation and manipulation. Thus the scientist's own nature impels him to develop the experimental method. The structure of intentional-functional behavior and the possibilities implied in this structure are uncovered by the experimental psychologist, therefore, in an experimental way. He is not satisfied merely with the observation of behavior as it presents itself to him; he organizes experimental situations in which he can propose certain questions about behavior. The answers presented to him during the experiment confirm or challenge directly the differential theoretical structures, and indirectly the comprehensive theoretical structures, which make up the science of psychology. Therefore, theoretical psychologists require the experiments of empirical and applied psychologists in order to develop theoretical structures which will organize as adequately as possible the phenomena observed in behavior. For this reason, the extension of the experimental mode of existence to as many areas of psychology as possible is a necessity.

When a psychologist devises an experiment, he begins with a differential theoretical point of view concerning behavior. This attitude may have been developed in a dialogue with comprehensive-theoretical psychologists. In this case, we may say that the differential-theoretical view is a postulate derived from the comprehensive-theoretical vision of psychology. But it is not uniquely characteristic of a differential-theoretical view that it be hypothetical. What makes a theory differential in the strict sense is its quality of being translatable into operational terms. The experimental psychologist thus devises an experiment on the basis of a differential-theoretical view in the strict sense. The outcome of the experiment affirms or challenges totally or partially the differential theory of the psychologist. The experimental results, therefore, may give rise to a new differential theory concerning the aspect of behavior under study.

A somewhat similar situation exists in applied psychology. Though the latter is experimental in a far looser sense than psychology pursued in the laboratory, one cannot deny its experimental aspect. For the applied psychologist aims at the solution of certain problems in human life, for example, in industry or in education. He does this only by utilizing certain possibilities of human behavior within given situations. He develops of necessity some differential theory which guides his attempts to utilize these possibilities in a way which will produce the desired effects. While doing so, he discovers that this differential theory is valid, invalid, or only partially valid. This knowledge may restructure his differential theory. New possibilities in behavior within a given situation may reveal themselves to him. His new differential theory in turn calls for experiment with the new possibilities which he has discovered. In this sense, we may say that the applied psychologist also engages in experiments which arise from and lead to differential theories.

It is clear that every experiment is rooted in an operational theory. Later in our discussion, we shall demonstrate that this operational theory may be rooted in turn in a phenomenological description of the situation under study.

Individual operational theories, when translated into actual observation, experimentation, or application within a certain area, give rise to a more complex operational theory. That is, the results of different operational theories within the same area of investigation give rise to the structure of a differential theory which integrates them. This differential theory, to be sure, must be broken up again into its constituent operational theories when the psychologist wishes to translate it into concrete operational procedures. Examples of more complex differential theories are learning theory, field theory, and Gestalt theory.

The comparatively new science of psychology, like physical science in its beginnings, is still largely a collection of differential-operational theories. The psychologist cannot build at once a structure of ideas which presents a comprehensive theory of intentionl-functional behavior. It is mainly through phenomenological descriptions and through experiments which test operational differential theories that the psychologist obtains the numerous fragmentary pieces of knowledge which will enable him ultimately to form a comprehensive theoretical structure. Early psychologists were forced to grope for understanding through phenomenological descriptions, observations, and experiments. This research enabled them to expand their store of fragmentary but nonetheless effective theoretical constructs. As we shall see later, the fragmentary nature of these constructs does not mean that psychology must abandon the quest for the understanding of the whole of intentional-functional behavior. Rather, the universality of man's existential quest implies that he will necessarily strive for a comprehensive theoretical view of psychology which will integrate partial discoveries and fill the gaps left by differential-theoretical structures. This new comprehensive structure of ideas will, in turn, illuminate and stimulate further development of the differential and operational psychological theories.

CHARACTERISTICS OF DIFFERENTIAL THEORIES

When we examine the characteristics of differential theories, we discover that they are not primordially reflective in the proper sense, that they are limited in comprehension, and that they are mastered by the actual performance of the operations concerned. We shall examine these three characteristics more or less in detail.

Reflection in the proper sense mans that man "bends back" on his own existence. When the psychologist reflects in this sense, he shifts his attention from the behavior which he has under observation to his own behavior as a psychologist. He then makes his own psychological mode of existence the object-pole of his investigation, and he develops a psychology of the psychologist. This reflection also enables him to hypothesize about the relationships between the psychological mode of existence, other modes of existence, and the primordial structure of existence itself. To further his understanding he may borrow comprehensive concepts from philosophers. He uses these as hypothetical constructs in his sytsem of ideas, suspending belief or disbelief in their ontological status. Moreover, he keeps his reflection on his psychological mode of existence in constant dialogue with the phenomena and the theoretical constructs developed by differential theorists. If the result of his reflection is clearly inconsistent with the phenomena, he rejects the borrowed constructs and revises his theory.

As we shall see later in our analysis, this theory of the psychological mode of existence is not the whole of comprehensive psychological theory. It is its necessary foundation. It may be called, therefore, fundamental or foundational theory.

In the strict or proper sense, differential and operational theories in psychology are not reflective. Differential theorists are not primordially interested in the psychological mode of existence as a whole. Reflection on the psychological mode and all its differentiations is not a study which lies within the realm of one or the other differential theory. On the contrary, it implies of necessity a study *about* all the differential theories from a general, independent, theoretical viewpoint. Such a viewpoint must remain outside the confines of one or the other differential theory. For a differential theory is only one limited approach to the psychological mode of existence as a whole. Therefore, it can never provide the ultimate basis for a total outlook on the whole psychological mode of existence.

The differential and operational theorist reflects, however, in a less proper or strict sense. Though he does not reflect on his own psychological mode of existence, he may reflect on the effectiveness of his empirical operations. He may also think about the operational translation of his hypotheses. Again, he may reflect on the possibilities of the integration of operational propositions into a logically consistent structure. Each differential theory selects its own constructs in order to develop a structure of ideas which represents the relationship of behavioral phenomena observed within its domain. These constructs, however, are determined by their usefulness for structuring the specific phenomena. They are not suitable, therefore, for an understanding of the psychological mode of existence itself.

In other words, differential and operational theories are not primordially concerned with the mode of existence of the psychologist himself. They are primarily oriented toward those behavioral phenomena which are the object of the theory in question. The so-called reflection of the differential or the operational theorist thus remains outside of himself.

The operational theorist is involved in a thoughtful consideration of the functional implications of the findings in a certain field of psychology. And the differential theorist is concerned with the systematic relationship of behavioral phenomena and operational propositions within a single area of psychology.

We should add here that some differential theories, such as the psychoanalytic and psychotherapeutic, imply a certain type of self-reflection. It differs, however, from reflection on the psychological mode of existence as a whole. First of all, self-reflection is not the primary aim of psychoanalytic and psychotherapeutic theories. Second, this limited self-reflection refers in practice to the analyst or therapist only in terms of a special purpose, such as the improvement of the therapeutic relationship. Finally, this self-reflection is not concerned with the psychological mode of existence in all its manifestations in differential theories. It refers only to the analytic or psychotherapeutic differentiation and not to the psychological mode of existence as such.

We may conclude that the differential theories never have self-reflection as a primary aim. Rather, they are an immediate outgrowth of man's spontaneous cognitive mode of existence.

Comprehensive theory, on the contrary, is a more remote development of man's cognitive mode of being. Man's spontaneous manner of knowing is not directed first toward knowing himself. He responds first of all to the phenomena which reveal themselves to his senses. Self-reflection is secondary. Another link between differential operational theories and man's spontaneous cognitive way of existence is the fruitfulness of both ways of knowing for subsequent activity. Our knowledge in daily life directs our activity. And the results of our activity supply us in turn with the knowledge of new phenomena. Differential and, more specifically, operational theories also lead to new experimental and observational activities of the psychologist. These provide him in turn with the knowledge of new phenomena. Comprehensive theory, on the contrary, cannot be translated immediately into operational terms.

The second main characteristic of differential theories is that they are limited in comprehension. They are not aimed primarily at a comprehensive knowledge of behavior. The most basic characteristic of every differential-operational theory is its commitment to a certain dimension of behavior. Such a perspective uncovers aspects of behavior while it covers up other aspects. These latter can be revealed only by a change of perspective. And changed perspectives imply other differential theories.

A differential theory aims at an integration of operational postulates and the phenomena that are discovered in the light of these postulates. The latter are determined by their capability of being translated into empirical operations. These operations are concrete, limited modes of experiment and observation. They always imply limited perspectives: only certain phenomena are revealed. Therefore, the integration of operational postulates and their corresponding phenomena is necessarily limited to that which is revealed in the light of particular perspectives. Differential theory can never seek the comprehensive integration of the perspectives of all other differential theories in the light of a total view. Logically, a differential theory *as differential* cannot possibly produce an overall view that transcends the perspective of every differential theory including its own. It may, however, seek to integrate in the light of its *own limited perspective* the findings of other differential theories.

Learning theory, for example, may consider phenomena described by psychoanalysis. But this consideration will of necessity be from the perspective of learning theory. This implies that it will not include the special aspects which reveal themselves only in the light of the psychoanalytic viewpoint. In other words, such an integration would not be a comprehensive integration but rather an absorption of the findings of one area of psychology by another. The differential theorist would merely demonstrate in such a case that he can consider from his own specific perspective the material that has been uncovered in another field of psychology. And he would imply that this material of the other field manifests not only its own particular profile but also the profile in which he is specializing.

This possibility of looking upon all phenomena of behavior from various viewpoints and of uncovering various profiles clarifies for us the very specific sense in which a differential theory can be comprehensive. That is, the differential-theoretical mode of existence in psychology is *comprehensive* in so far as it stands out toward the whole of behavior. But it is *limited-comprehensive* in so far as it views all behavior from only *one perspective,* such as the psychoanalytic, the organismic, or the psycho-physiological point of view. In the latter sense, each differential-theoretical approach will always remain limited or directed toward only one profile of behavior. Nevertheless, its contribution, incomplete as it may be, is indispensable for the understanding of behavior as a whole. The analytic approach to behavior, for example, cannot dispense with the necessity for sociological, genetic, and physiological psychology. Nor can these latter abrogate the need for the analytic method. No psychologist, whether comprehensive, differential, operational, or applied, should either underestimate or overestimate any differential approach to behavior.

The third main characteristic of differential theories is that they are mastered by the actual performance of the operations involved. The psychologist who specializes in a differential theory rooted in empirical operations conducts the necessary operations initially under competent supervision of a psychologist who is already an expert in the field. Empirical operations imply the use of experimental techniques which embody the theory concerned. When the student masters these techniques, he gains at the same time a concrete knowledge of the theory.

For example, one becomes a psychotherapist by practicing therapy under the direction of a supervisor who examines the strengths and weaknesses in the student's therapy sessions. The latter are tape-recorded or observed by means of a one-way vision screen. In this manner, it is quite possible to become an effective therapist without a profound theoretical insight into the meaning of therapeutic psychology and its relationship to the whole of psychology.

Again, a psychologist may conduct fruitful experiments regarding the learning ability of animals. He may draw valuable conclusions from these experiments. At the same time, he may have very litle theoretical insight into the relevance of these conclusions for certain aspects of human behavior. This lack of general theoretical insight does not invalidate the concrete worth of his experimentation. Sooner or later it may be evaluated by comprehensive psychologists and find its place in the whole of psychology.

Another psychologist may be trained in the administration of intelligence and aptitude tests. He is quite competent in computation. He engages in valuable research in the measurement of intelligence. It is not at all necessary, for the performance of these operations as such, that he reflect on the meaning of this measured intelligence within the whole of human behavior. To be sure, it would be rewarding for such a specialist to engage in such reflection. Indeed, most schools of psychology do stimulate insight far beyond that of mere operational technique. But a differential psychologist can perform effective, well-controlled research without being aware of its relationship to the whole of the object-pole of psychology.

Every expert in any differential-operational field of psychology becomes an expert by participating in operational research. While doing so, he develops a sensitivity for the kinds of questions raised by his specific field. He becomes keenly aware of the types of observational and experimental operations through which these questions may be answered. Differential theories, such as psychoanalytical and physio-psychological, develop their own complex of questions, methods, and operations so that every differential expert acquires a special orientation toward his own field. The psychoanalytically-oriented scientist knows by practical initiation, for example, that he cannot use the methods of cybernetics in order to understand the subjective qualities of the feelings of his patient. On the other hand, it is self-evident to the psychologist who works in the field of cybernetics that he cannot directly use constructs such as the *Oedipus complex* of Freud and the *shadow* of Jung to build a brain model.

We may conclude that the learning theorist, the client-centered therapist, the psychoanalyst, and the physiological psychologist all become experts in their differential and operational theories not by reflection but by action. They do not learn the meaning of psychology within their specific fields by means of a theoretical introduction. They learn their profession through practical experience in operational research. Practical training in a differential or operational theory develops in the student a specific interest in a particular profile of behavior and teaches him how to explore it. Reflection upon the more profound nature, meaning, and relationships of this specialized mode of psychological existence lies, as such, beyond the scope of differential and operational theory.

It should be evident by now that the theorizing of the differential psychologist is intimately bound to and limited by his concrete research. Differential theory is, therefore, essentially operational, immediately related to the concrete operations performed in research. The psychological mode of such a theorist is absorbed by one specific perspective of the object pole of psychology. He thus develops observational and experimental designs which enable him increasingly to discover new knowledge about his own area of interest. His mode of involvement with a specific profile gradually reveals its structure, variability, conditions, and functional relationships. But his concrete operations are limited in type.

Such specialization does not preclude communication and intellectual stimulation among various differential theorists. Characteristically, however, the differential-operational theorist is interested in other differential theories from his own point of view. He interacts with other theorists primarily insofar as they enlighten him in the study of the specific profile of behavior in which he is doing research.

CREATIVITY OF THE DIFFERENTIAL THEORIST

Despite the limitation of his field of research, the differential-theoretical psychologist is far from a technician without creativity. A series of significant experiments or observations is an organized elaboration of an original question posed to behavior. The theorist is aware that his series of experiments as such is not his decisive contribution to science. He knows that his creative contribution is the discovery of a crucial question and the embodiment of this question in observational and experimental operations. He realizes that it is possible for him to ask an unlimited number of questions. But he also knows that an infinite number of possible questions is relatively useless in the sense that they will not lead to deeper understanding of human behavior. He no longer shares the naïve optimism of certain scientists of an earlier period who tended to forget that they were profiting from centuries of speculation which helped them to eliminate many unfruitful questions. He realizes that tentative thought, observation, speculation, and argumentation are necessary before one can pose a question to behavior which opens up really new vistas or horizons.

Let us consider the case of the psychologist who is doing admirable research in psychotherapy. It would be naïve to believe that he could be capable of effective operational questioning without the benefit of countless years of practice of therapy, of reflection on processes, of talking, arguing, hypothesizing, and publishing about psychotherapy on the part of earlier psychologists. It would be impossible to do effective contemporary research in psychotherapy if other psychologists had not practiced long ago the infant science of psychotherapy and reflected upon it. The tedious labor of discovering the most valuable perspectives and questions can require years of concentrated creative endeavor. The differential-operational theorist cannot neglect this creative, pre-operational phase of his work. If he is wise, he knows that he may lose more in the long run by such neglect than he would gain by impetuously going through the motions of skillful measurement or experiment. His observations and experiments might be well controlled and executed without contributing in the least to the understanding of the profile under study. He might conceivably produce reams of accurate reports of useless experiments about trivia.

In a sense, the pre-operational constituent of the differential-theoretical mode of existence is the crucial one which determines the significance of the research itself. This constituent is at work not only in the first beginnings of a science, for it repeats itself as long as the science lives. Over and over again, the pre-operational discovery of a possibly fruitful question is followed by the translation of this question into operations. Behavior itself gives an answer to the operational question. The answer is hidden in the so called "data" gained in observation and experimentation. The scientist must interpret this answer creatively. The period of reflection on the data may be called the post-operational constituent of the differential-theoretical mode of existence. This post-operational constituent, however, is pre-operational in relation to the *next* related experiment or observation. The differential-operational theorist reflects on the data which he has obtained in order to formulate new effective operational questions. Therefore, the pre-operational mode of existence reactualizes itself continually in scientific existence. If it did not do so, science would die out as a dynamic enterprise. It would become a monotonous repetition of what has already been done.

REDUCTIONIST TENDENCY IN THE
DIFFERENTIAL-THEORETICAL MODE OF EXISTENCE

Having considered the chief characteristics of the differential-theoretical mode of existence, we should point out the dangers inherent in it. Every mode of existence endangers human existence as a whole insofar as it tends to identify the whole of life with itself. The same may be said of the various constituents of each individual mode of existence. Each of these limited approaches to one mode of existence sometimes attempts to absorb within itself the whole mode of which it is only one component. Differential theory, for example, is only one constituent of the whole of psychology. Yet there is often a tendency in the differential-theoretical mode to regard itself as the entire psychological mode of existence. We may carry this statement further. As we have seen, the differential-theoretical mode differentiates itself in many specific modes, such as the psychoanalytical, the behavioristic, and the physio-psychological. Observation of these specialized modes reveals that each of them sometimes tends to identify itself with the whole differential-theoretical mode or even with the entire psychological mode of existence. This phenomenon appears so frequently that it calls for explanation. We shall do this by describing some of the conditions which foster the appearance and reappearance of this phenomenon. These conditions are, first of all, the fundamental structure of our existence, which compels us to approach the object pole of psychology under certain profiles or perspectives; next, the possible seduction of successful psychological methods; and, finally, the seduction of sudden new breakthroughs in psychology.

REDUCTIONISM AND THE EXISTENTIAL STRUCTURE OF MAN

We must refer here to our earlier explication of implicit assumptions which have a hypothetical status in the science of psychology. According to these assumptions, man is a bodily existent, an embodied subjectivity. The fact that he exists in and through a body implies that he can attain to the universal or the totality only by many partial encounters with the multitude of phenomena. This general truth of existence must be predicated by the psychological mode of existence. Every differential-operational theory is in reality one of these many encounters with phenomena. Each one uncovers only certain phenomena insofar as diffential theory views the whole of behavior under only one perspective.

The differential theorist who is engaged in such a partial approach to reality is still driven, however, by his existential intentionality toward comprehension of the whole. The need to know the whole permeates, as it were, his quest for partial knowledge. This need may distort his awareness of the limitations of his differential perspective. It may even lead the psychologist to believe that his differential theory is a model for all behavior under all its aspects. The tremendous dynamic drive to be involved in all-that-is may even seduce him to believe that his differential theory is the model not only for all behavior but for all reality. This last distortion is called psychologism. It would seem that the existential dynamism toward comprehension is so pervasive in man that it renders the overestimation of differential theory unavoidable, at least from time to time. As we shall see later, an explicit attempt to develop a comprehensive theoretical psychology may lessen considerably this implicit attempt toward comprehension by differential theorists. For this implicit attempt to extrapolate beyond the data of differential theory can be very harmful to psychology. It could prevent a balanced understanding of behavior.

REDUCTIONISM AND THE
SEDUCTION OF THE SUCCESSFUL METHOD

We have seen that the differential-theoretical psychologist begins to master his areas of specialization by a thorough initiation into methodical research. The efficiency of his method is determined by the profile of behavior which he studies. A highly developed differential-operational theory presupposes a refined and efficient methodology which alone reveals the particular perspective desired. Such a methodology is fundamentally an experimental elaboration of one perspective which opens up a specific area of behavioral phenomena. Every other perspective, if it is well developed and embodied in an empirical methodology, should manifest a quite different methodology since it reveals a quite different field of phenomena. In other words, one criterion of the efficiency and precision of a differential-operational theory is its uniqueness. The very refinement of the psychological method of a differential field accounts for its impressive results within its own area.

The continual pressure of the existential need for universal comprehension, however, combined with the daily experience of the admirable achievements of a differential method, cannot but tempt the differential theorist to overestimate the power of this method. He may assume that the method which has been so successful in the special area of his research can also be applied, with necessary changes, in other fields of psychology. He may be seduced to believe that this method, if used in other areas, would lead to results similar to the successes in his own field. Consequently, the psychoanalyst, the learning theorist, the student of cybernetics, and the physiological psychologist may at times indulge in extrapolations beyond the confines of their respective differential theories.

This tendency may lead to the imperialism of certain theories at the expense of other possible ones. The various aspects of the object-pole of psychology can be revealed only by the development of as many methods as possible. The imperialism of only a few methods of research would imply the restriction of the whole object-pole of psychology to only those few profiles which could be explored by these methods. Such a methodical restriction of the psychological mode of existence might lead, unfortunately, to a considerable impoverishment of man's knowledge of intentional-functional behavior. It might also lead psychologists to mistake their thorough knowledge of certain aspects of behavior for a thorough understanding of behavior under all its possible perspectives.

The psychological mode of existence is a searching standing-out toward behavior by means of observation and experiment. Since the empirical or the applied psychologist cannot understand behavior from a single viewpoint, he seeks for such understanding through different viewpoints which he elaborates by means of observation and experiment. He cannot know *a priori* which specific phenomena will reveal themselves to him when he assumes a new approach and embodies it in a strict methodology. At times the results of his research are disappointing. Only through his assumption of a variety of viewpoints and their embodiment in observational and experimental methods does an unexpected realm of phenomena sometimes open up. The psychologist cannot foresee or plan this sudden disclosure of a new field of phenomena. He can only be faithful to his task of constant translation of operational hypotheses into concrete research. It is quite understandable that a sudden, unexpected breakthrough to a realm of phenomena never before revealed is an exciting event.

Frequently such a discovery changes our insights in a radical way. Then the inherent existential groping of man for universal comprehensive knowledge may unfortunately fixate itself on such a new realm of phenomena. He may be led to believe that this particular discovery is the key to the comprehensive knowledge of all behavior under all its aspects and conditions. He may be seduced into assuming, for example, that the unconscious, the libido, the stimulus-response bond, the striving for superiority, or the feedback mechanism is the ultimate explanation of all behavior. He may be inclined to forget that a discovery which is based on concrete operations can never be the last and ultimate explanation of the whole of behavior, because operations are limited in space and time. They embody a certain limited way of looking at reality, a circumscribed point of view. Therefore, they can never reveal more than a limited profile of behavior which corresponds with the limited perspective which they embody.

An explicit attempt at comprehensive theory would lessen this tendency toward over-evaluation of important but limited discoveries. Comprehensive theorists would evaluate the variety of incidental breakthroughs in the light of an open theoretical vision. Such a comprehensive theoretical psychology, on the other hand, would never attempt to obstruct the one-sided growth of differential psychologies. On the contrary, it would foster this growth as a desirable, limited specialization which enriches psychology. In the meantime, however, comprehensive theory would balance the impact of this one-sided growth by pointing out other possible profiles of behavior which have not been investigated. In other words, comprehensive psychology would foster one-sidedness *as one-sidedness.* Or, it would promote at the same time both one-sided specialization and the awareness that specialization is by definition limited, so that it can never be a basis for the understanding of behavior as a whole.

The science of psychology is of necessity dependent on the revelation of new phenomena. The order of this opening up of new profiles of behavior cannot be planned according to a hierarchy of importance of these phenomena. To be sure, psychology is in principle capable of revealing behavioral phenomena gradually and unceasingly. But the psychologist can never foresee which phenomena will reveal themselves first in the light of his research. Nor can he know *a priori* which phenomena are most important for the understanding of the whole of behavior. Therefore, the development of the science of behavior is necessarily many-sided and often unharmonious. Psychology is the result of the interplay of many one-sided differential theoretical activities carried on by numerous psychologists. It is obviously impossible for every psychologist to assume all psychological perspectives and their embodiment in empirical operations as his own. Some will inevitably devote their energy to phenomenological, experimental, or clinical research. Others will concentrate on the application of psychology to the improvement of behavior within concrete life situations. Others again will dedicate their lives as psychologists to theoretical reflection. And all of them will uncover new phenomena from their own particular, one-sided perspectives. Moreover, no authentic science of psychology is possible unless all modes of being a psychologist make their contribution to the whole.

To be really fruitful in his work, each psychologist must realize that his specialized psychological mode of existence has a relative value. He must be aware that the same is true of his psychological discoveries, no matter how exciting they are. The value of his specialized mode of existence and of the knowledge which it reveals is essential but not exclusive. It does not exclude the values of other psychological modes, of other differential-operational theories, and of the phenomena which they uncover. All differential theories and the dimensions of behavior which they uncover are of value, but we cannot determine *a priori what* their precise value is. New perspectives and new profiles of behavior will continue to open up in the future. In the light of these discoveries, the value of former discoveries may prove to be more or less than it originally seemed to be. The value of every differential-operational theory thus remains relative in so far as we cannot determine precisely what this value is.

Reductionism and the Two Main Differential-Theoretical Modes of Existence

The differential-theoretical mode of psychological existence divides itself into a variety of modes according to the diversity of aspects assumed by its theorists. While every viewpoint differs from every other, it remains possible that a whole series of perspectives may have characteristics in common. When we seek this commonality among the many perspectives studied in contemporary psychology, we discover that all these perspectives may be subsumed under two main categories. One series of approaches in differential psychology tends to reveal primarily the intentional-functional profiles of behavior; the other, the external profiles of behavior which are measurable in exact quantitative units. Examples of the intentional-functional differential theories are, among others, the psychoanalytic, the psychotherapeutic, and various clinical theories. The external behavior category of differential theories may be illustrated by the physiological, learning, sensuous-perceptual, and cybernetic theories. How are we to explain the emergence of these two main types of viewpoints which have characterized psychology from its beginning?

All science, to be sure, begins with the observation of externally perceptible phenomena. The particular phenomena with which the science of psychology originates are behavioral. The psychologist considers these phenomena from different viewpoints. He discovers that he can view behavioral phenomena under either their measurable, quantitative aspect or their qualitative, intentional-functional aspect. Both profiles of behavior, it should be noted, present themselves immediately to our perception. Even the pre-scientific observer in daily life is aware of this givenness of the two main profiles of behavior. Such awareness is commonly expressed in spontaneous questions. Somebody smiles. The observer of the smile may ask himself spontaneously: "What does it mean? Is the person who smiles pleased or is he laughing at me?" He reflects on the situation to find out which answer is true. The question reveals, however, that the observer is implicitly aware that a theoretical distinction can be made between external behavior and its intentional-functional meaning. It is to be noted that he does not make an *absolute* distinction between external behavior and its intentional-functional aspect. As long as what he observes is really behavior, it has to have some meaning, some intentionality, some function. The doubt in the questioner's mind is not a doubt regarding the meaningfulness of the behavior, but regarding *the kind* of meaning embodied in the behavior. Behavior immediately presents itself to the observer as meaningful.

When behavior is no longer intentional-functional, it ceases to be behavior. At the same time, it ceases to be the object-pole of the science of psychology. For example, the falling open of the mouth of a corpse is not behavior. It lacks the characteristic of intentional functionality. Therefore, no psychologist as psychologist devotes his time to the study of the automatic movements of dead bodies. If he observes such automatic movement at all, he does it only insofar as it is relevant to the understanding of behavior.

The spontaneous awareness of both an intentional-functional and an external measurable profile of behavior points to the two main differential-theoretical modes of existence in psychology. For science is ultimately a methodical and critical elaboration of our spontaneous awareness. Both types of psychology have produced effective scientists; both have led to discoveries which have enriched our understanding of behavior. Evidently, the comprehensive theoretical psychologist has no right to reject apodictically either one of these main types of differential psychology, since he is striving for the integration of the science of psychology as a whole. He cannot decree that either behavioristic or intentional-functional psychology is not truly psychology. He is a scientific theorist, not a philosopher. Regardless of his personal bias, he must theorize on the basis of what psychologists actually do and factually demonstrate.

On the other hand, the differential theorist, who is engaged in research that pertains to one of these two main types of psychology, may be seduced by his own need for universal knowledge. He may be inclined to perceive his own type of psychology as the only scientific one. He may expect that it alone will eventually offer a complete understanding of the whole of behavior in all its profiles. The success of the methods developed and the insights reached by his type of psychology may encourage his bias. Such unconscious extrapolation may even manifest itself in disparaging remarks about the other type. The representative of the behavioristic type of psychology may talk derisively of the "subjective nonsense" of analytical research. Such remarks spread more heat than light. No profile of behavior is totally irrelevant to the understanding of behavior. And every profile impels us to adopt a different method of investigation.

The danger of an unconscious imperialism is that one type of psychology attempts to absorb the other. Such an attempt tends to reduce the whole of behavior to one of its two main profiles. If carried out on both sides, it would inevitably lead to a dualistic conception of behavior. Such a conception can be avoided only as long as both types of psychology remain clearly aware of their limitations and maintain mutual respect. The differential-operational theorist of each type of psychology, however, is so absorbed in his concrete investigations that he has little time or energy left to immerse himself in the totally different language, methods, and problems which arise in the other type of psychology. Therefore, practically speaking, the unity of intentional-functional behavior can be safeguarded only on a higher level of theorizing which occupies itself exclusively with the respectful integration of the contributions of the two main types of psychological existence in a higher unity.

Once it is clearly understood that both main types of psychology are limited modes of standing out toward behavior, it may be confidently stated that each type extends itself in its *own* way to the *whole* of intentional-functional behavior. The approach of each type will always remain a partial approach directed primarily toward one main profile of intentional-functional behavior. Nevertheless, the contribution of each type, incomplete as it may be, is indispensable. Man is by nature bodily subjectivity or incarnated intentionality. Therefore, both the biophysiological and the intentional-functional aspects are indispensable constituents of his behavior. They are embedded in different languages, methods, and operations. They represent relative but indispensable values for our understanding of behavior as a whole.

CHAPTER FIVE

THE COMPREHENSIVE THEORETICAL
MODE OF EXISTENCE
IN PSYCHOLOGY

EMERGENCE OF THE COMPREHENSIVE-THEORETICAL MODE OF EXISTENCE

The psychologist studies intentional-functional behavior from a variety of aspects. Each differential mode of psychology opens up a specific area of concrete phenomena which, at first sight, seem endless in their diversity. The differential theorist, however, unites these phenomena by means of differential constructs which have an integrating function within his special field. These constructs embody the fundamental interest of his differential approach. In the last analysis, it is this theoretical perspective which unites diverse manifestations of behavior within his specific differential theory.

For example, behaviors as varied as walking, smiling, kissing, and boxing may be observed from the aspect of physiological psychology. The theorist may use a differential construct, such as muscle innervation, to indicate a physiological quality common to all these types of behavior. To be sure, a smile, a kiss, a boxing match are experienced in daily life as quite different kinds of behavior which reveal an inexhaustible richness of meanings. But in the example given, the richness of perspectives of each one of these concrete events is relegated to the background in favor of one profile—the psycho-physiological. This

130

profile represents an aspect of behavior selected because of a specific differential approach. Other differential approaches may place the same behavior in totally different contexts, such as the psychoanalytical, client-centered, or cybernetic theories.

This differential procedure, as we have seen, is absolutely necessary because our bodily mode of existence compels us to exploration by means of perspectives. We are incapable of grasping the whole of reality at once. The need to integrate these various profiles of behavior, however, leads to the emergence of the comprehensive theoretical mode of existence.

This mode of existence aims at the unification of the differential approaches. Man's spontaneous existential interest in intentional behavior as a whole necessarily gives rise to comprehensive theory. Thus man seeks to restore the concreteness and wholeness of behavior which has been broken up into profiles by the differential modes of psychological existence. The comprehensive and differential modes are thus related to each other as synthetic and analytic studies of behavior.

Something similar to the mutual influence of differential and comprehensive theory can be observed even in the pre-scientific dimension of existence. In daily life, for instance, when we must function in a pragmatic fashion, we may consider certain objects not in their full richness but under only a few of their profiles. When we move our furniture to a new house, for example, we perceive our tables, chairs, paintings, and carpets from a point of view which differs from our usual perception of them. We may consider our paintings, for example, under two perspectives—their size and fragility. Keeping these two points in mind, we seek a safe place for our paintings among the other furniture in the moving van. At this moment we do not enjoy their subtle pastels, harmonious forms, and beautiful perspectives. Afterward, however, when the paintings adorn our new home, we no longer concentrate on size and fragility but lose ourselves in their aesthetic meaning.

Differential theory dwells much more on such abstracted profiles, however, than man does in everyday life. In daily life the painting remains primarily a painting, even if it is sometimes placed in a different context such as that of object to be moved efficiently. In differential theories such as physiological psychology or learning theory, however, a smile, a kiss, and a boxing match are nothing other than processes of a physiological nature or of conditioning and reinforcement. And both differential theories are valid because both series of constructs consider phenomena which are observable in a smile, a kiss, and a boxing match. The same may be said of a variety of other series of constructs such as experiential, social, and motivational ones.

However, it is not unthinkable that concrete behavior as a whole may evaporate, as it were, and lose its reality for a psychologist who studies behavior only insofar as it is resolved into profiles described in specific languages pertaining to widely different perspectives. This danger of loss of contact with concrete behavior as a whole increases with the development of psychology, which implies a proliferation of the psychological mode of existence into an increasing number of differential modes. Each of these necessarily develops its own conceptual frame of reference for its special profile of behavior. Moreover, each is intimately linked to empirical operations and develops its own operational language. The language, constructs, and methods of full-grown differential theories are thus very different from one another. We may even say that a differential theory demonstrates that it has attained its maximum efficiency only when it has developed an idiom of its own. This idiom of the specialist is not comprehended by the psychologist of any other differential theory so long as he—as the representative of that other theory—thinks in constructs proper to his own exclusive area of psychology.

A unified theory of behavior cannot be attained, therefore, simply by securing the sum total of the conceptual frames of reference or of the idioms characteristic of the various differential theories in psychology. They have no basic similarity to one another. Some of the differential theories, to be sure, may share a formal aspect such as a mathematical, statistical, or experimental-instrumental sophistication. But obviously this formal, external similarity is of no practical value in the scientific unification of concrete behavior as a whole.

The wholeness of behavior as it appears in psychology can be approximated only by comprehensive theoretical psychology. Such a science develops so-called foundational-integrational constructs which represent a plausible hypothesis of what behavior may be like in its wholeness. Differential theories, on the other hand, develop abstracted profiles of behavior which must be reintegrated within this hypothetical model.

A dialogue is possible between the hypothetical model of the whole and its parts, that is, between integrational constructs and differential constructs. Comprehensive theory is precisely this open on-going dialogue. In order to understand the nature, aim, and conditions of this dialogue, we must first make explicit what is implicit in the comprehensive theoretical mode of existence which, like every mode, can be analyzed in its constituents. We may distinguish five relevant constituents—the foundational, integrational, hypothetical, creative, and communicative—of this mode of existence. The following discussion of these constituents proposes to clarify the meaning and purpose of the comprehensive theoretical mode of existence and thereby of comprehensive theory as well.

The Foundational Constituent

The comprehensive-theoretical mode of existence is foundational and integrational. Comprehensive theory insofar as it is *foundational* examines the foundations, assumptions, and basic constructs of the science of psychology. It does so, first of all, by making explicit what is implicit in the subject-pole and the object-pole of the psychological mode of existence. The results of this explication, however, are kept constantly in a dialectical relationship with the findings of the differential psychologies.

133

Comprehensive theory insofar as it is *integrational* aims at a continuous integration of the differential psychologies in the light of the foundations, assumptions, and basic constructs developed by foundational theory. The *integrational* constituent is thus primarily concerned with the comprehensive aspect, whereas the *foundational* constituent is primarily concerned with the basic aspect of comprehensive theory.

The psychologist who studies the foundations of his science engages in a reflective mode of knowledge which is essentially different from the direct mode of knowledge which characterizes differential-operational psychology. He studies that specific mode of existence itself which is called psychology. He examines it insofar as it manifests itself in the actual and historical endeavors of scientific psychologies. He observes what psychologists do in multiverse methods within diverse areas. He attempts to uncover the basic mode of existence which is revealed through their work. Once he has delineated this phenomenon, he goes further and endeavors to make explicit what is implicit in it. He strives in this way to arrive at a better understanding of the subject-pole and the object-pole of psychology and of their mutual involvement. Thus he discovers the foundations for an integration of the differential psychologies.

The center of interest of the comprehensive theorist differs from that of the differential psychologist. The latter has refined or specialized his psychological intentionality to an interest in one of the many profiles in which behavior can appear to the human observer. His attention is totally absorbed by this specific aspect of the object-pole of psychology. He is involved in the development and practice of methods which will enable him to uncover the structure, variability, conditions, and functional relations of behavior as they appear in this one specific profile. It is not his primary aim to discover how his research is related to the psychological mode of existence as such. Neither does he consider it his task to discover and describe how his special knowledge can be integrated with the findings of other differential theories. On the contrary, his theorizing is intimately bound to and limited by his concrete research. Therefore, it is essentially operational. This does not imply that he cannot study *all* behavior. It implies only that the differential theorist *qua* differential theorist cannot study all behavior from *all* viewpoints opened up by the various differential approaches. He can study *all* behavior, however, as it appears under the one specific profile which forms the object of his research. But he cannot, at the same time and with the same method, study all behavior as it appears under all other profiles.

We should point out here that neither can the comprehensive theorist study all behavior *exhaustively* under all possible profiles. This would be impossible. First of all, the number of profiles in which behavior can appear is inexhaustible. Moreover, comprehensive theory must be constantly in readiness for the limited number of differential studies of single profiles so that it may comprehend them together. What the comprehensive theorist aims at, therefore, is the continuous integration of those profiles which have been already studied by differential psychologists. He explores these in the light of his explication of the foundations of psychology.

Consequently, a comprehensive psychology can emerge only after the development of various differential theories. The comprehensive theoretical mode of existence is essentially a reflective mode which can arise only when sufficient matter for reflection is present. In the science of behavior, this matter consists of the activities, methods, data, and theories of the differential psychologists.

One might develop a philosophical psychology, to be sure, by reflection on immediate spontaneous experience. But it would be impossible to develop on this basis a comprehensive *scientific* theory of psychology. The latter is by definition a reflection on the discoveries of scientific psychologists. Comprehensive theoretical psychology can and should be enlightened by the insights of philosophical psychology. However, its basis, source, and criterion remain the concrete phenomena uncovered by differential psychologists. For this reason, the statements of comprehensive theoretical psychology are such that postulates can be deduced from them which are open to the empirical test. Comprehensive psychology is thus organized thought about and integration of what scientific psychologists are doing, discovering, inventing, formulating, and applying.

Reflection on the foundations of the psychological mode of existence can therefore never be separated from reflection on what empirical and applied psychologists are doing. It is precisely through consideration of their activities that the comprehensive psychologist becomes aware of his own specific mode of existence, which is the *reflective* scientific mode. This mode has many constituents. It is now clear that one of these is an awareness of the generally accepted, significant results of empirical and applied psychology.

The differential psychologist is not a foundational theorist. He is engaged in actual experiments, observations, and applications. He is so much absorbed by this operational activity that he has little time to reflect on the foundations of his science. Therefore, the necessary limitation of his work necessarily leads to the emergence of comprehensive theoretical psychology as a field of specialization.

The difference between comprehensive and differential theory in psychology may be simply expressed. Both types of theory are bound to the phenomena which manifest themselves in behavioral research. Differential theory cultivates research in psychology by systematically directing the critical attention of the scientist to a certain profile of behavior. Comprehensive theory, on the other hand, fosters the understanding of behavior primarily by concentrating upon the psychological mode of existence itself insofar as it is revealed by the differential psychologists.

The development of this foundational aspect of theory is the condition for the development of the secondary or *integrational* approach of comprehensive theory. In other words, foundational theory creates a frame of reference within which the scientist can integrate the phenomena which are revealed by the differential theories. Thus an introduction to a differential theory trains a student to perceive certain isolated profiles in critical, controlled, and methodical ways. This training leads him to operational research within his specialized field of behavioral study. But reflection upon the basis, meaning, and relationships of his work and of the profile which he explores lies beyond the perspective of the differential theory itself.

Foundational theory will reveal itself as ultimately useful not only for the general understanding of behavior but also for empirical and applied psychology. All theorizing, including comprehensive, means that the psychologist perceives behavior in new ways. A new comprehensive perception develops from reflection upon differential perceptions of behavior. Every new perception, including comprehensive, will uncover new possibilities of meaning in behavior. These discoveries, in turn, will sooner or later stimulate the empirical and applied psychologist to experiment with the newly perceived possibilities. Such experimentation and application will ultimately affect the practical course of human behavior and its conditions. A similar situation may be recalled in comprehensive theoretical physics. The new comprehensive perception of Einstein uncovered new possibilities in matter. Differential-operational theorists experimented with these possibilities and as a result were able to utilize nuclear energy. Similarly, the object-pole of psychology, "behavior," may change under the impact of comprehensive theory.

Another question now arises. Does the subject-pole of comprehensive theory also change under the impact of theorizing? Does the comprehensive psychologist gain new knowledge about himself and therefore about other subjects like himself? Any theorist who explores the foundations of his science necessarily learns something about himself. The foundational theorist in psychology investigates what the psychological mode of existence is. He discovers that it is one of the modes of human intentionality rooted in existence. Therefore, he will necessarily achieve knowledge about human existence which will sooner or later affect both his self-understanding and his own behavior.

This growth in self-understanding is not the primary aim of comprehensive psychology. Nevertheless, it is a necessary consequence of the study of the psychological mode of existence. We cannot overlook the fact that growth in self-understanding satisfies a deep urge in man. This need for self-understanding is usually an explicit or implicit constituent of the total motivation which sustains the activity of the comprehensive theorist in psychology.

The Integrational Constituent

The first constituent of the comprehensive-theoretical mode of existence is, as we have seen, the foundational attitude. A secondary constituent is the integrational attitude. The purpose of the integrational task in psychology is the comprehension of the findings of differential psychologies in the light of the constructs developed in foundational theory. An examination of the origin and meaning of the word *integration* may clarify this statement. The word is derived from *integratus,* the past participle of the Latin word *integrare,* which means to make whole or to renew. Integration, then, refers to the activity of restoring an integer, an original "untouched whole". This implies that in any attempt at integration, an original whole, an image of the totality, already exists or is given. It also implies that this whole has been split up into parts which must be reintegrated. It is therefore the task of the scientist to attempt to restore this whole and not simply to fabricate. In other words, a comprehensive scientist cannot merely piece together in an arbitrary manner a number of various parts. He must follow to the best of his abilities the structure of the whole insofar as it is known to him.

The originally given whole, in the case of psychology, is intentional-functional behavior. The split-up parts of this original whole are the profiles of behavior in so far as they have been investigated and elaborated by the differential psychologists. Foundational theory attempts to make explicit what is implicit in the originally given whole of intentional-functional behavior. The function of integrational theory, on the other hand, is to reintegrate into this explicated whole the profiles of behavior which have been abstracted by the differential psychologists.

PRE-SCIENTIFIC KNOWLEDGE OF BEHAVIOR AS A WHOLE

Every man has some pre-scientific notion of what intentional-functional behavior is. It would be impossible for him to respond to his fellowmen without some awareness of behavior. This is true of the psychologist as of all men. If he did not possess an implicit awareness of what behavior is before he began his scientific research, it would be impossible for him even to identify the object of his study. Without this awareness he could not, in fact, distinguish the movement of a machine from that of a child or a patient. In practice, all psychologists possess an awareness of intentional-functional behavior as a whole even though some formally deny it in theory. They demonstrate by their daily behavior in the laboratory, clinic, and classroom that they knew implicitly what behavior is even before they began to do research in it. They were aware of an originally given whole of behavior which calls for restoration. The isolated profiles which are abstracted from this whole can take on meaning only in the light of their source. In view of this fact, there is no experiential justification for the differential psychologist to maintain that he has no implicit awareness of behavior while he engages in research on one of the profiles of behavior. Psychology need not wait for innumerable phenomena revealed by single profile studies to be summed up to form the first human knowledge of what behavior is. We know implicitly what behavior is from the very beginning of our investigations. Phenomenology makes this implicit knowledge explicit.

Thus differential psychologists uncover operationally the lawful structures which become manifest when they observe behavior in certain profiles under varying conditions. Then comprehensive psychology reintegrates this newly gained knowledge within our primary awareness about the behavior of man which becomes less implicit and increasingly explicit during this scientific process.

THE PRE-SCIENTIFIC AND THE SCIENTIFIC TENDENCY TOWARD INTEGRATION

The tendency toward integration or *com*prehension is inherent in man's existence. Comprehensive psychology as integration reflects what each man does spontaneously in daily life when he attempts to organize his knowledge about his own behavior and that of his fellowmen into some kind of meaningful whole. In a sense, every man is a born integrational psychologist, at least in a naïve, uncritical, pre-scientific way. For every man attempts to integrate—in a primitive manner—his experience about himself and his fellowmen. To be sure, the differential psychologist disregards this natural inclination to psychological synthesis when he concentrates on one profile of behavior during his highly specialized operations. Efficient scientific concentration in one area can only be gained at the expense of concentration on the whole. It is interesting to observe, however, that the differential psychologist, like other men, is guided in his daily life outside the laboratory by some implicit apprehension of the whole of human behavior. To be aware of behavior as a whole is unavoidable. It is an existential: it belongs to man's existence.

Science, however, is the critical and controlled elaboration of the pre-scientific modes of understanding existence. And comprehensive scientific psychology is the outgrowth of man's natural striving for a coherent comprehension of his differential perceptions of behavior. The ultimate objective of all psychology is the understanding and explanation of behavior. This is only possible on the basis of an explicit discovery and formulation of the unifying factors and universal characteristics which bind the disconnected perspectives of the science of behavior into an ordered and comprehensive system of relations. Psychology cannot stop with a disorganized enumeration of phenomena which have been discovered and accumulated in experimental and clinical observation. Neither can it be satisfied with the mere enumeration of the profiles of behavior which have been investigated by differential psychologies. Therefore, comprehensive psychology as *integrational* strives to reduce this complexity and plurality to a kind of unity.

WHY COMPREHENSIVE AND NOT DIFFERENTIAL THEORY?

A differential theory is solely concerned with a particular aspect of behavior. Therefore it cannot integrate the perspectives of other differential theories. Freudian theory, for example, does not attempt to integrate discoveries concerning the role of conditioning in the learning process so as to change the main constructs of Freudian theory itself as a result of this open integration. Each differential theory maintains its own point of view. One of the perspectives in which Alfred Adler, for example, sees all behavior is that of striving for power. And all behavior can indeed appear in this perspective. It opens up a richness of phenomena which might have gone unnoticed if Adler had not taught us to "see" all behavior in this possible dimension. One of the differential perspectives of Freud, on the other hand, was that of man's striving for pleasure. Psychology would be the poorer if Freud had not opened our eyes to this particular profile in which all behavior can appear. Similar statements may be made about all differential theories. This situation in the science of psychology is necessary and should always be maintained. Differential-theoretical understanding of behavior is and should be the fragmentation of man's original, implicit understanding of behavior as a whole. Each differential theory should therefore concentrate on its own perspective to the exclusion of others in order to be more fruitful in its own area of psychology. The intrinsic impossibility of forming a comprehensive theory of behavior on the basis of one differential theory lies in the very nature of concentration on isolated profiles.

Existential Foundations of Psychology

FOUNDATIONAL CONSTRUCTS

How do we obtain unifying constructs which point to behavior as a whole? Foundational theory produces such constructs through a phenomenological explication of behavior, which is based on naïve, natural observation of behavior as a whole. The results of this type of observation can be reported in case studies, in literature, and sometimes in philosophy. Phenomenological explication clarifies what is essential in naïve experiences. The foundational theorist crystallizes these explicit descriptions into unifying constructs. Subjective distortions may creep in during the process of reporting on natural observation and during the phenomenological explication. Therefore, as we shall see later, intersubjective validation, experimentation, and constant checking and re-checking are necessary. Moreover, the constant dialogue between the foundational constructs and the conclusions of differential psychologies serves as a control.

INTEGRATIONAL DIALOGUE AND PHENOMENOLOGY

We may now ask how an integrational dialogue is possible between the constructs obtained in foundational theory and the conclusions of differential theories? This interaction is possible because foundational and differential psychology have a common ground, phenomenology. The differential psychologist, like the foundational theorist, necessarily starts from natural observation. He is necessarily engaged in some kind of explicit or implicit phenomenology, for he sees meaning and structure in natural observation. Following the process of observation, he draws conclusions concerning various phenomena. Then he investigates the lawful relationships among these phenomena. The final result of his research is never a closed system, but only a tentative one. This is necessarily so because his insight into the profile of behavior which he studies always reveals breaks in continuity. The differential psychologist fills these gaps, as it were, by means of hypotheses which bind the known facts together in his differential-theoretical model.

The comprehensive psychologist requires the help of the phenomenological psychologist in order to initiate a fruitful dialogue with the differential psychologies. The natural observation and the phenomenological explication of the differential psychologist is frequently implicit, uncontrolled, unreported, unchecked. One of the tasks of the specialist in phenomenological psychology is to perform in a critical, scientific way what has sometimes already been done in a loose, pre-scientific way by the differential psychologist. He may, for example, provide critical reports of the natural observations which have led to psychoanalytic constructs such as Oedipus complex and transference. By means of the phenomenological method, he may make explicit in a scientific way the fundamental structures of these phenomena observed by psychoanalysts. Following such a procedure, a dialogue between the phenomenological explications of behavior as a whole and those particular profiles of behavior is possible because both explications follow the same method and speak the same language. They shed light on each other. We have now arrived at a description of comprehensive and of differential phenomenological explications of behavior. A dialogue between the two provides our first insight into how they can be integrated. It gives us the necessary knowledge of the phenomena which must be integrated within a scientific system.

THE COMPREHENSIVE SCIENTIFIC MODEL

For a comprehensive scientific psychology, it is not sufficient to have a knowledge of the various relevant phenomena of behavior which are the basis of the system. An understanding of their mutual lawful relationships must be established by operational observation and experimentation. The comprehensive psychologist relates them to one another and finally to the integrational constructs which have been developed by foundational psychology. He attempts in this way to make intelligible the intentional-functional structure as a whole. He does not have at his disposal, however, all possible lawful relationships which exist among phenomena of behavior. There-fore, the only method which remains to him to make behavior as a whole intelligible, is to form an image, picture, or model of behavior which reflects the psychological knowledge which has been achieved at the present moment of the development of psychology. Such a scientific model is thus a theoretical image of behavior devised by the comprehensive psychologist. He attempts to explain and to integrate within its structure the contributions of the differential theories. The isolated pro-files of behavior uncovered by these theories may now be said to delineate themselves in this model as a "Gestalt" or a well articulated structure.

The comprehensive model explains observed behavior, but it *is not* itself behavior. Therefore, this cognitive structure is not a reproduction of behavior like a photograph, a movie, or a tape recording. The scientific model of the integrational theorist is a constructed model, a tissue of ideas. It will never *mirror* intentional-functional behavior in its full concreteness, for it is the result of an intellectual process of reconstruction or *re* synthesis. As we have seen, behavior as it appears origi-nally has been broken down into various profiles by many differential psychologists in clinics, laboratories, and consulting rooms. Therefore, the comprehensive structure of behavior which results from an intellectual *re*construction of these profiles is always one which, as such, is not given in concrete behavior. In other words, every comprehensive scientific model is projected by the theoretical psychologist on the basis of the limited knowledge produced by the differential psychologists. It is an attempt to *con*ceive and to *com*prehend the various profiles of behavior in their interconnection. It is never a direct perception of intentional-functional behavior in its own inner unity.

On the other hand, it remains true that the model of the comprehensive psychologist is existentially oriented to behavior presented to perception in the various profiles of behavior. The fact that this theoretical construction of the comprehensive psychologist points to behavior implies that the object-pole is never absent in comprehensive psychology. That is, the model is based on the givenness of the phenomena to which it points as an existential structure. It is not merely imagination; it is not a subjective configuration or synthesis in the mind of the theoretical psychologist. The integrational theory must be in conformity with the phenomena uncovered in the differential psychologies to which it refers. Therefore, the behavior to which the integrational model refers is always indirectly present in the comprehensive theory of the psychologist.

The integrational model, however, represents at the same time more than the perceptible phenomena. Its character is truly existential, for it is an intellectual, subjective grasp of phenomena which reveal themselves to the human existent. This existential character implies that it would be a meaningless structure if considered in complete isolation from the differential theories and their phenomena. The content and meaning of this structure can be better found in the differential-operational psychologies to which it refers than in itself. The more the student of psychology immerses himself in the richness of differential-operational theories, the more this comprehensive structure gains in depth and meaning for him. Therefore, the comprehensive theory of psychology can never replace the differential psychologies on which it is nourished. In a sense, it is an outline of what can be found in these psychologies. An outline is worthless if we do not know the material from which it is drawn. Comprehensive theory is for the student of psychology an instrument that enables him to comprehend the relationships between the variety of phenomena and differential theories which he encounters while immersing himself continually in the study of differential psychologies.

INTEGRATIONAL CONSTRUCTS

Integrational theory is a scientific structure or model that increases in complexity during the dialogue between foundational constructs and differential psychologies. The growth of this complex structure implies an increase in constructs and sub-constructs which integrate differential theories and phenomena both with one another and with the foundational constructs.

We may define an integrational construct as follows:

> *A concept—expanding continually in articulation and definition—that refers hypothetically to observed behavioral phenomena, and that can be used most adequately for the integration of the greatest number and variety of phenomena and lawful relationships observed and structured by differential psychologies.*

The construct is thus not a "mental thing" isolated from the phenomena to which it points. This view of a construct is idealistic or rationalistic. Neither is it a mirror of something that exists as such outside the mind of the scientist. Such a conception would be positivistic. Existential psychology considers a scientific construct basically as a subjective structure of reference through which the scientist stands out toward a group of observed phenomena. The construct is thus a subjective-objective unity. It is a subjective structure of the scientist who explains and organizes groups of phenomena on the basis of their observed similarities. The comprehensive theorist cannot consider his constructs as absolute and final explanations of those phenomena to which they point. For new phenomena may reveal themselves in the light of new perspectives of differential psychologists. The old constructs may then prove to be inadequate to explain the new phenomena. Moreover, the continuing dialogue between foundational and differential theories may necessitate the design of new constructs. These may explain the phenomena in question no better than the former constructs did. Yet they may better facilitate the integration of these phenomena with other phenomena in the expanding integrational theory.

Therefore, the integrational construct is never an ultimate, but a provisional or hypothetical intellectual structure. The theoretical psychologist designs, defines, and redefines these conceptual structures in order to increase their accuracy as pointers to the phenomena observed; also to prevent confusion with other constructs or with identical constructs used with different meanings in other differential theories. These constructs of comprehensive psychology are called integrational constructs, although it is true that differential constructs are also to some degree integrational. Differential constructs, such as homeostasis, conditioning, reinforcement, proprium, ego, and unconditional positive regard, also point to certain groups of similar phenomena which they explain and integrate.

However, the explicit addition of the word integrational to the constructs which are developed in comprehensive psychology implies that the comprehensive psychologist seeks the highest possible degree of integrating power in his constructs. This is necessarily so, for he must use them for the integration of the variety of phenomena and lawful relationships discovered in a multitude of differential psychologies.

Examples of such integrational constructs are: existence, mode of existence, modality of existence, existential conscience, functional conscience, self, positive existential transference, negative existential transference. An example of a provisional definition of such a construct is the following existential definition of the self: "The self is an intellectual structure devised by the scientific theorist which points to the hierarchical Gestalt of the behavioral modes of existence which are observed in the subject."

Many constructs which are developed by differential theories can be related to comprehensive constructs as sub-constructs. For example, conditioning, reinforcement, ego, super-ego, and complex are frequently used as sub-structures in a comprehensive theory of behavior. All constructs and sub-constructs, however, tend to change their meaning to some degree in mutual dialogue. This change frequently necessitates a careful redefinition of the constructs concerned. The dialectical process tends therefore to refine the intellectual instrument through which the psychological scientist stands out toward behavior.

SOURCES OF INTEGRATIONAL CONSTRUCTS

There are many possible sources for integrational constructs. The primary source is the personal reflection of the comprehensive psychologist during his foundational and integrational activity. This reflection may draw on other sources in its search for intellectual structures. We have seen that comprehensive and differential psychologies yield constructs such as existence, mode of existence, profile, or perspective. We have also seen that certain integrational constructs have been developed by phenomenological philosophies and that the psychologist may borrow them. Another source is personal creative observation. Alfred Adler, as a result of his observation of his patients, created the construct of inferiority complex to account for interrelated phenomena of behavior which seemed to manifest that the patients in question felt less worthwhile, powerful, and perfect than their fellowmen and used compensations to counteract these feelings.

A main source of integrational constructs for the comprehensive theorist is the differential theories with which he must work. Differential constructs may become useful in a comprehensive theory of psychology. The comprehensive theorist enlarges, in this case, the differential or relative integrational power of these constructs into a more comprehensive power by broadening and deepening their original meaning. Examples are Rogers' construct of the self; Goldstein's and Maslow's constructs of self-actualization; Horney's construct of the idealized self; Freud's constructs of repression, defense mechanism, transference, catharsis; Gordon Allport's constructs of the proprium, of the concrete and the abstract.

The comprehensive and differential theories of other empirical sciences such as physics, biology, and physiology have developed their own constructs which may sometimes prove useful for the comprehensive theorist in psychology. However, they must be carefully redefined with an eye to the typical behavioral phenomena which the psychologist must integrate. Examples of such constructs are field, vector, and purposive behavior. Constructs may also be borrowed from many other fields such as literature, theology, history, and anthropology. Each area of human knowledge enlarges the possibility for the discovery of efficient integrational constructs and sub-constructs. The chief caution to be taken is that these borrowed constructs must be cut off from the phenomena of their original field and then critically related to the behavioral phenomena.

QUASI-HYPOTHETICAL INTEGRATIONAL CONSTRUCTS

Foundational psychology may obtain some of its main constructs from a phenomenological-philosophical analysis of man as a whole. Concepts obtained by such analysis are descriptive and not explanatory. Ideally they are not of a hypothetical nature but are "true" descriptions of reality which, at least in principle, do not require experimental verification and in fact cannot be verified directly by experimental methods.

The psychologist *as psychologist* cannot declare that these concepts obtained from phenomenological philosophers *are* only hypothetical constructs; neither can he assert with certainty that they are not in some way "constructed" by philosophical ideas which influenced the observation and description of the philosopher. For he does not have at his disposal the training or the methods of the professional philosopher. He is compelled to abstain from any absolute judgment regarding the nature of these concepts, for he cannot support such a judgment by his own scientific methods.

On the other hand, *as a comprehensive psychologist* he must keep the structure of behavior as a whole hypothetical, always remaining ready to change it when new discoveries of differential psychologies compel him to do so. For this reason, he deals with the concepts developed by philosophical phenomenology *as if* they were hypothetical constructs. He calls them *quasi*-hypothetical constructs, which can be defined as:

Comprehensive concepts borrowed from philosophical phenomenology which are utilized in foundational psychology "as if" they are hypothetical constructs, without making any absolute statement regarding their status as concepts or constructs.

THE HYPOTHETICAL CONSTITUENT

Comprehensive psychology as an intellectual approximation of behavior is essentially provisional and hypothetical. Theoretical formulations of science are always incomplete, to be sure, as demonstrated by the revision of classical Newtonian physics. The theoretical model which seems valid today may have to be discarded tomorrow. Comprehensive psychology must therefore always remain open and dynamic. It should never succumb to the temptation to become a closed system. From this viewpoint, it may be defined as an *open progressive* integration of the historical and contemporary knowledge about intentional-functional behavior.

The hypothetical status of comprehensive psychology explains its mobility, which reveals itself in the continual emergence of new theories of behavior. Man himself is existence, radical openness to reality; he strives by nature for universal knowledge. In the psychological mode of existence, his need is for the comprehension of intentional behavior as it is in reality.

On the other hand, the comprehensive theorist knows that all psychologists are embodied subjects and are therefore placed in limited cultural periods, which call forth restricted viewpoints revealing limited aspects of behavior. The theorist also realizes that all differential psychologies combined could not possibly cover all perspectives of behavior, the number of which is inexhaustible. Consequently, he is aware that every new perspective which may be opened up by new differential psychologies may compel him to revise his comprehensive structures. Moreover, every new awareness of behavior may change behavior itself. Changes in behavior must be reflected in comprehensive theory, thus necessitating a revision of the theoretical model.

In other words, the comprehensive theorist is convinced that his theory is in principle provisional and incomplete. He realizes that comprehensive theory should never cease to develop, but should stimulate the emergence of new differential theories, which in turn will stimulate him to constantly revise his comprehensive structures. In more existential terms, the comprehensive psychologist feels dynamically driven by the existential tension between his actual limited psychological mode of existence and the comprehensive manner in which he would like to exist toward behavior. Therefore he is never satisfied with the incomplete psychological knowledge embodied even in his most advanced theoretical model. His tension reveals itself in his urgency to constantly revise his constructs and their interrelationships. Without this existential tension, both comprehensive and differential psychology would end in complacency, and there would be neither progress nor the need for progress.

It is now clear that differential theories are necessarily hypothetical with regard to the whole of behavior, for each theory is only one perspective of behavior in its entirety. It is obvious, too, that comprehensive theory under its *integrational* aspect is always open to revision, for new perspectives opened up by differential theories continually provide new material for integration. The latter may change considerably both the identity and the hierarchy of the subordinated constructs in the theoretical model. What may be less obvious is the fact that the *foundational* constituent of the comprehensive theoretical mode of existence is also hypothetical and neither absolute nor ultimate. A comprehensive theory is based on a primary foundational construct which enables the theorist to bring clarity into the complexity of differential phenomena and their relationships and to transcend their disorganized diversity. This construct helps him to reduce the plurality of differential theories to a kind of unity. To be sure, psychological integration will be successful only to the extent that this central point of reference is capable of making the multiplicity and complexity of differential theories transparent and of reducing them to unity.

What is the source of this basic construct concerning behavior? Evidently, it is not to be found in differential theories. The categories of differential psychologies refer in principle only to phenomena which are revealed under one limited perspective of a particular group of psychologists in a restricted cultural period. They are therefore essentially unable to comprehend without distortion the phenomena uncovered by other differential psychologies. Foundational categories should be sought, therefore, in the essential structure of behavior itself. Ideally, the categories obtained by the explication of the essence of behavior would be valid at all times for all people in all situations. Therefore, they would provide a lasting foundation for the organization of all phenomena of behavior revealed by all differential psychologies. Accordingly, the comprehensive psychologist attempts to establish as his primary principle of integration, an essential characteristic of behavior which is universally valid. Yet he may produce a comprehensive theory of behavior which differs from another comprehensive theory. The other psychology may claim that it too is based on an essential characteristic of all behavior. Moreover, this other may also prove that it is capable of integrating all the phenomena provided to date by differential psychologies.

The contradictions in such a case are only apparent. First of all, a comprehensive theorist may be convinced that he is explicating an essential characteristic of man, which is in fact only a characteristic of behavior in his own cultural situation but not of intentional behavior as such. It is merely quasi-essential. Or, under the pressure of his culture, the theorist may unduly emphasize one of the essential characteristics of behavior at the expense of another more basic characteristic. Yet it may still be true that the phenomena revealed by the differential theories can all be integrated without distortion in his comprehensive theory. These differential psychologies have also emerged in his same culture, which is pervaded by the same implicit view of behavior. Therefore, no differential theorist of this particular cultural period may have been impelled to adopt a perspective out of harmony with the implicit cultural view. Out of the inexhaustible number of possible perspectives, only those in tune with the cultural vision may have been selected. Thus the *Zeit Geist* may blind both the comprehensive and the differential psychologists to certain aspects of behavior.

Does this mean that a one-sided comprehensive psychology which emerges in a particular cultural period is worthless? By no means. Every successful comprehensive psychologist makes explicit a certain essential, or at least quasi-essential, characteristic of intentional behavior. He shows how the multiplicity of behavioral phenomena uncovered by differential psychologies of his culture can be integrated within this aspect. If his view is not most fundamental, then his integration can be subordinated later to a more comprehensive psychology when a more basic aspect of the essential structure is discovered. In this case, a one-sided attempt at comprehension proves to be a worthwhile stage on the road toward an increasingly comprehensive psychology. It finds a position between a differential and a truly comprehensive psychology. Moreover, such theory will provide later psychologists with an insight into the basic view of behavior which developed within a certain cultural period. Finally, when psychology discovers that a certain comprehensive theory of behavior does not work in reality, it is forced to discard it. It is able to do so only because the implicit comprehensive psychology of a cultural period has been made explicit by such a one-sided theory.

The possible and probable one-sidedness of a comprehensive theory, under its foundational aspect, makes it necessary to consider foundational constructs as provisional and hypothetical. The comprehensive psychologist should always be ready to question the foundations of his theory and to change them for more valid primary constructs which may be discovered in the evolution of human knowledge.

But how does the foundational theorist know when he should question his basic constructs? What is the criterion of the validity of the foundational constructs of a comprehensive theory? It is the primary experience of the theorist. But the theorist may easily distort his primary experience of human behavior by imagination, by anxious conformity, by ambition, by the need for the acclaim of fellow scientists, by one-sided over-apppreciation, or by other emotional attitudes imbedded in his own cultural period, which represents only a phase of the evolution of behavior. Therefore, the psychologist requires another test of the validity of his foundational constructs. This criterion is the fruitfulness of the dialogue between comprehensive theory of behavior and concrete real behavior as it appears in the development of history. A comprehensive theory tends to embody itself in concrete behavior by means of numerous explicit or implicit applications to behavior as it appears in society. The dialogue is between theory and praxis, between thought and action, speculation and reality.

If the fundamental constructs of the theory are valid, the dialogue between the theory and actual behavior will be fruitful and progressive. Theory will foster efficient and harmonious behavior. This behavior in turn will reinforce and develop the theory by its confirming answer to the tentative application of the theoretical views. Every application of theory to reality is an implicit question posed to reality. The question may be translated thus: "Are you really as we have described you? If so, manifest it by responding effectively to the application which flows from our description." Both comprehensive and differential theory are questions to reality, but the questions posed by comprehensive theory are more absolute and basic. Comprehensive theory pushes to the limit the views of behavior which underlie the differential psychologies of a cultural period. These more or less implicit concepts lead the differential theorists to pose limited questions related to the aspect of behavior which they are exploring. But comprehensive theories, because of their very comprehension, force these underlying views to reveal their limits in two ways: first, by making them explicit in foundational constructs; second, by exposing the full impact of all their implications for the whole of behavior. From this point on, a dialogue is possible between these fully explicit views of behavior and all actual behavior of people in daily reality.

The view of behavior expressed in foundational constructs may indeed be one-sided. In this case, it will be impossible at certain points to maintain the dialogue with concrete behavior. That is, at those points where other "sides" of behavior which are neglected by the "one-sided" theory of behavior reveal themselves in daily reality. Here there can be no response from reality because the theory is silent on aspects of behavior which manifest themselves in reality. Suppose, for example, that a comprehensive theory of behavior implies in its foundational constructs that human behavior is absolutely identical with animal behavior. Such a theoretical foundation is attractive, for it simplifies the process of psychology considerably and consequently promotes the "elegance" of the theory in question. But what is the result of the dialogue between this theory and the real behavior of men in daily life? As long as the psychologist poses only those questions which relate to what is animal-like and infra-personal in the behavior of man, answers will come forth readily and will reinforce the theory. When the theory is applied, for example, to the biological aspect of the behavior of hunger, a fruitful and satisfying dialogue will develop. But the comprehensive psychologist cannot restrict himself to questions related to only certain areas of behavior, for comprehensive psychology is a question to the whole of behavior under all its aspects. Therefore, as soon as the theory cited above attempts a dialogue with other human behavior such as prayer, love, faithfulness, and philosophizing, the answers of behavior will not conform to the biological categories which form the basis of this theory. The comprehensive psychologist must then admit that his basic constructs are somehow one-sided because they do not conform to reality. He experiences that a certain behavior escapes his theory, and consequently his foundational constructs can no longer be called comprehensive. In other words, the reality of behavior as it reveals itself in the history of human experience is the test of the validity of the foundational constructs of a comprehensive theory.

Ideally, differential psychologies claim only the validity of that limited aspect of behavior which they study operationally under controlled conditions. It is possible for such psychologies to test their hypotheses by experiment and controlled observation. A comprehensive theory, on the other hand, purports to explain behavior as a whole. And behavior in its totality cannot be put to experimental test, because empirical operations always presuppose the abstraction of controllable variables from the whole. How then are we to evaluate the foundational constructs of a comprehensive theory? One method is to derive from them hypothetical postulates which are then tested by differential operational psychologies. However, as we have seen, it may well be that the existing differential psychologies do not include certain profiles of behavior which have also been disregarded by the comprehensive theory. It is not unthinkable that the foundational constructs proposed in a certain culture are also implicitly present in the differential theories which emerge in the same period. In such a culture, comprehensive and differential psychologists alike may be blind to certain aspects of the reality of behavior.

The only source of evaluation possible for foundational constructs, therefore, is a close study on the part of the comprehensive psychologist of all manifestations of behavior in past and contemporary history. It is evident that concentration only on behavior reported by differential psychologies is insufficient for the validation of foundational constructs. The comprehensive psychologist should, therefore, be open to manifestations of behavior in history, literature, painting, sculpture, and other arts and sciences. These may open his eyes to aspects of behavior which are disregarded by practicing psychologists. As we shall see later, this is an area in which the comprehensive psychologist can be truly creative. By pointing out neglected aspects of intentional behavior, he can pave the way for new differential psychologies which will study these neglected profiles.

It may require a long period of time before comprehensive psychologists are able to see that their foundational constructs are one-sided in the sense that they do not respond to the full reality of behavior. The laboratory of history stretches itself over time and space. At times, entire generations of psychologists must pass by before it becomes clear that the dialogue between foundational constructs and the reality of behavior is halted, that their application is destructive rather than constructive. Then new foundational constructs must be proposed on the basis of a new explication of the primordial experience of behavior. This reconstruction of foundational theory is necessary to bring psychologists once again into contact with the reality of behavior.

It is evident that comprehensive psychology should remain hypothetical under its foundational aspect, because it is inevitable for the comprehensive psychologist to err. He is bound to be influenced in his explication of his primary experience of behavior by cultural viewpoints. No psychologist can escape his culture totally. Often the psychologists of a certain era are not even aware that their view of behavior has long ago reached an impasse. Sometimes an entire culture must die before the psychologist is able to recognize the deficiencies of his foundational constructs which have been formed under the impact of that culture. This human inclination to a one-sided way of interpreting reality teaches the comprehensive theorist to be humble in formulating his foundational constructs. He should become increasingly aware that his constructs are always subject to being proved false and that there is no substitute for the tedious test in the laboratory of history.

To understand more concretely the hypothetical character of comprehensive theory, let us look more closely at the effects of cultural influences on man's view of behavior. Man always reflects on his behavior; he communicates his thoughts to others and sometimes discovers that they share intentional behavior which he may have thought private and personal. The mutual communication of thought within a culture leads to a shared image of what behavior is like. Therein lies the beginning of a spontaneous psychology as a cultural concern. This psychology changes, to be sure, with the cultural situation. And this change in turn causes a change in intentional behavior itself, and likewise in the self-image which is embodied in it and which dominates the culture.

Man experiences himself and his intentional behavior differently in various periods of culture, for he is exposed to different historical situations. Each new situation implies a challenge to master its demands by the evolvement of adequate intentional behavior. Man's attempt to answer this challenge make him aware of latent potentialities which he actualizes in meeting the needs of the moment. The unfolding of particular types of intentional behavior obviously leads to the neglect of other possible types. As soon as the historical situation is mastered, man becomes aware that he has achieved a certain behavior but has disregarded other possibilities. This awareness is evoked especially in his encounter with other men who have actualized human capacities which he has disregarded. The Roman peasant, soldier, and administrator were made aware of the neglect of their potentialities for philosophy, oratory, art, and architecture by their clash with the Greeks, especially when this clash became a human encounter. On the other hand, the cultures of certain African and Indian tribes which did not encounter other cultures became frozen and petrified.

The original behavioral response of people when faced with a new situation is pre-reflective. Such intentional-functional behavior implies a new experience of self. When large numbers of people thus assume a new attitude toward themselves and their behavior, it permeates the culture by a process of pre-reflective interaction which may be compared with osmosis. This implicit, omnipresent view is not immediately expressed in an explicit psychology. Various other behavioral expressions

158

precede a more or less clear formulation of the view because they are closer to the original experience.

The first members of a culture who are able to express a new intentional behavior and the aspect of self inherent in it are the artists of the age. They experience a refined sensitivity, a kind of radar that scans the world of meaning in which they live. Within this world of accepted meanings, they are aware of the slightest stirrings which reveal themselves in the intentional behavior of people. They are able to express these responses in poems, novels, music, and painting. Literary and artistic expression is always very close to the original intentionality expressed by a people.

Another revelation of the intentional behavior of man is the philosophical one. The philosopher of an era attempts to express the essence of all that is under the impact of the first stirrings of the new period of culture which announces itself to his alert intuition.

Although psychology is at first embodied in literature, art, and philosophy, it gradually shows distinctive characteristics which set it more and more apart. The orientation of psychological research thus depends on the implicit view of behavior which permeates a culture. Every differential and comprehensive psychologist is under its influence. He is imbued with an implicit view of behavior and of self from his earliest years, simply by living in his culture and by being immersed in its language. When a culture becomes increasingly aware of itself, the implicit view of behavior becomes explicit. Comprehensive psychology in its foundational aspect is one form of this awareness. It opens up the possibility of critical evaluation of the view of behavior inherent in the differential psychologies of the culture.

We have said that one possible evaluation for foundational constructs is the close study by the comprehensive psychologist of manifestations of behavior in past and contemporary history. Openness to all past and present revelations of behavior may lead to new insights into foundational constructs.

In fact, a pre-scientific openness to human behavior in its revelations of disturbances recorded by psychotherapists and sociologists may provide a real possibility of escape from cultural determination. Such study may lead the comprehensive psychologist to the discovery of those aspects of intentional behavior which are neglected in the contemporary foundational view of man, since their repression could well have led to disturbances in patients. Another possibility of transcending the contemporary scene may be an involvement in the foundational views of man which have dominated other periods of culture. Finally, an open study of the psychologies of man implicit in other cultures may foster the awareness of the relativity of our own foundational constructs.

We may conclude that the hypothetical nature of comprehensive psychology, even under its foundational aspect, calls for the following:

1. The study of the contemporary self-experience of man as it is embodied in his intentional behavior and implicitly present in contemporary psychologies and their orientation of research.

2. The study of the self-image expressed in cultural endeavors other than psychology, such as art, literature, social customs, language, philosophy, science, education, and patterns of worship.

3. The study of the impact of the contemporary self-experience of man on his intentional behavior, through explication of records of therapeutic, educational, and other social situations.

4. The study of behavioral indications of dissatisfaction with the dominant views of man, even though slight, and of the new self-experiences which manifest themselves in this newly emerging behavior.

5. The study of the situations which have influenced the various forms of self-experience embodied in the behavior and the behavioral products of contemporary man.

6. The comparative study of the self-image of man embodied in the behavior of the present period of our culture and those of other periods of our culture.

7. The comparative study of the foundational self-image of man which dominates the development of our whole culture in all its periods and the foundational self-images that have dominated totally different cultures in their various periods.

The type of research just proposed is demanded by the hypothetical constituent of the comprehensive-theoretical mode of existence. For this constituent compels the comprehensive theorist in psychology to respond to the whole of intentional-functional behavior in constant wonder. This sense of wonder translates itself, among other ways, as an endless questioning of his constructs and models.

THE CREATIVE CONSTITUENT

The comprehensive theoretical mode of existence, as we have emphasized, is not merely a mode of registration of data and constructs developed in differential psychologies. The integration of seemingly opposed constructs requires the continual shaping and reshaping of a theoretical model in its structure and substructures. This constant change in theoretical vision enables the psychologist to comprehend with inner consistency the ever-increasing number of phenomena and laws uncovered by the growing number of differential psychologies. A comprehensive model is not given as such in the reality of intentional behavior. It arises from systematic thought about that which is uncovered in intentional behavior by differential psychologists. It is therefore a creation of the theorist.

However, the careful and "playful" consideration of the various perspectives of psychology is necessary but not sufficient for the creation of a consistent theoretical model. First of all, the number of profiles which are uncovered by differential psychologies is limited and does not necessarily represent the most fundamental aspects of intentional behavior. Further, the constructs and data of differential psychologies may be so disparate that it is impossible to relate them in some kind of theoretical unity without resorting to views opened up by other disciplines. Therefore, the comprehensive theorist—in so far as he is able— also studies philosophies and theologies of man, anthropology, sociology, literature, and art with special reference to behavior. He may involve himself in psychotherapy, which provides an opportunity to be in direct contact with intentional-functional behavior as a whole. Nourished by all these sources of constructive thought, he ponders creatively the contributions of differential psychology. His constant creative consideration of possibilities of integration implicit in the data and constructs leads him to the creation or re-creation of his theoretical model.

Such creativity presupposes an attitude of both presence to and distance from its object. The theorist is intimately *present* to the differential psychologies and to other disciplines; he steeps himself in their thought. He is *distant* insofar as he does not allow himself to be seduced by one or the other differential psychology, so as to become himself a differential psychologist who considers the whole of intentional behavior predominantly from the viewpoint of one profile. He keeps himself similarly distant from philosophy. The ideas developed by philosophers are for him, *as an empirical scientist*, quasi-hypothetical constructs, some of which he uses as integrational constructs as long as research and observation do not refute them. This attitude of presence and distance keeps the comprehensive theorist free for a never-ending creative "play" with phenomena and constructs.

The comprehensive psychologist is creative not only in developing constantly new structures and sub-structures to embody the contributions of differential psychologies, but also in suggesting new hypotheses to be tested by them. In order to unify the variety of differential constructs and data, the theorist is forced to create integrational constructs which can be used as a sufficient explication of seemingly unrelated data. In other words, the comprehensive theorist must fill in the "gaps" left by differential research. The differential psychologists may be stimulated in turn to new investigations by his proposed theoretical solutions. They may deduce testable propositions from his theory and put them to the empirical test.

The comprehensive theorist is also creative insofar as he points out neglected aspects of research which may lead to the emergence of totally new differential fields of psychology.

Finally, comprehensive psychology is the point of departure for the clinical psychologist and psychiatrist who in their fundamental concern for the human person as a whole are disinclined to approach their clients from merely one or the other differential viewpoint. This attitude stimulates the comprehensive psychologist to formulate creative hypotheses for clinical psychology which the clinician in turn tests in his practice.

The Communicative Constituent

The comprehensive theoretical psychologist responds to the whole of behavior not only in order to express this totality in a theoretical construct, but also to communicate as an organized whole that which is seen in isolation by differential psychologists. This implicit aim of communication influences the attitude and the verbal expression of the comprehensive psychologist. He must present the contribution of psychology as a whole to his fellow psychologists, to students of psychology, to students of the arts and sciences, and to the human community at large. The growth of psychology implies an increasing differentiation in fields of specialization which develop their own language and methodology. The latter are at times difficult to understand, even for psychologists when they are not specialists in the area concerned. It is also difficult for both specialists and non-specialists to comprehend what the relevance of minute discoveries may be for the understanding of intentional behavior as a whole. Differentiation may even lead to a loss of insight into the whole if the comprehensive psychologist does not keep himself continually informed of the increasing insight into intentional behavior achieved by the painstaking labors of his colleagues in the differential psychologies. One of the functions of comprehensive psychology is thus a two-way communication of the changing structure which represents the increasing knowledge of psychologists as a community of specialized scientists.

The applied psychologist in the clinic, in education, and in industry also feels the pressing need for this type of communication. He deals with intentional behavior as a lived totality among the groups and individuals who come to him for guidance, diagnosis, and therapy. He does not have the time to acquaint himself thoroughly with the numerous reports of research submitted by the disparate differential fields in psychology, all written in their own peculiar idioms. He desires to know whether or not this research substantially affects his insight into intentional behavior, and how this changed insight may affect his treatment of his clients. When comprehensive theory has emerged into a field of psychology in its own right, pursued by many scientists all over the world, it will ideally provide the applied psychologist with this knowledge.

New students of psychology should first of all be given a general view of the science to familiarize them with the fundamental intellectual knowledge of behavior which has been achieved by comprehensive psychology at the time that they enter the field. After this, it is less difficult for them to study, in the light of this structure, the overwhelming number of differential psychologies and to assess their relevance to the whole. Comprehensive psychology communicates to them a fundamental structure.

The findings of comprehensive psychology are also relevant for other arts and sciences, for the political administration of government, for church and school, and for the public at large which obtains much of its psychological information from magazines, pamphlets, and newspapers. It is impossible for the community at large to develop a coherent insight into the significant developments in psychology by reading the inexhaustible number of published reports on isolated observations and experiments. Such a piecemeal type of knowledge may lead to confusion and to a dangerous over-estimation of certain well-publicized differential approaches at the expense of a balanced insight into the whole. In the possible future, communication specialists may be able to report with competence new discoveries in psychology within the perspective of comprehensive psychology and thus prevent harmful distortion of insight.

CHAPTER SIX

THE STUDENT AND THE STUDY OF ANTHROPOLOGICAL PSYCHOLOGY

It is one of the themes of this book that all sciences are rooted in man the scientist, and that consequently each one of them can be understood on the basis of the specific mode of existence of the scientist which led to the emergence and development of the science in question. Therefore, before developing a more concise consideration of the function of anthropological psychology in itself, we shall first reflect on the student and the study of anthropological psychology. In order to do so, we must first present an outline of the central idea of anthropological psychology which will concentrate chiefly on the scientist and his study, while in the next chapter we shall concentrate on anthropological psychology in and by itself. Because both aspects of anthropological psychology are inter-related, some overlapping will be unavoidable.

We may begin with a provisional descriptive definition of anthropological psychology which will serve our special purpose. The discussion of the various terms of this definition in relation to the student and his study will lead to an initial under-standing which will find its necessary complement in the next chapter on the function of anthropological psychology. For our purposes here we may describe anthropological psychology provisionally as: *an open, personal, progressive integration of the historical and contemporary psychological knowledge about man—in the light of a phenomenological explication of the fundamental psychological structure of his personality—in order to understand his psychology.*

OPEN, PERSONAL, PROGRESSIVE INTEGRATION

We shall first reflect upon the expression, "an open, personal, progressive integration." As we have seen, the Latin word *integratio* is related to the verb *integrare*, to make whole. Verbs reveal a basic characteristic of the human personality, namely, his becoming, his growing towards, his reaching out, his going beyond what he is and what his world is at this moment, his humble readiness to change, his original plasticity and fluidity. This capacity for growth is one of the properties that distinguishes man from the things which surround him. The walls of his home or the stones in his path do not manifest a spontaneous inner dynamism urging them to perfect themselves. Genuine free growth, however, pervades the whole human person and embodies itself in all his activities and relations. This characteristic of becoming also imbues the persistent need of man to integrate meaningfully all that he knows about man. The developing result of his innate search for the rediscovery of the integral wholeness of man will be authentically human to the degree that it is permeated by the human characteristic of becoming, of creative, never resting openness. Unfortunately, his attempt at integration may lose its aliveness and openness when its provisional results are printed and then disregarded. The human attempt may become a fossil somewhere in a museum of books which will come to life only when another man humanizes it again by infusing new life into it. The reader or student does so by his participation in the search of the original thinker or theorist of personality, and by making it live on through his personal creative search. Sometimes, libraries are like cemeteries rather than sources of the wonder of new life. Many printed attempts at the integration of our knowledge of man remain dead because we who open the records are lacking in authentic humanness, in openness to the spontaneous search for wholeness present in our life. Under the impact of an objectivistic mechanistic education, we may perceive ourselves

167

as objects with qualities, or as well-organized study machines. Then we are unable to infuse human life into the books which cover our desks. A printed attempt at integration of the science of man becomes for us nothing more than a finished, unchangeable "thing" that we can read, memorize, or quote, or to which we can refer as we would refer to the North Pole, the Indian Ocean, Chile, or Bagdad. We may be naïve enough to believe that this is the best way of understanding or of honoring the author.

If we ever hope to understand the author in his very act of attempting to integrate, we have to share his attempt, we have to become as it were his co-creator. We have to undergo his wrestling with thought, his moods of elation and despair, his delight when he achieves fresh observations, and above all his dynamism of becoming. Only then will we meet him; only then will we be able to recreate his work. Then we can humbly participate in the great human effort to understand the psychology of the human personality. When we experience the tentative integrations of Freud, Jung, or Adler as holy texts which can never be changed, we will never understand their creators in their act of creating, and we will never be able to participate in their work. This is why we insist that the search of anthropological psychology must be open, personal, and progressive.

Therefore we are not distressed but delighted at the appearance of so many antagonistic theories of personality. Disagreement is an encouraging sign of search, of readiness to change, of the wonderful plasticity of life, on condition, of course, that this disagreement is authentic and open and not the result of a dogmatic entrenchment in one or the other closed and final integration. Authentic disagreement is the fruit of the complexity of the problems we are faced with. Some students, comparing the unshakeable data of controlled experimentation with the ever-changing attempts to attain an integral theory of personality, may shake their heads in pity and wonder. When a new integration appears, they may ask impatiently: Is this finally "the" anthropology of man, "the" conclusive theory of person and personality? The psychologist of man will answer that there never has been and never will be such a "thing" as "the" psychology of man. If there would ever be "the" psychology of man, there would no longer be any true psychologists, for the perennial human effort to grow in the understanding of man would be buried in a closed system. This would spell the destruction of the humble awareness that we still do not know and that we never shall know perfectly all that is knowable about man's psychology. Needless to say, the extinction of this humility would be the death of science as a creative enterprise.

Indeed, the beginning student may be dumbfounded by the variety of psychological integrations and their manifold contradictions. Therefore, to commit onself unconditionally to one or the other psychological anthropology would be unwise and presumptuous. For on what basis would one decide that one phychology of man is better than the other? But even if "the" conclusive anthropology really existed, it would still be unwise to learn this integration in the same way as one would learn the structure of the nervous system or the scoring of the Stanford-Binet, for the comprehensive theory of personality expressed in this supposedly exhaustive integration would not be the truth of the student himself. The psychology of man can never become *his* psychology if he limits himself to simply learning the integration expressed by others without experiencing in his life and in the lives of others the reality of this psychology. For being a psychologist of personality is a personal enterprise, a questioning, a reply of the student himself. It is life itself which raises the question of the psychology of personality, and it is life which urges me on to rediscover and to restore the original wholeness of my own personality. My life, my existence, my being a person is mine. When I study how other men have restored the original whole of human personality, I cannot simply put my own personal existence aside as if it does not concern me, for they are talking about me, and they are integrating *my* personality. I am necessarily interested in myself because it is characteristic of man that he is in relationship to his own personality. Therefore, every man is born a true psychologist of man at least in a naïve and pre-reflective way. In the same sense every man is, by force of his very being, always attempting to restore the original whole of his being. One way in which he tries to do so is by the integration—at least in a crude and primitive way—of all his experiences about himself and his fellow man. He is always searching for the meaning of his life, and if he cannot find an integrating meaning he becomes neurotic or psychotic.

Again, one or the other specialist of certain measurable aspects of man may pretend or even believe that he is free from this human need for meaning—that he is not interested in the whole man. On closer investigation, however, we should discover in him also a psychology of man, though perhaps a very primitive one on the unconscious or half-conscious level of his existence. This natural inclination to anthropological synthesis which belongs to man's fundamental personality needs may be repressed by him in the laboratory, but it guides and directs him in his daily life even if he would be ashamed and disturbed by so unscientific a tendency.

Moreover, in spite of his protest, even his behavior in the laboratory itself and his choice of experiments is done under the impact of his unconscious anthropology. Even his disdain for the psychology of personality, or his contention that physiological-biological data obtained by experiment will sooner or later make crystal-clear the whole reality of human existence, betray his hidden view of man, for it is impossible to escape being an implicit anthropological psychologist. It belongs to man's very personality; it is greater than man is, and it is present even in the angry denial of its presence. Apparently, man must care about himself and must be a dialogue with his psychology.

This implicit psychology of man, when it becomes explicit in anthropological psychology, is authentic only when the student *himself* observes man in himself and in others; when he *himself* ponders the results of his observations; when he *himself* attempts to reply; when he *himself* clarifies his insights;

and when he *himself* searches explicitly for the restoration of the original whole of man's fundamental personality structure.

The questions and answers of the printed attempts at integration of personality knowledge, such as Freud's or Jung's, Murray's or Allport's, are not *mine*. To learn their questions and answers would no more contribute to the making of a psychologist of personality than the enumeration of the various glands or the memorizing of the rules of controlled experimentation. Only an open, personal, progressive integration will enliven and enrich the treasures of the past with one's own experience. Personal integration makes for a progressive integration which is never finished but is always open to the past, the present, and the future. This personal assimilation will make the student a "living" therapist, a "living" teacher of psychology, and a creative contributor to the science of man.

INTEGRATION OF HISTORICAL AND
CONTEMPORARY PSYCHOLOGY

After this elaboration of the expression, "an open, personal, progressive integration," we must consider a further qualification of our definition of anthropological psychology which states that it is an integration "of the historical and contemporary knowledge about man." The anthropological psychologist is characterized by a *personal* search for the integral understanding of the human personality. There is no psychologist, however, who can ever begin to understand man as if there were no previous understanding of man, for many others in the course of history have tried to understand man psychologically before him, and he lives under the impact of their understanding. The psychologist is born into a community of men which communicates to him a language. Therefore, he is imbued with the historical ways of understanding man insofar as those ways are embodied in the language which he has learned to speak. It is impossible for a psychologist to try to understand man without language, and also impossible to understand man without tradition. It is interesting, for example, to realize how our language has been influenced by certain romantic, rationalistic,

171

and religious concepts which express certain ways of seeing man in particular periods of history. More recently, certain Freudian, Adlerian, and Jungian concepts have become part of our Western languages. Such embodiments of psychological understanding have taken place throughout history in all languages. The same is true of art, monuments, and social institutions; they are all imbued with the psychological understanding of past generations.

Moreover, during all centuries great men have concentrated on the secrets of man's psychology, and they have expressed their growing understanding in classical theories and descriptions. The psychologist is under the sway of this embodied history of the understanding of man. But this does not mean that he has to abandon his quest for a personal integral understanding. On the contrary, he has to infuse new life into history. The theories of personality developed by the great psychologists of all centuries and cultures are the expression of *their personal* understanding of man. Their mission is to make us sensitive to their experience. They enable us *personally* to see something to which otherwise we would have been blind. If there had been no Freud, our conception of certain dynamics of man would have been much more naïve and superficial; or rather, we would perhaps not understand what we now do when we encounter man. Without Alfred Adler, we would not be so sensitive to the meaning of inferiority feeling and the need for compensation in man when he is placed in certain life situations. Without Hippocrates and Galen, perhaps we would not be aware of that aspect of the reality of man which has been called temperament. The psychologists of all centuries speak to us to make us capable of personal experience or observation, to make us aware of the wealth contained in the totality of man's personality. Once this is understood, there is no reason to be disturbed by the existence of many contradictory attempts at integration in the history of psychology and psychiatry. What matters is not the theory of person and personality, but *man*. In every one of the "attempts-at-integration" some aspect of man's psychology finds expression. Every truly great psychologist was struck by a certain aspect of man, such as his libido, his will to power, his religious need, the impact of his biological substructure, his observable behavior. Sometimes he was so impressed by a certain minor aspect of man's psychology that he made it the exclusive basis of his understanding of the whole of man. It became the core of his attempt at integration. In this case, the resulting integration was distorted, but nevertheless we cannot do without his special message. We cannot do without Galen, Freud, Jung, Pavlov, Watson, and all the other psychologists of man. Accordingly, the psychologist must take up the past in a creative way. He must endow the past with a new life. Evidently, he *himself* has to do this. Although anthropological psychology is an intersubjective and historical enterprise, each psychologist of man has to understand man on his own. Even those anthropological psychologists who for historical and personal reasons are inclined to favor one or the other school of psychology or psychiatry, will not *a priori* believe this or that psychological statement about man, but at most suspect its truth. The authentic psychologist of man does not accumulate knowledge of psychologists of the past, but he listens to man no matter from whom the message comes. Therefore, while studying the historical integrations of human knowledge about man, the psychologist may attempt to return to the human experience or observation which is explicated in a psychological statement. Only in his personal presence to man, or in experience or observation, is it possible for him to see and accept the meaning of this statement personally.

INTERSUBJECTIVE AGREEMENT AND
VALIDATION OF THEORY

We have stressed that the psychologist is authentic to the degree that the knowledge of the psychology of personality becomes his personal insight. Does this mean that the anthropological psychologist is forced to limit himself to a kind of monologue that expresses only his strictly personal experience or observation? The beginning student is indeed struck by the fact that the findings of experimental psychology seem much easier to agree upon than the insights of man as a whole as revealed by the various psychologies of man. This difference, however, does not mean that the latter is *only* personal, or is not open to intersubjective agreement and intersubjective validation. It is true that *in fact* there exists more agreement in the realm of physiological and biological psychology than in the realm of the psychologies of personality. There is more general agreement among physiological psychologists about the number of reinforcements needed to condition a rat than there is agreement among the psychologists of man regarding the meaning and function of man's anxiety or his sexual needs. This is so because it is easier to verify the results of an experiment with rats than the explication of the meaning of a deeply human experience, for as soon as the psychologist transcends the realm of research on the infra-human level, he cannot subject the phenomena which he studies to direct factual verification and precise control. Therefore, it is *in fact* far more difficult to come to agreement. We shall need the long and acid test of the laboratory of human history in order to come to factual agreement concerning the rightness or wrongness of our explication of man.

But the more we explicate in a scholarly way the implicit anthropology of man, the sooner we shall be able to detect our falsifications and to open the discussion which might correct these self-deceptions. The impossibility of testing these explications in the laboratory is not a reason to avoid the explication of man's psychology in as scholarly a way as possible, because mankind can never avoid harboring implicit anthropologies which guide and direct the orientation of experimentation and clinical work in psychology. These implicit anthropologies will make for a longer period of blindness to their imperfections or even falsities than a scholarly confrontation of them. By bringing them into the open, we shall be more ready for the signs in man and society which seem to indicate that our explication was not the right one because in principle the truth about man is intersubjective. Therefore, sooner or later we shall bridge our factual disagreements if they are clearly stated and thus more open to clear repudiation or confirmation by history.

Accordingly, *in principle,* the personal insight of the psychologists of personality does not mean an arbitrary insight.

We have explained that the further qualification of personal integration is an integration "of historical and contemporary knowledge about man." We have shown that this openness to all historical and contemporary knowledge about man does not exclude the personal character of our integration, and finally that our own personal integration can be taken up in the stream of the historical human enterprise of integration because personal integration does not exclude potential historical intersubjectivity.

FUNDAMENTAL STRUCTURES OF PERSONALITY

We have now to consider the next qualification of integration which has been formulated in the definition as "in the light of a phenomenological explication of the fundamental structures of his personality."

In elaborating the first terms of the definition, we have seen that "integration" means restoring or renewing the original, untouched, integral whole. This expression implies that anthropological psychology presupposes an originally given insight into the totality of man which has been broken up, as it were, and has to be restored. But what is breaking up this original whole? An organic whole is broken when we make one of its aspects the center of our attention in such a way that we forget about the embeddedness of this aspect in the total organic whole. Yet we are forced to break up the organic vague totality of our knowledge about man and to concentrate on certain aspects of this knowledge in order to grow to better insight into these aspects, and indirectly to a sharper view of the whole to which these aspects belong. The historical growth of the understanding of human personality is a two-way process. One pole of the process is the concentration on certain aspects of man's psychology; the other pole is the constant reintegration of the studied aspects within the whole of the original insight after their elucidation. One or the other psychologist may object and say: "We do not have an insight into the totality of man's fundamental psychology; consequently, the only way open to us is the performance of a great number of experiments. Then in the far future all the results of these experiments will be added and will reveal to us the whole of man's psychology, unknown to us up to that moment." This is an abstract theoretical conception which is at odds with the elementary phenomena of experience. Imagine for a moment that there is no awareness of man's personality structure before we start to collect data about man by means of controlled experimentation. Not having any awareness of human personality, how can we be sure that we are not studying a dream or a fantasy or a plant or a river? However, no student of human psychology has ever made such a mistake. This proves that there is some directly given notion of human psychology guiding us in our research. The psychologist is protected against mistaking the sky for man, a tree for man, the walls of his laboratory for man, by an immediately given overall knowledge of what human psychology is, what a wall is, what a tree is. In other words, there is an experiental knowledge of human psychology given to the psychologist immediately, directly, inescapably. This knowledge is not obtained by experimentation, but presupposed. The methods of experimental psychology do not determine what human psychology is, but are directed by what human psychology is. They are true to the degree that they are in accordance with this given knowledge of man's personality structure. They are worthwhile to the degree that they differentiate more clearly what we already know vaguely about man's personality structure by experience of the immediately given. This point is basic for the understanding of what anthropological psychology is.

The original integral whole for the anthropological psychologist is the fundamental personality structure of man, and it has to be restored by constantly relating all detailed studies of man to the integral whole given in his primary experience. This will not only make for a richer understanding of the whole man but also for a better understanding of various aspects of man.

The Student and the Study of Anthropological Psychology

The understanding of the integral components of a whole can only lead to a better understanding of this whole if our understanding of these components increases in the light of the knowledge of the whole itself. Thus a better understanding of the part gives a better understanding of the whole and vice versa. Consider a person who is interested in knowing what a house is. He already has a vague experience of a house. This given knowledge has to lead him to further understanding. Therefore, he first reflects on his original given knowledge and makes more explicit his implicit awareness of what a house is. He finds by means of this process of explication that a house is a place for people to live in. Now he can deepen his knowledge of house as a whole by the study of certain segments of the house, but always on condition that he studies them in the light of the explicated whole—a place for people to live in. He studies, for instance, what the door of a house is. He can understand this only in the light of the whole. The door of a house is a connection between the inside and the outside of the house. We need a door because people living in a house can move around and need to move around and, therefore, need an opening. Moreover, people who live in a house are also bodies that have to be protected against weather conditions. They are, moreover, personal selves that need privacy. They have property that they like to protect. These are some of the reasons why they place an object called door between the opening of the house and the outside world. This explication helps the person to understand at the same time what a door is and what a house is. We could never understand what a door in a house meant if we described it as totally independent of any idea of house whatsoever. We could then describe the door only as wooden, square, and so on. But nobody reading this information would be able to discover the meaning of "door" and at the same time obtain a more differentiated meaning of "house".

Similarly, anthropological integration is the continual restoration of the elucidated aspects of man's personality within the original whole of man's fundamental personality structure. Only

177

a study of aspects of human personality in the light of this structure can lead to a deeper understanding of human psychology. Finally, this knowledge of fundamental personality structure is given in immediate experience in a vague, implicit way and therefore has to be explicated.

Are we not contradicting ourselves? We stress the aim to understand the personality as an integral whole and at the same time we talk about explication of our immediate experience of the human personality. Is this explication not a division of the personality which destroys the integration of the given totality? Not necessarily, because we can divide in many ways. Some of these ways respect the immediately given whole; others do not. Take, for instance, a painting by Rembrant. I see the whole of the painting in one swift glance; then, admiring the painting, I "dwell" for a moment on this, then for another moment on that detail, but all the time I am relating the particular detail of the painting to the whole and to all other details, and vice versa. When I ask myself how I select my details in such a way that they can teach me about the meaning of the whole painting, I discover that there is some kind of natural articulation present within the whole of the composition itself. In Rembrandt's painting, "Midnight Round", I dwell on the colors of the uniforms, the little drummer in the foreground, the walking attitude of the men, their rifles, the dark background from which they emerge. Continuously relating these integral parts of the composition to one another and to the whole makes me experience that this painting really means a "Midnight Round" characteristic of Amsterdam at a certain period. When I am open to the meaning of the painting, when I allow the painting in its given totality to open itself to me, then I discover a natural articulation inherent in the composition itself. I could do something else; I could refuse to allow the painting to reveal itself to me. For instance, I could divide the painting into cubic inches, and then I could handle those cubic inches statistically in terms of their equality. Or I could abstract one characteristic of the painting, for instance its colors, and make a division only according to color—so many black spots, so many grey spots, so many golden spots. In both cases, I could collect an amount of separate data. But this information could never teach me the meaning of the painting as a whole. I would know much about the measurements of the painting and about the number and the quality of the paints which were used. I would know more about other wholes, such as the "conceptual whole" of measurement or the "conceptual whole" of the color scale. But I could never directly restore those spots or measurements of painting to the meaning of the whole. The same is true of the psychology of personality. Any division by measurement alone, any division according to only one type of personality characteristic (for instance physiological ones), will make it impossible to reintegrate these units into the meaningful whole of a unique personality.

Therefore, it is not division as such that harms the understanding of personality, but the fact that a division is made independent of the fundamental structure of personality. There is a natural articulation of human personality which is given; for if human personality were not an organic unity of many natural articulations, there would be no difference between a homogeneous mass and an organism. Human personality is not like a collection of sand or a heap of stones or water in a swimming pool. The fundamental human personality is a structured whole, well articulated in the light of a unifying principle of organization. We have to find this principle of articulation and organization, and then in the light of this principle we may study certain articulations which come to the fore. For a time these articulations may gain in individuality; they may stand out in our attention; but after that they will have to be reintegrated within the whole if we wish to prevent distortion. We could compare this with the process of biological differentiation.

When we study, for instance, the genesis of the human embryo, we are faced in the first stages of its development with a rather diffuse phenomenon which does not show much differentiation. The unsophisticated observer will not recognize this embryo as a potential human child. Gradually, however, differentiation begins. Various parts emerge from the vague diffuse totality and gain dramatically in individuality and distinction. An initial trunk, arms, legs, and a head are shaping our impression of the whole of the fetus. At certain times, some parts are gaining so much individuality that they threaten to dominate our vision of the whole. The head of the fetus, at a certain phase of development, is out of proportion to the rest of the body. For a time it seems to distort the human appearance, but then it falls back into the totality of the fetus and comes into proportion with the rest of the body. This development may serve as an example of what happens in the differentiation of our initial experience of the human personality and the later study of some of these differentiated aspects of our initial experience. First we "dwell" on our initial experience of personality which is diffuse like the original human fetus. Dwelling on it reflectively, we become aware of how this initial awareness of human personality implies various organic differentiations or articulations. We try to explicate faithfully these articulations which are given in our experience without imposing on this given phenomenon our prejudices or our emotional distortions.

In the course of our explication, some aspects of human personality may temporarily gain in individuality and distinction at the cost of the view of the whole, as the head of the fetus did. Nature itself took care that the disproportionate head of the fetus acquired proportion with the organic totality from which it emerged. But the psychological knowledge of man is partly man-made. Therefore, there is no natural organic principle of organization which forces the "enlarged" aspect into proportion. This entails the possibility that our knowledge of the psychology of personality may become distorted by our losing sight of the whole; it implies also the possibility that we may start to force our distorted view of man's psychology on the reality of man himself. Then the whole process of study would be reversed. Instead of being a humble fidelity to "what is", to the psychology of man which reveals itself to us, science becomes some distortion imposed on psychology. And because of the fact that reality is more than we are, we shall necessarily lose this battle between our petty impositions and reality. Not *reality*, but we will be crushed.

SPECIALISTS OF THE WHOLE

This danger of a distortion of the whole of man's psychology is the necessary consequence of the fact that modern research is so perfected, so onesidedly directed, and therefore so time and energy consuming that it is impossible for the researcher who works in limited areas of personality to relate his findings to the explicated fundamental structure of human personality and to all the findings of all the studies of personality. Therefore, there is only one choice for humanity today: either to develop on a global scale specialists of the whole personality who counterbalance the process of individualization of certain aspects of personality, or to resign itself to an otherwise inescapable distortion of our view of man. The last course will mean our gradual destruction because we will lose contact with our own psychology. There is only one choice today: to integrate or to perish.

This necessity implies that a tremendous amount of time, energy, specified talent, skillfulness, and scholarship will be required to perform the integration of all the fields of psychological study. How can we find a solution for this problem of time, energy, talent, and special training? There are three conceivable solutions: the genius solution, the local psychology solution, and the cooperative specialist solution. The genius solution rests on the hidden assumption that it is possible to educate a sufficient number of psychologists who combine in their personality the talents and training of the phenomenological explicator of man's initial awareness, of creative theoretician and interpreter, of astute translator of differentiations into operational concepts, of skillful collector of data for detailed study, of clinical experimenter, clinical observer, perfect master of statistical measurement, and finally integrator of this detailed study within the frame of the explicated fundamental structure of personality in comparison with all the studies that have been done in the course of history in all countries and cultures. This super-psychologist would not only combine in himself these talents which usually do not go together, but also find time and energy to accomplish all these things. No psychologist can be so naïve as to believe that such genius can be produced in sufficient numbers.

Another solution, the so-called local psychology solution, suggests a division of labor in which psychologists in various countries concentrate on various phases of the knowledge of man. In an over-simplified, and therefore inaccurate example, one could imagine that the local psychology of certain countries would produce Freuds, Adlers, Jungs, Binswangers, Buytendijks, and Merleau-Pontys who would take care of the integrative phases of science, and the local psychology of certain other countries would specialize in operational translations of some of their discoveries on the infra-human level which are open to operational manipulation, measurement, and experimentation. This solution too seems inefficient—still more so when the countries concerned use different languages. When these respective psychologists do not have much direct contact with one another, the gap between the specialists of the whole personality and the specialists of certain measurable aspects of personality becomes very wide—especially when the latter had no contact with the former during their graduate study in their own national universities.

A third possibility, the cooperative specialist solution, does away with the genius psychology concept and the local psychology concept. According to this solution, no country specializes in the exclusive production of psychologists of the whole personality or of psychologists specializing in one or another measurable aspect of personality, but rather every university makes room for both talents and stimulates them without discrimination. In this case, one could obtain one's degree in any university of any country concerned by means of integrative theoretical, experimental, or clinical research. This relationship of the future specialists in the psychology of the whole man and the psychology of certain measurable aspects of man in the same countries and at the same universities would make for more efficient cooperation and would gradually contribute to the restoration of the knowledge of the whole personality. We need scholars who specialize in the integration of our knowledge of personality in the light of a phenomenological explication of man's fundamental psychological srtuctures.

VARIETY OF PERSONALITY THEORIES

When the psychologists of personality attempt to integrate our knowledge of personality in the light of a phenomenological explication of man's fundamental personality structures, how can they explain the fact that there are so many integrations, such as Freud's, Jung's, Adler's, Binswanger's, or Frankl's anthropology? A first answer would be that some of these men were not trying to integrate on the basis of the fundamental structure of the human personality. If the basic categories of integrating the data and insights regarding human personality are not sought for in the explicated fundamental structure of personality, the categories will be able to contain only the phenomena of a certain group of men in a certain culture. Only the fundamental personality categories obtained by the explication of the basic structure of man's personality are valid at all times for all people in all situations, and are therefore broad enough to provide a basic organization for all psychological data, even of relative data, because their relativity has to be shown against the background of categories which are universally valid.

We must add, however, that even when anthropological psychologists are really basing their integration on the basic categories which are implicit in the primary awareness of fundamental personality structure of man—even then we may see different kinds of integration. Every integration of the psychology of man is pervaded by an original intuition, an all-illuminating light. This primary intuition enables the anthropological psychologist to bring clarity into the complexity of psychological data. This is true of the anthropologies of Freud, Jung, Adler, Horney, Binswanger, and Sullivan. There is no psychologist of personality who is satisfied with the complexity and plurality of data which are collected in experimentation and clinical observation and who is resigned to their disorderly enumeration. An anthropological psychologist is always trying to reduce the plurality to a kind of unity; he tries to discover structures; he wants to comprehend. A man such as Freud, or Jung, or Adler, or Binswanger attempting this integration does not know *beforehand* how the unity will be brought about or which structures will be discovered. The light by which he studies the psychology of man and thinks about the mutual relationships of the phenomena which he discovers is not first decided upon and then put into operation. It may perhaps be said that every new anthropological psychology begins with the vague suspicion that a certain approach will be fruitful before the psychologist of personality realizes precisely what he is doing, by what principle he is guided, by what light he is proceeding, or what fundamental intuition he is using. Usually the evident fruitlessness of a certain way of thinking about the psychology of personality in the past gives rise to and guides a new mode of thinking, but provisionally it is not at all clear in what this new mode consists. Thus, for instance, a psychologist of personality came to the conclusion that an explanation of the phenomenon of repression as involving only the need for pleasure is insufficient. Psychologists then tried to proceed along new paths; Jung pointed to the repression of the spiritual needs of the Self, Adler to the repression of the need for power. What these men are first of all interested in is a broader explanation of repression, and not reflection on the light in which they consider repression. Only much later does this light become the theme of investigation. Often such investigation is not performed by him who first made use of the light but by other anthropological psychologists. In this sense, it can be said that the psychologies of Jung, Freud, Adler, and others are much better understood by later anthropological psychologists than by these psychologists themselves.

Evidently, a psychological integration will be fruitful to the extent that its central point of reference, its basic idea of man's psychology, is capable of making the multiplicity and complexity of the psychological phenomena transparent and of reducing them to unity. For instance, we can reach no results at all in the integration of the knowledge of man's behavior with the idea "nails," while the ideas "nervous system", "libido", and "learning" offer at least some explanation.

Why is it that even when the anthropological psychologist attempts to choose as his central point of reference, as his basic principle of integration, a truly fundamental personality characteristic, he may still develop an anthropological psychology which is different from another one which was also based on a fundamental personality characteristic? First of all, an anthropological psychologist may be convinced that he is explicating a fundamental personality characteristic, while it is actually a characteristic of his own personality and of many who are in the same contemporary cultural situation, but not true of human personality as such. Or he may unduly emphasize one of the fundamental characteristics of human psychology at the cost of the others. In this case the anthropological psychologist misjudges the true character of his own fundamental personality because he has no eye for the other fundamental aspects of his personality. We may ask why this psychologist is so impressed by one aspect of his fundamental personality at the cost of the other aspects? Here only a psychological analysis could give an answer. The historical growth of his personal existence may have brought about his distorted explication of his fundamental personality, or it may have been the *Zeit Geist* which made him blind to certain aspects of his own reality.

Does this mean that such a onesided anthropological psychology is meaningless for psychology? By no means. For such a onesided psychology explains a certain fundamental aspect of the human personality and makes clear in what way the multiplicity of data about personality are integrated in this aspect. The participation of such a onesided personality theorist in the ongoing conversation of psychologists of personality helps his colleagues to transcend their own onesidedness. Secondly, when we are able to discover what type of distorted outlook made for this particular view of personality, we may learn about those people who share more or less the same emotional affliction in a certain period of culture. Their anthropological representative depicts for us their distorted world of resentment, despair, and rebellion. Finally, when we find out in reality that such a personality theory does not work, we shall be forced to question the theory concerned. This is the very moment in which we shall be born as psychologists of man. Now we are personally participating in the dialogue of mankind about the psychology of personality by means of discussions, publications, dissertations, and lectures.

CRITERION OF ANTHROPOLOGICAL PSYCHOLOGY

This brings us at once to the critical question: What is the criterion in the light of which I can see that my explication of man's basic psychological structure is true and valid? The criterion of truth is the presence of what I experience or observe. However, there is a difficulty in that I may distort my real primary experience or perception by imagination, anxiety, or by other emotional attitudes which may be ingrained in me or in my contemporary culture because of past traumatic experiences. Therefore, I need another criterion of truth for my explication of the fundamental structure of human personality. This criterion is the fruitfulness of my dialogue with the fundamental human personality in myself and in others. If this dialogue is based on a onesided explication of the fundamental psychological structure of human personality, sooner or later it will be impossible to keep the dialogue going at certain points because it will no longer touch reality, and therefore there will be no answer. Imagine, for instance, that I have explicated the fundamental structure of human personality as being absolutely identical with animal life, and that as a result of this explication I deal with the other as an animal. As long as I put only questions to him that will touch in him what is animal-like and infra-human (for instance, the biological aspect of his hunger drive), everything will be satisfactory. As soon, however, as I attempt to have a dialogue with this human person about his prayer, his love, his faithfulness, noble ideas, his philosophy, and I attempt to do it on the basis that the psychology of man is absolutely identical with that of the animal, his answers will not fit my biological categories. I will have to admit that my explication of the fundamental psychological structure of man is onesided because it does not work in reality.

In other words, the reality of the psychological life as revealing itself in collective and personal psychological history is the test of the truth of our explication. Here again, it is far easier for the psychology of the measurable aspects of man to apply the test of reality by means of experimentation. Some of these tests may indirectly prove that the implications on the infra-human level of certain explications on the formally human level are mistaken, and thereby foster a new explication. However, this proof is not usually sufficient because the reality of the psychological personality itself transcends that which can be tested by means of laboratory equipment or statistical measurement. Personality experiences such as responsibility, dread, anxiety, despair, freedom, love, wonder, or decision cannot be measured or experimented with like the infra-human aspects of personality. They are simply there and can only be explicated in their givenness. How can we find out that this explication is not a distortion? Close attention to history may be the only possible way. Entire generations of psychologists of personality may pass before it becomes clear that a certain psychological view is onesided and does not correspond to the full reality of the psychology of personality. It may become gradually clear that the prevalent view of personality contradicts reality, and a renewed explication of man's personality structure must be be attempted in order to come into contact again with his psychology. As an example, we may refer to orthodox reflexology and behaviorism. Their implicit anthropology was that man was a bundle of conditioned and unconditioned reflexes. That explication was in tune with the predominant anthropology of our most recent cultural period: man is a thing, something to be conditioned, organized, manipulated, experimented upon. At the moment, however, we see the consequences of the large scale imposition of this view of man in increasing neuroticism, self-estrangement, loneliness, despair, and boredom. Therefore, there are signs everywhere of an awakening interest in a renewed explication of man's fundamental psychological structure; other aspects of personality are emerging—man's human face is coming to the fore.

It is inevitable for man to make mistakes, to err in his psychology of personality. The psychologists of personality are always influenced in their explication by their cultural viewpoint. Often the men of a certain period of culture are not even aware that long ago they reached an impasse, and sometimes an entire life or an entire culture has to be a failure before man will recognize the deficiencies of his personality theory. This inclination to human onesidedness inspires the psychologist of personality to be modest in forming his views. To live up to the responsibility of being a psychologist of personality means a lifelong task of scholarly work.

As we have said, the explication of man's fundamental psychological structure—in the light of which explication the psychologist integrates the human knowledge about the psychology of man—is always in danger of falsification. The test of our collective history is necessary to prove the correctness or incorrectness of our explications. Humanity has no substitute for the painful test in the laboratory of history. Humanity can only prevent this test from taking longer than is necessary by making anthropological psychology the concern of sensitive scholars all over the world. These scholars must be the ears and the eyes of mankind, detecting the slightest indications that certain personality theories lead to deformation. They have to expose these indications in order that we may revise our directions when we discover that we are in blind alleys. It is not the psychologist of the measurable aspects of contemporary man in the laboratory or clinic who can assume this function. Experimentation and clinical research do not orient themselves; they are already oriented by an implicit or explicit view of personality. Therefore, it is only exceptional and accidental when they go beyond the prevalent theories of personality. Experimental research as such, and theories immediately linked to this research, cannot provide a viewpoint outside and above themselves from which to judge themselves critically. Therefore the specialist of the psychology of personality should abstain from too strong an involvement in detailed clinical or experimental research which could affect his impartiality. He has to be faithful to his unique function of being an impartial integrator of psychological knowledge in the light of man's fundamental psychological structure. The experimental or clinical psychologist is always measuring something. The comprehensive psychologist of personality is always integrating some measured aspects of the human reality and some aspects which are not measurable. Experimental and integrational research are the two poles of the axis on which turns the fascinating historical process of the discovery of the psychology of man.

UNDERSTANDING HUMAN PERSONALITY

The end of our descriptive definition, "in order to understand his psychology," announces the final aim of the anthropological endeavor: the growth in understanding of the psychology of man. The aim of any study guides the study in all of its phases. In this sense, the end is present in the very beginning and remains active as a background against which the psychologist of personality continually selects when reading, thinking, comparing, writing, or collecting data. The aim of the psychology of man is to understand man. But what is the usefulness of a psychology which makes us understand but which does not help us directly to "predict and control"? We are obsessed today by the image of the psychological laboratory, the computer, and the testing room. When we are doing things that are not directly convertible in the processes that go on in these sanctuaries of the natural sciences, we feel guilty. We tend to be disturbed when one of the highpriests of natural science in his symbolic white coat points his accusing finger in our direction and declares that we are not dedicating all of our scientific life to the service of experimentation. We feel that he may expel us from the community of scientists because we do not contribute to the increase of prediction and control.

This dogmatic attitude is due to the onesided view of personality that enslaves our society. The Gestalt of the technical prevails on the globe today.

Experimental psychology and the theories linked to it can never rise above this contemporary view of man's psychology because they are part of it. Therefore, this kind of psychology is so well accepted in our culture that it evokes guilt feelings in the psychologist of personality. In self-defense, the psychologist of personality could be tempted to demonstrate the usefulness of the comprehensive psychology of personality. He could attempt to find something in his work that equals the usefulness of motivational research, telling us which kind of package sells best; or perceptual research, informing us about the optimal conditions for vision on the road; or of human engineering, telling us how to construct an instrument panel to be used in a rocket with which we will shoot people to the moon. All these things seem far more practical, far more sound, than to talk about the psychology of personality. The effort, however, to prove an equal kind of usefulness of the psychology of personality would be in vain. A comprehensive theory of personality can never be justified by its *immediate* usefulness. Such a psychology can only justify itself by its appeal to that in man which forces him to search for an integral insight into himself and his fellow men and to grow through this understanding. The usefulness of psychology for this inner growth is frequently not understood by many psychologists of the measurable aspects of man. Many of them know only the usefulness which they experience in their laboratory or clinic or in their daily practice as industrial, educational, or motivational psychologists.

"What can you do with it?" "So what?" "How can you apply it?" "Can you translate it into an *operational* definition?" These are the questions, and the terms "do," "apply," and "operational" have a very definite meaning, limited as they are by the perspective of the world of the worker. The psychotechnics of the measuring psychologist are useful and necessary for the world of labor in which they are integrated. But the theory of personality as such seems useless to this world of labor. This psychology goes beyond the world of labor. An anthropological psychology which would be completely integrated in our contemporary world of labor would be "useless" in a higher sense. It would be useless as a means of transcending contemporary and local forms of of psychology through the integration of the psychology of men of all cultures and all centuries in order to grow in the understanding of the psychology of man as he is. An anthropological psychology which would be an integral component of the culturally and locally determined world of labor would be unable to assume a standpoint from which to view the relativity of the different kinds of psychology. The attempt to understand personality in the light of its fundamental psychological structure and of the explications of this structure during all centuries goes far beyond "usefulness" as it is strived for in the psychologies of the measurable aspects of man. The understanding of the psychology of personality as a whole is characterized by a "usefulness" which it cannot abandon under penalty of ceasing to be the unprejudiced understanding of the psychology of personality. If technical usefulness becomes our last and only guide and criterion in the understanding of personality, we will no longer be able to understand personality as personality, but we will measure personality only insofar as it can be used in the world of labor, of manipulation, prediction, and control. To know the psychology of personality from this viewpoint is important for the anthropological psychologist because it reveals an aspect of personality. But the study of the psychology of human personality as "technically useful being" can never become the exclusive basis of understanding the psychology of the whole personality, never the basis of an open comprehensive personality theory. Many introductory courses in our colleges introduce the personality not as a whole but from the viewpoint of a technocracy. The psychology of personality as personality goes beyond man's testable abilities, beyond his similarity to animals, and beyond his possibilities for adjustment to the huge glittering antiseptic buildings of our technocratic society.

We can also use the term "useful" in a sense which is totally different from its technocratic meaning. The technical usefulness of the psychology of the measurable aspects of man is that this psychology helps man to improve himself and his conditions in such a way that he becomes a better adjusted and more efficient producer and consumer in our gigantic collectives. But the usefulness of the psychology of personality is that it improves man precisely in his being man, as an independent growing self. Anthropological psychology is an aid to his self-actualization by means of participation, by making him aware that he is more than a sum of technocratic determinations by his civilization. Precisely because our society tends to treat man as a "technically useful being", this psychology of man is not only humanly useful but even necessary. This psychology of man has a really therapeutic significance in the oppressing atmosphere of a technocratic universe. The humane usefulness of the psychology of man cannot be proved outside the practice of understanding man as man. One could compare this usefulness for living with that which is proper to psychotherapy and art. Their specific kind of usefulness for man's very existence cannot be proved outside the experience of therapy itself and outside the experience of art itself. In the same way, one cannot prove the usefulness of human love. From the viewpoint of the world of labor, love is a highly impractical and time consuming affair. Its humane usefulness in a deeper sense is known only to the lovers themselves in the act of loving.

One can only understand the humane usefulness of the psychology of personality when one is "present" to the reality of the whole man. This being present to the reality of man as man is the primary experience of the psychologist of personality. Many psychologists are not present to man as man, wholly absorbed as they are in the experimentation of the laboratory, or in the psychotechnics of the testing room, or in social psychological research "about" certain aspects of man. Therefore, they are unable to understand "what this anthropological noise is all about." It cannot make sense to them. As a rule, therefore, pleas for the humane usefulness of a psychology of personality fail to convince the psychologist who is not anthropologically oriented. On the other hand, the psychologists, clinicians, or experimentalists who are already anthropologically oriented do not need such a plea because the value of this psychology clearly reveals itself in their psychological understanding of themselves and others. Only by attempting to understand oneself and one's fellowman as human can one experience what the psychology of personality really means.

Therefore, the only way in which the student can experience the value of anthropological psychology is by the actualization of his own potentialities and his own need for a continual integration of this understanding. A tremendous wealth of questions, tentative answers, anxieties, and delights are evoked in the student who confronts his own psychology and the psychology of others. Only by means of this actualization is it possible to make the student experience "true to life" what the psychology of personality really is and how incomparable is the value of the "useless" understanding of the anthropological psychologist. We are convinced that the development of our modern society and of the psychology of measurable aspects of man within society is in dire need of anthropological depth. Modern man, whether Marxist or Capitalist, is more and more in danger of becoming the victim of a technocratic mentality which pervades our society and its psychology. The more this mentality advances and extends itself in psychology, the more difficult it becomes for man to be in harmony with his psychology, with his real self, and to assent to his fundamental personality structure. The basic questions which arise in this situation are always of an anthropological nature.

CHAPTER SEVEN

ANTHROPOLOGICAL PSYCHOLOGY

Comprehensive psychology requires constructs sufficiently fundamental to integrate the contributions of various psychologies which embody isolated viewpoints in the study of intentional behavior. This variety of differential approaches can be reduced to three main categories, namely subject-oriented, object-oriented, and situation-oriented psychologies.

One series of perspectives considers human behavior in its subjective, experiential aspect. The subjective experience of man is embodied in quantifiable behavior and always refers to an object-pole in a situation. The psychologist, however, can limit his research exclusively to the subject-pole of this behavior. Many of the theories which have developed from psychiatry and psychotherapy demonstrate this perspective. The constructs and idioms of the psychologies which are predominantly subject-oriented differ from those which are oriented towards the bodily objectifiable, measurable aspects of behavior. This relative difference in method and idiom is not necessarily a difference in functional, mechanical, quantitative, process-like approach. The psychologist who specializes in the study of the subject-pole of behavior abstracts certain aspects from this behavior and isolates them for empirical study. For this differential theory he may very well use functional, mathematical, and mechanical constructs. Such an isolation of subjective variables is evident, for example, in the studies of the early introspec-

194

tionists. The use of a mechanistic model is also common in psychoanalytic studies of the subject-pole of behavior. As a third category, the differential psychologies which are concerned with the situational approach to behavior have developed their own methods, constructions, and formulations. The situational aspect of behavior encompasses those social, interpersonal, environmental, cultural, and historical features which enter into behavior as a whole and without which human behavior would be unthinkable.

Comprehensive psychological theory aims at the integration of these three types of differential psychologies in an open scientific model. This model can subsequently operate as a provisional guide in the development of the field of psychology as a whole. Comprehensive theory can pursue this main purpose only when its fundamental constructs are not exclusively subject-, object-, or situation-oriented. It must transcend these three dimensions of behavior by means of constructs which represent behavior in its entirety. Comprehensive psychology thus requires a type of concept which can bridge the gaps between the three series of perspectives. Constructs are needed which are capable of reintegrating conceptually the subjective, objective, and situational aspects of intentional behavior, and which point to the original unity of behavior as it manifested itself before scientific research isolated profiles from behavior for investigation.

The transcendence of the three main types of differential constructs does not imply a devaluation of them. On the contrary, continual development of differential psychologies will remain the condition for the constant growth of comprehensive psychology. For the scientific mode of existence expands by means of an increasingly differentiated concentration on isolated aspects of its object of study.

The type of construct which transcends the three differential types is called *anthropological,* and the comprehensive theory which utilizes such constructs is named *anthropological psychology.* Anthropological constructs deal with the subjective-objective-situational Gestalt of human behavior which is rooted in the very nature of "anthropos", or man.

In this chapter we shall first discuss the meaning of the term "anthropological" and then describe the necessary and sufficient constituents of anthropological constructs in psychology.

The Term "Anthropological"

In current usage the meaning of "anthropology" is restricted to the "science of man in relation to physical character, origin and distribution of races, environmental and social relations and culture." (*Webster's New Collegiate Dictionary*, Springfield, Mass., G&C Merriam Company, 1960, p. 38.)

This restriction of the term anthropology stresses only one of the three main dimensions of "anthropos" or man, namely the cultural-social one. Etymologically, the term anthropology does not have this restricted meaning for it is derived from the Greek words, *anthropos*, which means man, and *logos*, which means word or science. Therefore, every concept, construct, word, or science which refers to man as a whole can properly be called anthropological. Man in his entirety, however, appears to us under many aspects. For example, we may refer to man insofar as he appears physically, racially, socially, and culturally. In this case, we speak of cultural anthropology. We may also perceive man in the light of other sciences or disciplines, such as medicine, history, sociology, philosophy, or theology. In these cases we can rightly speak of a medical, historical, social, philosophical, or theological anthropology. The psychologist may study man insofar as he appears to us in the entirety of his intentional-functional behavior. Such a study may be called anthropological psychology. It presupposes, however, the development of many differential psychologies through the gradual uncovering of different abstracted aspects of behavior by experiment and observation. Consequently, an anthropological psychology is possible only after this differential unveiling. The main method of such a psychology is the dialectical integration of the results of these differential approaches. In other words, anthropological psychology is a comprehensive theoretical psychology which studies *human* behavior. This concern with *human* behavior does not imply a neglect of the insights gained by the study of animal behavior. On the contrary, the contributions of animal psychology are integrated within anthropological psychology insofar as they shed light on certain aspects of human behavior which are similar to those of the behavior of animals.

Human behavior, to be sure, can be conceived and formulated in many ways. The constructs which specify the meaning of human behavior must reveal certain characteristics in order to be truly anthropological. We may call these characteristics the necessary and sufficient constituents of anthropological constructs. Briefly, anthropological constructs must transcend the predominantly subjective, objective, or situational connotations of differential constructs; they must represent fundamental human characteristics; they should be rooted in experience; they should be person-oriented, not function-oriented; and they should be appropriated by the student of human behavior in a personal way. The remainder of the present chapter will be given to a consideration of these constituents of anthropological constructs.

The First Constituent: The Transcendence of the Predominantly Subjective, Objective, or Situational Connotations of Differential Constructs

Anthropological constructs should transcend the exclusively subjective, objective, or situational connotations of the constructs of differential psychologies. These latter specialize in the study of one of these three dimensions of behavior because of scientific-methodological reasons which have already been explained. The cultural development of Western thought in the last three centuries, however, has tended to transmute these methodological distinctions into absolute ones. This absolutism leads to subjectivism, objectivism, and situationalism. Because of this unfortunate historical development, it is necessary for us, first, to discuss what we mean by an anthropological construct, abstracting from the term all possible subjectivistic, objectivistic, or situational connotations; second, to consider the development in our culture of the absolute dualism we have mentioned above;

and finally, to assess the impact of this dualism on academic and psychoanalytic psychologies.

The term "anthropological" as we shall use it excludes all subjectivistic connotations. The subjectivism which has dominated recent periods of Western culture has tended to reduce the full meaning of the term "anthropological" to only the subjective dimension of man's being. From such an impoverished viewpoint, man is explained as a subject who is initially separated from the reality in which he lives. Such a view is not rooted in our spontaneous, full experience of man as a meaningful, intentional whole who is self-evidently present to reality. It posits *a priori* that man is first of all an isolated entity. This concept implies that there must be in principle an absolute split between man and reality. This position that man is an isolated object in the world forces us to far-fetched hypotheses to account for the indisputable fact that man manifests abundantly in his daily behavior a lively intimacy and familiarity with reality. None of these hypotheses is satisfying, however, once we have started from the presupposition that man is essentially a cut-off, schizoid being who has initially no commerce whatsoever with reality as it reveals itself.

When we use the term "anthropos" or man, then we imply that man lives in an original openness for reality or, even better, that man *is* fundamentally openness for reality. This radical openness makes man different from trees, mountains, or rivers which do not have this initial understanding and freedom. We may consider man's intimacy with reality the most fundamental anthropological characteristic and the basis of all other human qualities. Man is thus a fundamental orientation or openness toward that which is not himself. Subjectivism denies or disregards this basic truth about man. A psychology which perceives the human being as fundamentally out of contact with reality can never transcend its initial subjectivism. For all later perceptions of reality will necessarily be products of this isolated subjectivity, and it will never be possible to know whether or not these products are really "out there" or merely subjective projections.

Such a fundamental subjectivism leads necessarily to just as fundamental an objectivism, which holds that man can represent in his consciousness only isolated objects from which he is absolutely separated. But man is from the beginning of life, by his very being, open for the fullness of reality, which will appear in the light of his understanding to the degree that he is faithful to his fundamental openness. Being man, therefore, does not mean being first of all an isolated self or subjectivity, whch later transcends its isolation in order to represent to itself (like a camera) isolated objects of a completely foreign reality "out there".

Psychology studies intentional behavior of man in its concrete givenness, which is always a particular realization of his original openness for reality. Therefore, psychology always studies, in the last analysis, some behavioral relationship of man to himself, to others, and to things. For man can develop only what he fundamentally is; basically he is always a behavioral relationship with reality. This relationship modifies itself according to both the inexhaustible variety of situations in which reality manifests itself and the stand which man takes toward reality. For the appearance of reality in the light of man's openness differs when man stands out toward reality as a perceiving, a thinking, a remembering, a loving, a theorizing, an imagining, a dreaming, a depressed, a paranoid, or a utilitarian subjectivity. Every mode of existence reveals a different aspect of reality. But all these modes are modifications of the fundamental "enlightening-relationship-to-the-world" which man *is*. They are special actualizations of man's existential belonging to the world, of his already-being-in-the-world.

Although man is fundamentally open for reality, at each moment of his life only certain aspects of reality enter his concrete awareness. The selection and the availability of these aspects are dependent on his attitude. The scientific attitude, for example, reveals other appearances of reality than the poetic or the philosophical one.

All-that-is can emerge and reveal itself to man in this wide-open area of reality or being. If man were not in this original open contact with reality, it would be difficult to explain how he has succeeded in coming into contact with the appearances of reality which were supposedly separated from him. This concept would necessarily lead to the idealistic explanation that man must first—in an unexplainable way—transfer the things in the world to his mind. Everything would then happen in his mind, and we could never be sure that the things outside corresponded with the "mind-things", or even that they really were "out there".

The foregoing considerations may enable us to define further our use of the term, "anthropological psychology". It is a comprehensive theoretical psychology of human behavior. Behavior is conceived as a Gestalt of observable differentiations of an original intentional-behavioral relationship of man to the world. Behavior is thus the observable differentiation of man's intentional relationships. For reasons of method, we may emphasize in this behavioral relationship: first, the intending subject-pole, man; second, the embodiment of this intentionality in measurable behavior; finally, the "situated" object-pole of this intentional behavior.

Every differential psychology should concentrate on one of these main profiles of man's existence. This concentration presupposes a temporary abstraction of the aspect concerned from the whole of man's behavior. This methodological restriction will give rise to similarly restricted constructs. Such a limitation should be distinguished from an absolute limitation. An *absolute* restriction of the object of psychology to one of these abstracted profiles would foster the conception that *only* the subjective intentionality, or *only* measurable behavior, or *only* its "situated" object-pole should be the exclusive object of psychology. Some differential psychologists, though they do not concede that they believe in an absolute limitation of the object of psychology, seem to be convinced that their own restriction is absolute. This attitude betrays itself implicitly in a "lived" refusal to consider seriously approaches to intentional behavior other than their own. Such an absolute restriction of the object of psychology, whether implicit or explicit, is not scientific but philosophical, for it is a universal and absolute statement. Any such statement on the nature of man and of his behavior is fundamentally philosophical because it can never be proved to be true or false in its absoluteness and universality by means of the scientific method itself. Psychology, to be sure, like every other science, presupposes philosophical assumptions. But the assumptions which enable an anthropological psychology to develop must be sufficiently comprehensive to allow for the integration of subjective, objective, and situational psychologies. It is evident that the assumptions which underlie the absolutism of certain differential psychologies would be useless for a comprehensive psychology, for they would defy its very integrative purpose by excluding at the start the contributions of other psychologies.

A comprehensive theoretical psychology can never use differential constructs as fundamental constructs, even if they are used in a non-absolute sense by the differential psychologist. The meaning of a differential construct is methodologically restricted to only that aspect of behavior which is studied by a particular differential approach. Anthropological psychology can utilize such constructs only when they are purified of their limited connotations. Even then, it is difficult to view them as foundational constructs because of the inherent quality of their restrictive connotations. They may be useful, however, as subconstructs or as "bridges" between foundational constructs and the discoveries of differential psychologies.

Anthropological psychology, on the other hand, requires differential psychologists who create constructs with their own *methodological* restrictions. The differential way is the only way for the psychological mode of existence to develop. Anthropological psychology resists, however, the tendency toward absolutism found in these restricted constructs. Such absolutism would hamper the development of psychology as a whole and would keep the differential psychologies in principle isolated, defensive, and mutually exclusive. It is an essential task of anthropological psychology to unmask differential constructs which are paraded as absolute symbols of the *whole* reality of human behavior.

The backgrounds of modern psychology reveal how and where the philosophical tendency to transmute certain methodologically restricted constructs into absolute ones arose.

DUALISTIC PHILOSOPHICAL PSYCHOLOGY

The French philosopher, scientist, physiologist, and mathematician René Descartes conceived of mind and body as two distinct substances. Both mind and matter in his thinking are complete and self-sustaining. Mind is a thinking thing and body is an extension thing. Toward the end of his life Descartes attempted a re-unification of the two. His original dualistic view, however, was in tune with the temper of his time and therefore destined to influence subsequent developments in philosophy and science, specifically in psychology and psychiatry.

The idea of the separation of mind and body turned philosophical interest toward the conscious subject. This consciousness was believed to be divorced from both body and world. Reliable knowledge was not based on an original union of the subject with the world through his body, but was merely an accurate mirroring of a world that was out there by itself, i.e., separate from the subject.

This view gave rise to two mutually exclusive starting points, namely, mind on the one hand, and body and world on the other. Each philosophical system which arose after Descartes adopted one of these starting points and denied or neglected the other. Idealistic philosophies stressed consciousness, while empiricist philosophies emphasized only body and world, which were considered to be of the same order. Idealism eliminated the world entirely as a source of knowledge and made consciousness itself—separated from the world—the absolute origin of clear and distinct ideas. Empiricism, on the contrary, held that all knowledge originates from the experience of reality which imposes itself on the perceiving consciousness. Idealism made consciousness an active, spontaneous force existing in itself in spendid isolation. Empiricism made the perceiving consciousness a passive registering apparatus determined by outside stimuli.

202

Anthropological Psychology

Almost every scientific psychology was rooted in either an idealistic or empiricist view of human nature, because it emerged in a cultural atmosphere satiated with Cartesian dualism and its implicit presence in both idealism and empiricism. Idealism led in psychology to introspectionism, which considered the contents of consciousness the legitimate and exclusive object of the new science. Empiricism, on the other hand, gave rise to behaviorism, which saw quantifiable bodily behavior isolated from the consciousness as the exclusive subject matter of a scientific psychology.

Originally, neither type of psychologist understood that the restriction of his attention to one aspect of behavior should be merely one of method. Each of them was inclined to posit his restriction of the subject matter of psychology as absolute and exclusive. Fortunately, this onesided dogmatic view contributed to the rich development of the two main groups of differential psychologies. The findings and theories of both idealistic and empiricist psychologies are of great value. When purified from a narrow philosophical dogmatism, they may be integrated within a comprehensive theory of behavior.

Introspectionism, which was the dominant scientific psychology until 1912, holds that psychology should develop by means of introspection or a looking-into-consciousness which reveals "contents" of consciousness. These mental contents should subsequently be described in terms of elementary sensations. Wundt and Titchener modified this development of psychology somewhat by combining the experimental method with introspection. Nevertheless, the basis of their psychology remained the method of introspection, and they shared the idealistic assumptions of the earlier members of that school. The introspective psychologist described the inner aspect of man, his consciousness, and his self-awareness. All "lower" functions or bodily-measurable, behavioral aspects were reduced to "contents of consciousness."

Behaviorism, on the other hand, excluded "consciousness" from the subject-matter of psychology and neglected the subjective aspect of behavior. This one-sided concentration on one aspect of behavior also gave rise to a large group of differential psychologies which will provide a substantial contribution to the integration of scientific knowledge of human behavior. We may cite the differential theories of such psychologists as Weiss, Lashley, Hebb, Guthrie, Hull, Spence, Skinner, and Tolman. As we have seen, the introspectionists chose to study in isolation one of the two aspects of man separated by Descartes, namely the *res cogitans,* the thinking consciousness. The behaviorists, meanwhile, concentrated their efforts on the other isolated aspect, the stimulus-response body machine, the *res extensa.* Both neglected the inherent "worldly" aspect of man's behavior. This aspect, too, became split off from the original whole as an isolated entity and gave rise to social psychologies of an environmental and cultural nature which originally tended to treat the environment as a factor in itself, insulated from intentional behavior.

Introspectionism views all bodily and measurable behavioral functions and also the world of situation of man in the light of consciousness. Like every differential psychology, it can be "differential-comprehensive" in so far as the aspect of behavior it studies is in some way present in all behavior. Consequently, introspectionism can study all behavior from its specific perspective. It errs, however, when it becomes a closed and exclusive psychology which denies the valuable knowledge gained from other differential approaches such as behaviorism and social psychology. Introspectionism alone cannot provide comprehensive psychology with the constructs required for the total integration of psychology. Comprehensive psychology cannot concentrate on consciousness to the exclusion of all other aspects of intentional-functional behavior.

The other group of differential psychologies, initiated by Watson, is based on the abstraction of the quantifiable, external aspects of behavior. Watson and some of his immediate followers adopted a radical philosophical position instead of a methodological one. Their philosophical absolutism considered behavior and consciousness as mutually exclusive. It denied the validity of any approach to behavior other than the abstracted and isolated measurable aspect. This one aspect was made absolute and was substituted for the whole. To be sure, it is worthwhile to study all behavior in the light of its measurable, external characteristics. But this "differential-comprehension" should never be confused with the "comprehensive comprehension" which integrates all differential aspects insofar as they are known at a particular point in the development of the science of behavior. Differential constructs developed by behavioristic psychologists, while valuable, are not sufficiently comprehensive to cover, for example, the contributions of introspective psychologies under their specifically "intentional" aspect.

We may conclude that a truly anthropological psychology should use fundamental constructs which are neither introspectionistic nor behavioristic, but which transcend the methodological limitations of both in order to integrate their findings into a higher unity without distortion. Only such constructs will create an open theoretical field of inquiry with stimulating interchange of ideas among all differential psychologies.

ANTHROPOLOGICAL PSYCHOLOGY AND NON-ACADEMIC PSYCHOLOGY

Scientific anthropological psychology cannot overlook data or constructs presented by any school of psychology. To be truly comprehensive, it must encompass non-academic as well as academic psychologies. A crucial development outside the academic setting of the university was initiated by the psychoanalytically-oriented psychologists. The extra-academic origin of psychoanalysis is one cause among many which sometimes lead to strife between academic and psychoanalytic psychologists. The comprehensive psychologist should transcend, however, the defensive and mutually excluding attitudes maintained by certain representatives of both groups. He must seek for unity in diversity and foster the highest possible development of all psychologies. Consequently, he should give his attention to psychoanalytic as well as to behaviorist and introspectionist theories.

We have already discussed the Cartesian influence which led to the dualistic split between behaviorism and introspectionism in academic psychology. We concluded that the contructs of these psychologies are methodologically useful within the realm of differential psychology, but not to be used as fundamental anthropological constructs in a psychology which aims at synthesis and comprehension. The question now arises as to whether psychoanalytic theory is also influenced by Cartesian dualism. The answer to this question will reveal whether or not psychoanalytic constructs are sufficiently comprehensive to provide a basis for an anthropological synthesis.

An appraisal of the basic constructs of psychoanalytic theory will determine whether they encompass human behavior as a whole under all its aspects or deal with it from perhaps broad but still limited differential viewpoints. The aim of such a candid appraisal is not to discredit the contribution of psychoanalytic theory, but to assess the relative value of its findings from the viewpoint of comprehensive theory. Only the respectful integration of all contributions to psychology will lead to an understanding of the fundamental principles of the individual, social, cultural, and economic behavior of man, and to the improvement of his position in the universe. Psychologists must pool their resources. Isolationism of the differential psychologies can only render them less effective.

An evaluation of Freud's contribution from the viewpoint of comprehensive psychology leads to the conclusion that he too worked within the contemporary framework of Cartesian dualism. His view of man is obviously not based on the assumption of an original existential unity between man and world. Man in Freudian theory is biologically fixed as a pattern of innate instinctive drives prior to his having any relationship with a world which is in principle alien to his being. The world is not constitutive of his existence, but rather a collection of foreign objects to be reacted to by his fundamentally fixed biological structure. Man is not primarily an existence, a standing-out with others toward being, a participation in reality; he is fundamentally and innately a narcissistic, pleasure-seeking subjectivity. His basic libidinal and aggressive drives do not impel him to participate freely in reality, but rather to make use of objects in his world merely for instinctive gratification of his subjectivity. In other words, reality does not have an intrinsic value to be participated in respectfully, but only an utilitarian value for the subjective ego. All sense of the world "out there" is consequently determined by the isolated, subjective, instinctual forces within the organismic box. All other meanings uncovered in reality, whether personal, ethical, religious, or political, are simply imposed on reality by the absolute libidinal subject in the form of "sublimations." Man's experience of such meanings in reality is simply an illusion. He is the victim of sublimation which hides from him the fact that the only meaning of reality for him is gratification of instinctive needs. In all these viewpoints Freud mirrors, on the biological and psychological planes, the philosophical dualism introduced by Descartes.

The isolated world out there, as Freud sees it, is only "reacted to" with a pre-structured instinctive impulse which is ready to grasp it in a pre-determined way. This subjectivistic view of man led Freud to the notion that civilization was a menace to the wholesome development of the autonomous subject, and that neurosis was fundamentally a conflict between the instinctual subjectivity and any form of culture. Not only did Freud divorce the subject from his world, but he "objectivized" this isolated subjectivity as a "psychic apparatus." This apparatus comprised a host of processes and mechanisms concerned with the quantitative regulation of instinctive tensions within this now "objectified" subjective realm. Thus Freud created the constructs of release, repression, and sublimation to account for the economy within this endopsychic universe. Neurosis and criminality are expressions of the "natural and vigorous" pregiven instincts of the isolated subject, who feels painfully limited in the expression of his instinctive subjectivity by the alien cultural world in which he lives as a suppressed stranger. The basic implicit assumption of an essential split between man and his world leads necessarily to the view that social life, culture, and civilization have no real roots in the very existence of the subject.

While Freud elucidated important characteristics of the sub-ject-pole of existence, he disregarded the possibility that man's neuroses may be due to a psychological factor which affects his existence as a whole, that is, the "situated" object-pole as well as the subject-pole. Is destructive aggression, for example, a primary instinct to hurt or destroy which is already pregiven as such in the isolated subject? Or should it be considered as a response evoked by an existential situation which is experi-enced as obstructive, thwarting, and interfering? The over-whelming asexual and aggressive impulses found in certain neu-rotic patients seem to be not merely innate forces in isolated subjects, but responses to a frustrating life situation embedded in the structure of the patient's existence during the history of his development. But Freud did not envision the development of the personality in terms of a differentiating encounter of sub-ject and world in which both are constitutive of man's actual being. He thought of his patients much more as victims of a constant search for release of subjective tension in a strange and hostile world which they had to use for the highest pos-sible fulfillment of their needs.

In reality, man as a whole is constituted as much by his world as by his consciousness. Man's consciousness is not separated from the world as Freud, under the impact of Cartesian dual-ism, believed. Consequently, Freud's viewpoint forced him to fill the isolated subjective boxes called "consciousness" and "unconsciousness" with all kinds of furniture called "internaliza-tions" in order to explain the undeniable interaction between these subjective areas and the world. Soon the psyche was filled with a host of "internal psychic objects." The relationship of Freudian theory to the Cartesian Ego, to idealism and intro-spectionism, is evident in this development. To be sure, one could not have expected Freud, in spite of his genius, to eman-cipate himself wholly from the dualism that permeated his cul-ture. His acute observations compelled him, in fact, to recog-nize the impact of significant life situations on the developing organism. But his dualism forced him to internalize these out-side influences within the subject in such a way that they lived there, as it were, a dynamic life of their own. The superego was a construct which represented these totally internalized forces. Freud thus created an inner mental world of the individual divorced from the "real-world-out-there." Soon he required the constructs of projection and introversion to account for the contacts between this so-called inner world and the outer world. Impulses and emotions are not, however, isolated objects which exist in themselves within an isolated "psyche," but dynamic aspects of man's modes of existence in the world. Conflict is not an endopsychic affair, but a clash between two or more incompatible modes of existence.

Freud's theory—especially his later ego theory—was further developed by Anna Freud, William Reich, Melanie Klein, Hartmann, Kris, Alexander, Loewenstein, Winnicott, and others. These later developments reveal considerable growth toward a less dualistic view of man and his world, but they seem to be still unable to transcend completely the original split between man and world on which psychoanalytic theory is based. Nevertheless, the contribution of psychoanalytic theory to our understanding of man is monumental and should be carefully integrated within an anthropological synthesis.

Carl Jung, also, is subjectivistic in his approach to psychology. To be sure, he fills the subject box with other objects than Freud did; for example, archetypes and a racial unconsciousness. Human development becomes for him a wholly internal, somewhat mystical process within the isolated subjectivity. However, he points to significant experiences, the formulation of which is capable of being purified from the dualistic theoretical influence.

A British group of psychoanalysts, notably Melanie Klein, Fairbairn, Winnicott, and Guntrip recognized the impact of culture on behavior. At the same time, their sophisticated theory of psychic internalization of the environment fell back on the isolated subject-box-theory. The Cartesian split is revived in their theory to such a degree that man is conceived to live in two worlds at the same time, inner and outer, psychic and material. The "internal objects-psychology" of this group can also be seen as a result of the selection of the imaginative aspect of human behavior as their perspective. In their theory, imagination is not considered as world-oriented and world-revealing in principle, but as part of a relatively insulated and autonomous subjective structure. They reveal a tendency to stress the endopsychic situation and internally generated conflicts at the expense of the impact of the outer world here and now. Melanie Klein, for example, views the experience of the outer world as secondary and subordinate to the "internal" experience. Her view develops into a theory of inner psychic reality and its structuring in terms of internal objects and internal object-relations. Day and night dreams and the play of children become expressions of this relatively autonomous inner world. In the same vein, Fairbairn even concludes that the original distinction of Freud between the conscious and the unconscious now becomes less important than the distinction between the *two worlds of outer reality and inner reality*. As a result of Melanie Klein's theory, the super-ego becomes a construct which covers a whole inner world of internalized objects.

The quality and quantity of clinical material presented by this British group compels respect; so does the quality of their theorizing. They represent an original and unusual contribution to psychoanalytic and other theories. Their refreshing insights and discoveries lend themselves to integration within a comprehensive psychology of human behavior. Their constructs, while valuable and necessary from the differential viewpoint, are not sufficiently comprehensive to provide a basis for an anthropological psychology.

"SITUATIONAL" ANALYTIC PSYCHOLOGY

The Cartesian split, as we have seen, led to introspectionism and behaviorism in academic psychology, while an analogous development took place in non-academic psychology. In addition, the cultural interpersonal school of psychoanalytic thought represented by Alfred Adler, Harry Stack Sullivan, Karen Horney, and Erich Fromm gave rise to a series of differential theories bound together by the viewpoint of the culture, the civilization, the "others", the world. These psychologists rejected the idea that man's impulsive and emotional behavior emerges from innate instinctive drives within the organismic box. They substituted the perspective of environmental conditions, social pressures, cultural patterns, for the perspective of autonomous instinctual subjectivity. This series of differential psychoanalytic theories stresses that culture molds character and that neurosis arises from disturbances in human relationships. These theories tend, however, toward an exclusively cultural explanation of behavior which implies an underestimation of the relatively free subject who interacts with his culture. This development mirrors the situation in academic psychology in which introspectionism was one-sidedly concerned with the processes "within" the subject, while original behaviorism was geared to the perspective of the outside stimuli. Fromm, for example, sees the inclinations of man simply as the result of the social process which creates man.

Harry Stack Sullivan views the human personality as the product of the personal and social forces acting upon man from the day of his birth. The social pressure of the culture-pattern molds the personality. Sullivan recognized, however, that it is a person-integrated-in-a-situation-with-another-person-or-persons whom one studies in psychology. Such a fortunate formulation tends to transcend the Cartesian split. However, when Sullivan further outlines his theory of behavior, it becomes evident that he promotes the culture-side of the split at the expense of the subjectivity of man. His psychology is a penetrating differential study of one aspect of the human reality, namely the acculturation of the conscious and preconscious ego in relationships with the world. As a result, he evolves a theory in which the real subjectivity of man has no place, but is replaced by a social self dependent on a need for approval and acceptance. His statement which most strikingly reveals this aspect of his theory is: "The self may be said to be made up of reflected appraisals." A necessary consequence of this one-sided attention to the "situated" object-pole of human existence is a one-sided appreciation of the "real self"—just as limited as the vague entity described by Horney, Fromm, and Jung.

The series of differential psychologies initiated by the perspective of the "situated" object-pole of existence illustrates strikingly the importance of differential psychologies. They elucidate one aspect of human existence in a most remarkable manner. They are capable of viewing the whole of human reality in the light of this one perspective, because this "situational" aspect is everywhere present in man, even in the innermost reaches of his being. This one-sidedness is laudable and fruitful as a methodological principle and should be maintained as a source of insight into one aspect of human existence. It is impossible, however, to use the differential constructs of these psychologies for a comprehensive theory which is the very transcendence of these aspects. Such a theory respectfully aims to discover the appropriate place of these differential constructs in a conceptual comprehensive structure which points to human behavior as a whole.

THE SECOND CONSTITUENT: THE REPRESENTATION OF FUNDAMENTALLY HUMAN CHARACTERISTICS

Differential psychologies deal with various isolated profiles of human behavior. Many of these profiles when taken in isolation from man as a whole are characterized by features, processes, and laws that can also be observed in animals, plants, and inanimate objects. These common aspects are abstracted, however, from the whole of man's behavior and objectivated for methodological reasons of research. The *full* meaning of these isolated features of human behavior can be grasped only when they are reintegrated within the whole by comprehensive psychology. Their meaning becomes clear when perceived again in the light of those properly human qualities of man which characterize all profiles of his behavior and their mutual interdependency.

These comprehensive, all-pervading, specifically human qualities cannot be forced into the mechanical models of certain differential psychologies such as stimulus-response, punishment-reward, tension-reduction, or homeostasis. Such frames of reference are equally applicable to nonhuman beings. Consequently, these "sets" of mechanistic constructs "catch" precisely that in man which is not specifically and exclusively true of human behavior as such. The foundational constructs of anthropological psychology should point, therefore, to precisely those unique qualities that make man distinct from every other type of being. Such unique qualities, which pervade all profiles, features, and processes of human behavior, will provide the synthesizing ideas which can inter-relate the data and theories of differential psychologies. Only such comprehensive constructs will facilitate a systematic integration, explanation, and understanding of human behavior.

This necessary concern of comprehensive psychology for man in his characteristically human qualities does not imply an underestimation of the methodological usefulness of mechanical models in certain differential psychologies. A differential mechanistic approach to certain isolated aspects of behavior remains methodologically justifiable as long as the interpretation of the results of such an approach does not go beyond the specific differential profile of behavior which is its object.

PHILOSOPHICAL ANTHROPOLOGY

Comprehensive psychology has thus to create constructs which represent the human characteristics of behavior. The discipline which is traditionally concerned with the fundamental characteristics of man is philosophical anthropology. This discipline studies the being of man, his nature, or his essence. It does so in the light of ontology, which may be defined as the study of Being as such. The anthropological psychologist, in so far as he is a foundational theorist, is necessarily interested in philosophical anthropology, and consequently in the underlying ontology on which it depends.

In every cultural period, philosophical anthropology and its underlying ontology reconsider the perennial problems of the philosophy of man in the light of contemporary knowledge and experience. The anthropological psychologist who has to deal with contemporary man in clinic, hospital, and consulting-room must integrate not only the past but also the most recent discoveries of differential psychologies. He is necessarily interested in formulations of contemporary philosophies which verbalize the contemporary predicament and self-awareness of man. However, he does not assume philosophical concepts blindly, but evaluates them in the light of both historical and contemporary contributions of differential psychologies in order to judge their applicability to these psychologies and their concomitant usefulness for the construction of comprehensive theory. Many ontological concepts are useful for comprehensive integration because of their universality, that is, their applicability to all behavior of all men. When constructs about behavior are obtained by a merely empirical study of a specific group in a particular culture, then they are useful in integrating only the data which pertain to that group. Only constructs which are obtained from an explication of man's very essence are in principle broad enough to integrate all psychological data obtained by all differential psychologies and concerning all classes of men in all periods of human history.

Certain differential psychologies, on the other hand, may develop their own implicit philosophical anthropology which is suitable only to the specific aspect of behavior which they study. The integration of the contributions of these differential psychologies presupposes, therefore, that the integrational theorist will make explicit their specific ontological assumptions. Only then is a dialogue possible between the fundamental philosophical anthropology represented in the foundational constructs of comprehensive theory and those ontological assumptions which underlie the differential psychologies. This dialogue will clarify whether or not the philosophy of man which underlies a particular differential psychology is sufficiently comprehensive to be adapted to discoveries of other differential psychologies. If it is not, the integrational theorist must purify the differential contribution of all unwarranted extrapolations arising from its implicit philosophy of man. Only such a purification will clarify precisely what the differential psychologist has established through scientific observation. Such an operation, on the basis of comprehensive anthropological constructs, is performed in comprehensive theory by means of the foundational dialectical method. This method is based on the principle that scientifically established data of differential theories can never exclude one another and are always open to integration. If the implicit philosophical anthropologies underlying the differential psychologies prove to be incompatible with one another, then the theoretical psychological interpretations may also be incompatible insofar as they are influenced by these contradictory concepts.

This dialectical activity of the comprehensive theorist does not imply that he can call himself a philosopher. First of all, he does not create philosophical concepts, but only uses them as another psychologist might use certain concepts of physiology. A differential psychologist does not become a professional physiologist because of this intellectual borrowing; neither does a comprehensive psychologist become a professional philosopher because of analogous borrowing. Furthermore, the comprehensive theorist uses only those philosophical concepts which prove relevant to the integration of the data of differential psychologies. His whole intellectual procedure is essentially different from the manner in which a professional philosopher approaches his own discipline. Finally, the comprehensive psychologist does not have the professional background in philosophy which would qualify him to construct a philosophy with authority. To continue the comparison given above, the use of philosophical concepts by a psychologist does not imply that he himself is a professional philosopher any more than the use of physiological data implies that a psychologist is a physiologist. In each case, there is only a highly selective borrowing from another discipline on the basis of discoveries in the field of psychology. This borrowing is therefore fundamentally a psychological and not a professionally philosophical or physiological activity; it presupposes, however, a previous professional activity by philosophers or physiologists. The results of this activity are assumed by the comprehensive psychologist. We may define such an assumption as a conclusion or judgment borrowed by one professional field of study from another, the intrinsic validity of which cannot be proved or disproved by the specific methods of the discipline which appropriates it. A borrowing science can prove only that the constructs borrowed are relevant to the explication and integration of its own discoveries and do not contradict the established scientific data within its own field. For example, the science of optics assumes that the laws of mathematics are valid and makes use of them to explain and integrate its own findings. However, optics makes no direct effort to prove or disprove the laws of mathematics.

The comprehensive theorist is especially interested in what psychology implicitly or explicitly borrows from ontology. For these ontological assumptions shape the basic frame of reference of psychology as a whole. The explication of ontological assumptions in foundational theory, and in the differential psychologies which are to be integrated, should not be understood as an operation which is to be performed once only. For foundational constructs should point clearly and precisely to the fundamental characteristics of man. And the insight of man concerning his basic characteristics continually grows richer, deeper, and more specific as history develops. An anthropological psychology which is open and vital profits from this growth of insight by constantly questioning its fundamental constructs and categories. Moreover, differential psychologies may be influenced in their theoretical formulations by newly emerging philosophies of man. This influence will impel the comprehensive theorist to a constant investigation of the possible presence of new philosophical elements in the formulations of differential psychologists. If such ontological changes are not clarified, they may obscure the contributions of differential observation and experimentation, and thus hinder their smooth integration within the wider frame of reference of anthropological psychology.

The Principle of Applicability

We may conclude that one necessary constituent of the comprehensive constructs of anthropological psychology is their representation of fundamental characteristics of man or those basic human qualities which characterize the meaning of human behavior as a whole. The comprehensive psychologist carefully selects and formulates his anthropological integrational constructs during the dialogue which he maintains between all differential psychologies and anthropological philosophy. This dialogue is not an arbitrary comparison between two fields of study; it is oriented by its purpose of integrating the contributions of the differential psychologies within an innerly consistent, comprehensive, anthropological frame of reference. This purpose provides the criterion of selection for the comprehensive theorist and assures a degree of inter-subjective agreement or convalidation.

In other words, for the comprehensive psychologist the criterion for the selection of foundational constructs is extrinsic to the philosophical judgment itself, but proper to his own science, by which he can determine the usefulness of these constructs for the integration of the differential contributions. When the comprehensive psychologist calls these borrowed philosophical constructs *assumptions,* he means only to indicate that they are assumptions *for him* as a scientist; he means that they are useful to him in the integrational dialogue. He cannot assert that they are *only* assumptions for he is not competent to prove such a statement by means of his own scientific methods. However, it may well be that various statements assumed by psychologists are certitudes in the disciplines from which they are borrowed.

The criterion which determines the selection of anthropological constructs is therefore the *principle of applicability.* This principle states that *the comprehensive scientific theorist of human behavior should borrow only those philosophical assumptions or constructs which can be used most adequately for the explanation and integration of the greatest number and variety of the findings of the various differential psychologies because of applicability to those findings.* This judgment concerning the usefulness of an assumption is thus psychological and not philosophical.

217

Not only comprehensive psychology but also differential psychologies borrow philosophical assumptions and constructs. Their criterion, however, is applicability not to the integration of *all* differential psychologies, but to the *specific* operations in which differential psychologists study certain profiles of behavior. Frequently, these constructs are limited; they are adequate tools for the explanation of behavior only insofar as it appears in the isolated perspective of a differential psychology. A stimulus-response learning theory, for example, is a differential psychology which studies the measurable stimulus-response aspects of behavior. This differential psychology may select as its philosophical concept that man is only a passive organism which is subjected to stimuli and which can be explained under all its aspects in terms of stimulus and response.

As we have seen earlier, a variety of human behaviors can indeed be perceived in the light of the perspective of a differential psychology. For this aspect may reveal itself somehow in all behavior. Such a consideration of the whole of behavior under this specific approach is not only useful but necessary for the growth of comprehensive psychology, which depends on the contributions of differential psychologies. It is clear, however, that the underlying philosophy of this one differential psychology is not necessarily applicable to many other differential psychologies which study totally different aspects of behavior. These aspects cannot appear as such in the perspective of one theory such as the stimulus-response learning theory. The ontological assumptions of the latter are useful only to the differential psychologist who attempts to perceive all behavior under only one specific aspect.

A contrast may clarify our position. Rogerian theory rests upon the assumption that man is worthy of respect and capable of assuming responsibility for his own existence. These philosophical constructs have proved useful for Carl Rogers and his students. However, a differential S-R psychologist, *as* differential S-R psychologist, cannot use Rogerian theory in his specific study because the latter does not imply aspects of behavior which reveal respect and personal responsibility.

Anthropological Psychology

It is necessary for the comprehensive scientific theorist to
keep the dialogue open not only among all contemporary differential psychologies, but also between contemporary and past
psychologies. Otherwise, the pull of a successful psychology
may be so strong that the comprehensive theorist succumbs to
its fascination and accepts its implicit philosophy of man which
is in tune with the *Zeitgeist*. The openness for all psychologies
of *past* and present protects him, at least to a degree, against
the seduction of the prevalent spirit of his age. Sometimes the
psychology of an era will be mechanistic and deterministic; at
other times, humanistic and personalistic, or environmental, or
religious, or aesthetic. Every one of these psychologies may
highlight one or another essential or quasi-essential aspect of
human behavior. Comprehensive psychology attempts to integrate them in the light of the principle of empirical applicability to the findings of differential psychologies. This principle
limits the essential task of comprehensive theoretical psychology
to the creation of a useful model for the integration of scientific psychology and removes from it all pretense of creating
an integral view of man as such. The latter task, which is proper
to philosophy, could never be based merely on the principle of
empirical applicability.

It should be clear at this point that comprehensive psychology
proposes its anthropological constructs as purely provisional. On
the one hand the anthropological psychologist is conscious of
the limitations of the human intellect. He knows that all scientific statements are approximations at best and are always open
to revision. On the other hand, he is aware of the dynamic
richness of personality and the fact that the behavior of man
can never be adequately encompassed by any theory.

DIFFERENCES BETWEEN ONTOLOGY OF MAN AND COMPREHENSIVE
PSYCHOLOGY

Our consideration of philosophical concepts and psychological
constructs may be better clarified by a statement of the ways

in which the ontology of man and comprehensive psychology differ in their fundamental purposes, criteria, and methods. As a primary object, philosophy of man studies the nature of man in the light of Being, whereas theoretical psychology investigates man's intentional- functional behavior in the light of the empirical findings of differential psychologies. Theoretical psychology borrows concepts from the philosophy of man which are used as principles of integration only insofar as they prove in some way applicable to empirical material. With respect to the reliability of their knowledge, many philosophies claim certitude, but the knowledge of comprehensive psychology is merely provisional because it is dependent on the discoveries of differential psychologies. The basic purpose of the philosophy of man is essentially non-utilitarian, but theoretical psychology is influenced by the pragmatic intention of integrating the empirical knowledge of the behavior of man so as to foster the authentic growth, development, and integration of his behavior in concrete life situations.

The criterion for the philosopher of man is whether or not a judgment provides an insight into man's nature considered in the light of Being; the criterion for the theoretical psychologist is whether or not a judgment proves capable of integrating meaningfully and consistently the *empirical* data and constructs concerning *concrete* human behavior in *concrete* life situations.

The method of the philosopher is a dialectical one in which the main voice is that of ontology. The ontologist examines empirical findings which may subsequently be used as only one minor fragment of an overall ontological view of man's nature. The method of the comprehensive psychological theorist is dialectical too, but the main voice is that of empirical data and constructs. In their light the theorist discovers the usefulness of certain philosophical concepts for the integration of the empirical data he is examining. These selected philosophical concepts become a fundamental part of a comprehensive scientific system which does not claim an overall view of man's nature, but only a provisional integration of empirical data regarding concrete ways of behavior in concrete life situations.

Anthropological Psychology

The criterion of empirical applicability to *all* past and present differential psychologies directs the selection and choice of basic constructs by the scientific theorist. This criterion limits considerably the possible constructs which can be used without doing injustice to any differential contribution. Ideally, when a sufficient variety of differential psychologies has been developed in the course of history, all theoretical scientists would use practically the same anthropological constructs. This would necessarily be so if the theory comprehended the variety of psychologies in all their diversity without distortion or exclusion of any insight offered by them. The slightest deviation from the criterion of empirical applicability would immediately be evident in the incapacity of the theory proposed to integrate one or the other differential psychology not covered by the deficient foundational construct. Concomitantly, the theory proposed would fail to be a comprehensive theory.

However, it would seem that a sufficient variety of differential psychologies has not yet been developed. Consequently, comprehensive theorists are not yet compelled by the variety of contributions to adopt fundamental constructs which are basically the same. Actually, then, differences in fundamental constructs are still possible. Instead of new differential psychologies, there are still many cultural and sub-cultural concepts which influence the theoretical psychologist in the form of implicit philosophies. The comprehensive theorist should be aware of these implicit philosophical influences and of the danger of their conflicting with the principle of empirical applicability. In the present stage of the development of psychology, then, various comprehensive theories are still possible, all of which may apply to contributions of all the differential psychologies. However, the increase in differential psychologies will decrease the number of empirically applicable comprehensive theories.

THE THIRD CONSTITUENT: ROOTEDNESS IN EXPERIENCE

An anthropological construct points to a fundamental human characteristic as it is found in real life. Consequently, it is crucial

221

for such a construct to be based on our experience of man himself and not on wishful thinking, subjective imagination, or theoretical prejudice *about* man. In other words, anthropological constructs must be purified of all that is in disharmony with our fundamental experience of the human reality. Therefore, the first task of the foundational theorist is to study, in the light of actual experience, constructs available to him from various philosophies and differential psychologies. He will ask himself precisely what conforms with experience in these constructs and what is only hypothetical conceptualization. If the construct proves to be erroneous or distorted by prejudice, then it should be either corrected or rejected. An anthropological construct expresses at best only an approximation of fundamental human qualities. Nevertheless, experience must be the root of the construct and can never be replaced by hypotheses, models, or unverified philosophical, social, or political views. The comprehensive psychologist will build his theory on anthropological constructs, to be sure, but the constructs themselves should never be rooted in theory but in the firm ground of actual experience. It must be emphasized that the comprehensive theorist borrows from philosophy only those concepts which are rooted in experience and verifiable in experience.

The development of anthropological constructs should be an explication of that which is implicit in the human experience which they express. As we have already seen, the integration of the contributions of the differential psychologies also presupposes a basis of real experience. Only then is a dialogue possible between the experience of human behavior as a whole expressed in anthropological constructs and the experience of isolated profiles of human behavior as discovered through a purification of the formulations of differential psychologies.

In order to root both anthropological and differential constructs in real experience, natural observation and the phenomenological method are used. Natural observation enables us to describe phenomena in their immediate appearance. The phenomenological method leads us to the inner structure of these phenomena and liberates our perception of this structure from personal bias.

Anthropological Psychology

The requirement that anthropological constructs should be rooted in our experience of characteristically human qualities implies that one type of philosophy seems to be preferable to others in the matter of borrowing anthropological constructs. The kind of philosophy which seems to be most useful is that which is rooted in a critical phenomenology of human experience. Only such a philosophy attempts to develop, on the basis of experience, concepts which relate in principle to all that is necessarily true of all human qualities. We shall develop this subject in a later chapter on existential psychology and phenomenology.

THE FOURTH CONSTITUENT: PERSON-ORIENTATION AND NOT FUNCTION-ORIENTATION

Anthropological constructs differ distinctly from the constructs of differential psychologies in terms of personal versus functional orientation. Various differential psychologies which study certain aspects of behavior in isolation from man's behavior as-a-whole state their theories in the form of impersonal functions or equations. Such psychologies follow of necessity an analytical, objectivating procedure because of their dependency on empirical operations. Such operations can be performed only with abstracted isolated variables which are objectivated from the results of analysis of the reality under study. For the same reason, differential theories considered in terms of these isolated aspects of behavior form together a heterogeneous collection of explications of abstracted profiles of behavior without any inner relationship to one another.

Anthropological psychology, therefore, must begin with human existence in its wholeness if it is ever to reintegrate these unrelated, abstracted profiles into a meaningful, self-consistent synthesis. This specific task of comprehensive psychology requires a terminology proper to itself, for it cannot function on the same lines as the differential psychologies. The system of constructs of an anthropological psychology must refer to existence as a "living," personal, intentional whole—as it appears in real life situations. Only on such a basis of foundational constructs will comprehensive psychology be able to create a synoptic view of human behavior from a synthesis of the knowledge available in the differential psychologies. The human or personal qualities and dynamics which are characteristic of man in his natural union with the world cannot be adequately represented by a terminology which is peculiar to physiology, physics, or mathematics. Any attempt to do this would force anthropological data to fit an impersonal, infra-anthropological theory instead of developing a theory suitable to the data. Anthropological psychology transcends differential psychologies precisely at the level where the human person emerges as the unique, all-encompassing, intentional Gestalt. On this ultimate level of integration the statistical, physical, physiological, neurological, biological, biochemical, or mathematical constructs are of no avail—regardless of how well they are adapted to differential psychologies on lower levels of integration.

The use of mathematical constructs, for example, on this highest level of integration of intentional behavior would alter the identity of the subject matter. For the expression of behavior in mathematical symbols would necessarily change the conception of the personal nature of the subject. Human intentional behavior as a total dynamic structure cannot be represented by a mechanical, but only by a personal model. The anthropological constructs which compose this model must develop a new terminology capable of representing phenomena of human behavior as personal, existential, or qualitative, and not as mechanical, functional, and quantitative. These constructs are qualitative in nature and refer to the intentional presence of man in a world which has personally significant meanings for him.

Certain differential psychologies must depersonalize their abstracted profiles of behavior to determine to what degree these profiles are influenced by specific biochemical or physical laws. Such a depersonalization would be impossible, however, for a comprehensive science which studies man precisely in his very distinctness from the objects of physics, chemistry, biology, and neurology. In other words, anthropological psychology studies the intentional-functional behavior of persons who actually exist together with other people in a meaningful world. To be sure, this behavior reveals certain process-like, mechanical features which can be abstracted for close observation and study by differential psychologists. But these features are peripheral; they are not the unique core of intentional behavior. Nevertheless, they should be taken into account and reintegrated by the anthropological psychologist in his comprehensive synthesis.

Anthropological constructs, when compared with the functional thought forms in which most differential psychologies cast their facts and theories, are indisputably more personal. It would be unscientific to represent human-behavior-as-such with constructs of differential psychologies which point only to certain physiological, biological, functional, or physical attributes which human behavior has in common with other species, but which precisely for this reason are, as such, not specifically human. To do so would be to transfer a construct from an object in differential psychology to which it properly belongs to the object of anthropological psychology to which it does not properly apply.

Such an animal-morphism, bio-morphism, or machine-morphism would be highly metaphorical and would imply an artificial impersonification of the human. While such a metaphorical use of language is interesting from a literary point of view, it would be misleading in science where we expect objective statements of fact. The literary statement that man is *like* an animal or *like* a subtle machine or *like* a plant which responds to the stimulus of light is metaphorically true and based on resemblances which are really present and found by comparison. Certain differential psychologies make some of these resemblances the total isolated objects of their investigations. In such cases, these constructs are *literally* valid for these differential psychologies within their isolated areas of investigation. But the statements made by such differential psychologies about isolated impersonal aspects of behavior become metaphorical when applied to human existence in its personal wholeness.

The structural differentiations of behavioral existence which are studied in isolation by differential psychologies are perceived in anthropological psychology as *personal* differentiations. That is, they are necessarily permeated by the unique human characteristics which are represented in the fundamental anthropological constructs. In anthropological psychology, each differential aspect of human behavior is perceived in a person who is existing intentionally, not as an impersonal function going on in isolation. The impersonal aspects discovered by differential psychologies are not denied, to be sure, but respectfully integrated within the view of the whole person. All impersonal human states are pseudo-impersonal in the sense that we can always find some meaningful personal presence behind them which uses, abuses, submits to, is indifferent to, rebels against, neglects, affirms, denies, or represses them. In other words, these functions and features, which are available to man in his organism and environment, follow certain biochemical, neurological, and physical laws to which the intentional agent must adapt himself.

The total human self and its existential differentiations can thus be cast in anthropological and in differential constructs. The former represent the human reality as a whole in so far as this unique humanity is present in its existential differentiations. The differential constructs represent the reality of the many resemblances between the human reality and other physical and biological phenomena in the universe. The latter differential constructs can never represent that in which the human reality differs essentially from other realities. Both types of constructs are, in different ways, close to experience.

It would be unscientific, however, to attempt to describe the reality of the whole in terms which apply only to certain features of its dependent parts. A differential psychology of the nervous systems of body and brain can efficiently use terms such as "electric potentials" and "neuronal circuits," but it would be impossible to do justice to the total intentional presence of man to reality by means of such terms alone (except when used in a metaphorical sense). Therefore, two different languages are necessary in psychology: the anthropological language to describe man as an existing Gestalt or person, and the functional or process language to account for the functional resemblances between man and other objects. These resemblances reveal themselves most clearly when studied in isolation from man as a whole. Psychologists may well be bilingual, but they should be careful not to mix the two series of constructs by speaking metaphorically about man as a living person through the use of terms appropriate only to the differential study of certain aspects of behavior. Nor should the differential psychologist, on the other hand, apply anthropological terminology to the abstracted profile of behavior which he studies. If he did so, the anthropological terminology would become as metaphorical as the differential terminology when applied to man as a total living existence. To describe a neuron as a person is just as metaphorical as to describe a person as a neuron.

We have already stated that each differential psychology should consider the whole of behavior from its own perspective because the latter can probably be uncovered in all human behavior. This implies that every differential psychology can probably cast all behavior in its own functional constructs. At the same time, all other constructs which are used by comprehensive psychology or by other differential psychologies would become metaphorical if applied to the specific perspective of this differential psychology.

We have also pointed out the tendency toward imperialism inherent in every differential psychology which is due to the innate tendency of man toward universal comprehension. Thus highly successful differential psychologies sometimes tend to overlook the fact that their functional differential constructs cover all behavior under only one aspect, even when that aspect is related to infra-human appearances in nature. In such an attitude of perceptual blindness, a differential psychology may be tempted to identify itself with all psychology and claim that its differential constructs explain all behavior under all possible aspects.

Observation of human behavior as a whole and of functional aspects abstracted from behavior yields data which both the anthropological and the differential psychologist must ponder.

The differential psychologist who in principle deals with isolated processes may experiment with these in his laboratory and thus collect data about isolated functions *as such*. He should be careful, however, not to make unverified inferences regarding these functions when they participate in the living totality of an intentional person in a meaningful situation. It is the task of the comprehensive psychologist to study what changes these processes undergo once they are perceived as living differentiated parts of human existence.

The anthropological psychologist cannot collect data about persons as existing totalities in meaningful life situations by the method of laboratory experiment in the strict physical sense. Such experiment presupposes as a necessary condition the objectivating isolation of variables. The psychologist can collect data, however, by means of observation and experiments in personal relationships in which he can verify his anthropological constructs. Both the comprehensive psychologist and the differential psychologist must detach themselves temporarily from their data in order to examine them and to arrive at theoretical formulations of them. In both types of psychology, these data are gathered by observation. In anthropological psychology, the observation is a personal attention to an individual or individuals who move intentionally in their life situation. In certain differential psychologies, the observation is a non-personal attention to specific impersonal, isolated aspects of human and animal behavior in relation to "stimuli" in the environment.

In anthropological observation, the emerging theory should be stated in terminology appropriate to the personal nature of the phenomena studied. In differential psychologies, however, the theory should be stated in impersonal terms, the isolated aspect being impersonal because of its very objectivation.

In both cases, then, the collection of the data is by means of observation, and the constructing of theory is through intellectualizing by a temporarily detached observer; with this difference, that in differential functional psychology the observation is impersonal, while in anthropological psychology it is personal. Both theories are objective: one is the objective study of human behavior as an intentional meaningful whole; the other is an objective study of isolated behavioral aspects.

Functional or mathematical differential terminology throws no light on psychological phenomena *as psychological,* i.e., on the nature and motivated appearances of behavior *as human behavior.* Differential constructs illuminate, however, the many non-human aspects of behavior without which the whole of human behavior could not be understood or adequately explained. Therefore, comprehensive anthropological psychology requires the constant development of functional differential psychology, the discoveries of which it should respectfully integrate within itself. This work of differential psychologies cannot be done by physiologists, physicists, neurologists, or biologists because they are not concerned with the relevance of their constructs and findings to the understanding of the non-human aspects of behavior. Only the differential psychologist performs this task so necessary to the growth of the field of psychology as a whole.

The concern of differential psychologists with the mathematical, physiological, neurological, physical, or biological properties of behavior does not make them mathematicians, physiologists, neurologists, physicists, or biologists. Their primary interest is in behavior insofar as it appears under and is influenced by these different functional aspects. Other sciences develop constructs and methods which deal with these functional aspects. The differential psychologists borrow these constructs from other fields, just as the foundational theorist in psychology borrows some of his basic constructs from anthropological philosophy without becoming for this reason a professional philosopher.

Anthropological psychology deals with human intentional behavior that becomes differentiated and organized in dimensions, modes, and modalities as a result of the ever expanding development of man's "lived" personal relations to reality. Within the anthropological description of this differentiating human behavior, comprehensive psychology integrates the description of those physical and biological features which human behavior

229

has in common with other species and which have been studied in isolation by differential psychologies. For this scientific task, anthropological psychology cannot use metaphors. It requires terminology appropriate to its subject-matter, which is the personal, motivated, intentional behavior of human beings. Anthropological constructs should not be reified as if they were things existing in themselves. They are pointers to reality. Some of the important constructs in anthropological psychology are: existence; dimensions, modes, and modalities of bodily behavioral existence; intentional behavior; human motivation; freedom; self; self-project; meaning; sense; and sign.

Various differential psychologies, on the other hand, abstract from the personal whole those characteristics which resemble features found in non-human phenomena, and must therefore express in impersonal ways the characteristics which they isolate. Comprehensive psychology proposes to be a theory of the behavior of man in terms appropriate to his personal or existential nature. However, such a theory can never be truly comprehensive if it does not have available for integration the impersonal aspects of the personal, which are rooted in the fact that human existence is also essentially a bodily, material existence in a material world. In other words, a truly comprehensive anthropological psychology would be impossible without the constant growth of functional differential psychologies.

CHAPTER EIGHT

ANTHROPOLOGICAL PHENOMENOLOGY
AS MODE OF EXISTENCE

In our discussion of anthropological psychology, we have concluded that anthropological constructs must be rooted in the observation of behavior. The anthropological psychologist can fulfill this condition only through the phenomenological method. Since human experience is varied in kind and degree, there are many types of phenomenology, or the study of experience, to correspond with this variety. The subject of this and the two following chapters is mainly one type of phenomenology: anthropological phenomenology, by means of which the psychologist lays the foundation of his constructs about behavior.

Because phenomenology was first developed by philosophers, every type of phenomenology reveals this origin in its fundamental features. The non-philosophical phenomenologies study experience, however, with other purposes and under other aspects than philosophical phenomenologies do. Thus the distinct features of anthropological phenomenology emerge from its unique purpose, which is intentional behavior insofar as it is relevant to comprehensive scientific psychology and psychological praxis. Therefore, the anthropological phenomenologist does not explore the phenomena of behavior under all ontological and factual perspectives. He limits himself strictly to those aspects which are relevant to his goal: the integration of the scientific differential knowledge of behavior into a comprehensive psychology which is pertinent to psychological praxis. This purpose presupposes the use of two kinds of anthropological phenomenology.

First of all, an anthropological phenomenology is needed which examines the structure and meaning of human behavior as a whole. Such a phenomenology provides the psychologist with a matrix from which comprehensive constructs can be derived. Because these constructs are rooted in human behavior as a whole, they serve as a comprehensive model within which the differential psyychologies can be integrated. This anthropological phenomenology of the factual whole of behavior is called comprehensive or existential anthropological phenomenology.

Comprehensive psychology presupposes, however, not only a comprehensive but also a differential phenomenology. The latter is a phenomenological study of the profiles of behavior that have been formulated by differential psychologies. The anthropological psychologist must know the structure and meaning of these profiles of behavior. He should be able to establish the "reality-of-behavior" which is indicated in the abstract formulations of differential psychologists. Only then will he be able to integrate knowledge of partial behavior with knowledge of behavior as a whole.

The distinction between comprehensive and differential phenomenology, however, is not the only one to be made in anthropological phenomenology. We must also clarify anthropological phenomenology both as a fundamental mode of existence and as a method which emerges from this mode. The *mode of existence* is most relevant for the praxis of psychology. The *method* is of primary importance for the development of theoretical and experimental psychology. To be sure, the mode of existence and the method are interrelated. One cannot be understood without the other; one cannot develop fully without the other. For the sake of clarity, however, we propose first to circumscribe and discuss anthropological phenomenology as mode of existence. In the next chapter, we shall consider it as method. Both circumscriptions are provisional and open to modification.

Anthropological phenomenology is fundamentally a mode of existence of a psychologist who seeks a comprehensive or a differential knowledge of intentional behavior as it manifests itself, with the least possible imposition of psychological theory or method, personal and cultural prejudice or need, and language habit.

Discussion of the Terms of the Definition of Anthropological Phenomenology

The term "phenomenology" is derived from the two Greek words, *phainomenon* and *logos*. *Phainomenon*, the neuter present participle of *phainestai* (to appear), means "that which appears." *Logos* means "word," "science," or "study of words." Therefore, etymologically, phenomenology is the study of that which appears. Etymological analysis gives us some initial understanding of the meaning of phenomenology. However, the term requires further definition.

Philosophical Phenomenology and Science

Phenomenology was originally a development in philosophy. The present chapter does not deal primarily with philosophical phenomenology, for an evaluation of this subject and its prolific development into many branches falls outside the scope of a study of scientific theory in psychology. Nevertheless, it is necessary to stress from the beginning that philosophical phenomenology does not oppose science. The philosophical phenomenology of science attempts to clarify the foundations of science, its meanings, and its situation in the whole of reality. Philosophical phenomenology goes beneath science, as it were, in order to disclose its experiential roots found in the original contact between man and reality. This phenomenological quest of the philosophers of science has led us to the insight that the world of science is not the world of man's first experience. The primary world of man's original experience is not at all identical with the world of science. The latter is a secondary world, a derived construction, an abstraction. This constructed world of science is removed from the primary world of lived experience. It is, however, rooted somehow in this world of man's original experiences, for without these first experiences man could never have attained to the construction of the abstract, theoretical world of science.

Differential psychologists use mechanistic models, for example, like the stimulus-response sequence. But such a model is not experienced directly as such by man in his spontaneous life. It is a construct that is secondary, derived, abstract, fashioned by the differential psychologist himself. This useful abstraction is somehow dependent on the psychologist's experience of behavior. If he had never experienced some aspect of a situation which somehow influences behavior, as well as some aspect of behavior which is elicited by this influence, he never would have been able to devise the stimulus-response model. This dependency on experience is characteristic not only of differential-scientific but also of comprehensive-scientific models of behavior.

Philosophical phenomenology thus makes explicit the fact that science is dependent on prior experience. It denies neither the value of science nor the necessity for the constructs which science derives from experienced reality. It recognizes that the use of secondary constructs is required in science. It maintains, however, that these constructions of the scientific imagination should be rooted in the experience from which they are derived. Otherwise, science could deteriorate into a free-floating, airy enterprise, out of touch with reality.

PHILOSOPHICAL AND ANTHROPOLOGICAL PHENOMENOLOGY

The preceding discussion of the relationship between philosophical phenomenology and science helps us to clarify the relationship between philosophical and anthropological phenomenology. *Philosophical* phenomenology aids the anthropological psychologist in the discovery of the ontological foundations of both comprehensive and differential psychologies. *Anthropological* phenomenology, on the other hand, enables him to discover the ontic or factual structures of behavior. The scope of this book does not allow extensive philosophical reflection on the meaning of the terms "ontological" and "ontic." We shall indicate briefly the difference between the ontological goal of philosophical phenomenology and the ontic one of anthropological phenomenology.

The ontic analysis of anthropological phenomenology is an exploration of observable behavior in order to discover its factual structures. Such ontic clarifications are performed in order to serve the actual practice of psychology; they guide the psychologist in his conduct when he deals with behavior in clinical or private practice. Anthropological phenomenology is concerned, therefore, with only a limited set of profiles of behavior, namely those which have been or are to be investigated by differential psychologies or dealt with in psychological praxis. Even when anthropological phenomenology studies behavior as a whole, it does so on the basis of the discoveries made by differential psychologies. It seeks the underlying meaning and structure of behavior as it is revealed in this variety of profiles. It always limits itself to the study of a certain number of manifestations of behavior under the aspect of their probable mutual relationships. Consequently, anthropological phenomenology of itself can never grasp the "ontological" structure which underlies behavior as such.

This ontological structure of behavior is clearly more basic than its ontic factual structure. In fact, the ontological structure of behavior makes factual structure or actual meaning of behavior possible; it is a manifestation of Being in intentional behavior. The ultimate concern of philosophical phenomenology is thus not limited to the structure of observable behavior; it includes all manifestations of Being. Philosophical phenomenology is not concerned primarily with the actual behavior of individuals, but with the underlying ontological structure of behavior as such. It does not aim to direct people in their actual conduct, but to analyze the hidden structures and guiding concepts which are basic to all possible patterns and manifestations of any behavior whatsoever. We should add to this statement of ultimate aim the fact that some philosophical phenomenologists refer at times to ontic analysis of behavior. They do so because they realize that a grasp of the factual structure of behavior may facilitate their penetration into its ontological structure.

We may conclude that philosophical phenomenology does not restrict itself to those aspects of intentional behavior which are explored by the differential psychologists. It goes beneath this factual structure in order to find its ontological basis. We have also seen in the preceding chapter that anthropological psychology requires the explication of its own ontological assumptions and of those of the differential psychologies. This implies that the comprehensive psychologist requires the assistance of the philosophical phenomenologist who makes these assumptions explicit. The psychologist uses the conclusions derived from these assumptions if they are relevant to his ontic phenomenology of intentional behavior. The comprehensive psychologist is thus dependent on philosophical phenomenology for the explication of ontological assumptions. His main function in this realm is a selective one, namely the choice of assumptions of philosophical phenomenology in the light of their applicability to the data of the differential psychologies which he integrates. The comprehensive psychologist is thus engaged in a dialogue between the outcomes of philosophical phenomenology of behavior and those of an ontic, anthropological phenomenology of behavior.

THE AIMS OF ANTHROPOLOGICAL PHENOMENOLOGY

The distinction between philosophical and anthropological phenomenology aids in the clarification of the specific goals of anthropological phenomenology, both comprehensive and differential. One of the goals is to help the comprehensive psychologist to root his theoretical constructs in experienced behavioral phenomena. If he has obtained these constructs from philosophical phenomenology, he must still ground them explicitly in concrete behavior as revealed by differential psychologies. Ontic phenomenology also helps him to root the constructs of the differential psychologies in behavioral reality. The comprehensive psychologist must ask himself to what experiences differential psychologists really point when they use such constructs as Oedipus complex, reinforcement, feedback, repression, ego, self, and individualism.

Anthropological phenomenology thus goes beneath both the constructs of differential psychologies and the scientific and "intuitive" insights of psychoanalysts, psychotherapists, and other practising psychologists; it searches for the foundations of these constructs, statements, and intuitions in behavior itself. What the differential psychologist and the practising psychotherapist take for granted, the comprehensive psychologist studies critically. Anthropological phenomenology may therefore be called a "genuine positivism or realism," "a return to behavior itself," "a true psychoanalysis," an "authentic behaviorism." We may now return to the discussion of the terms of our original definition of anthropological phenomenology.

ANTHROPOLOGICAL PHENOMENOLOGY IS FUNDAMENTALLY
A MODE OF EXISTENCE

Is Fundamentally—This phrase in the definition denotes that anthropological phenomenology is *primarily* a specific attitude or mode of existence which the psychologist assumes toward his subject matter, "intentional behavior." "Fundamentally" indicates that the phenomenological attitude is basic while methods are secondary. The specific appproach of anthropological phenomenology is, therefore, fundamentally different from other valid and necessary approaches to behavior. Among the latter are the theoretical, experimental, clinical-intuitive, and applied approaches; these presuppose attitudes in the psychologist which are fundamentally different from those of the phenomenological position. These various positions, however, presuppose and complement the phenomenological one. The distinction which we make here between existential mode or attitude and method is important for at least three reasons.

First of all, the method of phenomenology when successfully applied to a specific phenomenon lends itself to a clear codification of the steps taken to penetrate this particular phenomenon. Now, the history of science teaches us that students may memorize and blindly apply methodical rules without developing the basic attitude from which these codes have emerged. The consequence of such a development for phenomenology might be a stultification of original standards, which would then be routinely applied even in situations where a new kind of phenomenon might require modifications in the steps to be taken. Such stultification would mark the end of phenomenology as a dynamic enterprise. The development of an authentic phenomenological attitude, however, would prevent such degeneration.

A second motive for this distinction is the fact that many practicing psychologists such as diagnosticians, psychotherapists, psychoanalysts, and industrial psychologists develop a phenomenological attitude in the encounter with their clients. They attempt to understand the intentional behavior of their patients with the least possible imposition of psychological theory or method, personal and cultural prejudice or need, and language habit. In fact, certain types of training expressly instill this attitude in practicing psychologists. If such psychologists, outside the hour of encounter, engage in a controlled phenomenological explication of the intentional behavior of their clients, they are using the method of phenomenology.

A third rationale for the above distinction is found in the contemporary development of psychology and psychiatry. The pressure of cultural evolution in the Western world is stimulating in many areas a new openness for the original data beneath complex theoretical structures and superstructures. This return to phenomena has manifested itself initially in forms of psychology and psychiatry to which a controlled phenomenological method has not yet been applied. They manifest, however, a promising phenomenological attitude from which the method may emerge. In other words, the phenomenological method may be said to be present in an implicit way in these incipient phenomenological psychologies. The distinction between attitude and method will thus facilitate the appraisal of development in contemporary psychology and psychiatry.

"Fundamentally" also connotes the position of the phenomenological attitude in the hierarchy of modes of existence. It is the most fundamental scientific mode of existence. This means neither that this mode is the most valuable one in every phase of the science of behavior, nor that it is the only useful one for the investigation of every profile of behavior. On the contrary, in certain phases of scientific study and for certain profiles of behavior, other modes such as the experimental and the statistical are necessary. When we say that the anthropological phenomenological mode is most fundamental in psychology, we mean that it deals strictly with the basis of all other scientific operations, namely with lived intentional behavior itself. From this point of view, other scientific psychological modes can be said to presuppose the phenomenological mode, for the latter concerns itself with the foundation of all succeeding statements or operations in psychology.

MODE OF EXISTENCE

Man is existence; it is characteristic of man to involve himseld in reality as it reveals itself to him. Existence differentiates itself in various modes-of-existence. This differentiation takes place in the course of man's encounters with concrete life situations. Each mode-of-existence integrates various modalities-of-existence such as perceiving, feeling, touching, and thinking. Thus every mode-of-existence is a multi-dimensional unity of various modalities of interest or contact. These modalities constitute the structural unity of a mode-of-existence. A common purpose, interest, or project organizes different modalities in such a way that they constitute one mode-of-existence.

In this way, the phenomenological mode-of-existence in psychology integrates various modalities of existence. The phenomenological psychotherapist, for instance, feels, perceives, understands, thinks, speaks, and behaves differently when he encounters a patient than does a psychologist whose primary aim is to implement a psychological theory. One common interest characterizes all the different modalities of behavior of the phenomenological therapist. They all manifest his purpose of reaching an initial phenomenological understanding of the intentional behavior of his patient. This means an understanding of the underlying structures of behavior with the least possible imposition of psychological theory, methodology, personal and cultural prejudice or need, and language habit. This common project organizes the various modalities which constitute phenomenological-therapeutic behavior. This example illustrates how a mode-of-existence initiates, to a great degree, "how" and "what" one sees, experiences, or encounters. For every mode-of-existence inserts man in the world in a certain manner which influences his dealing with the world. The phenomenological mode-of-existence determines to a large extent what the psychotherapist listens for and how he manages the therapeutic situation. Similar statements can be made about other forms of applied psychology.

When this open phenomenological mode-of-existence is developed in the *academic* psychologist, it stimulates him to develop strictly controlled methods in its service. These methods are directed toward the unprejudiced, non-subjectivistic discovery of behavioral phenomena themselves before they are subjected to experiment, measurement, and theory formation.

Of a Psychologist Who Aims

This phrase indicates that the phenomenological mode of existence is rooted in a personal mode of life, which is that of an individual psychologist. We are not speaking, therefore, about a phenomenological mode of existence which is rooted in other personal ways of life such as the philosophical, artistic, sociological, or theological. A personal mode of being, moreover, is influenced by personal and cultural history, and by individual interests and projects. This influence co-determines which aspect of intentional-functional-situational behavior the psychologist chooses for his own phenomenological approach. A phenomenological therapist, for example, may be interested only in emotionally disturbed college students or hospitalized patients. Similarly, other practicing psychologists have individual interests. Therefore, the personal mode-of-being-a-psychologist determines to a degree the psychologist's phenomenological mode of existence. On the other hand, the phenomenological mode itself impels him to be aware of the implications and the limitations imposed by his own choice. This same awareness leads him to observe the selected behavioral phenomena with the least possible imposition of theory or method, personal and cultural prejudice or need, and language habit. The involvement of the psychologist as an historically situated subject is, of course, unavoidable. What should be avoided is subjectivism or the unchecked influence of theoretical or methodological prejudice which would distort the behavioral phenomena.

AT A COMPREHENSIVE OR A DIFFERENTIAL UNDERSTANDING

The phenomenological mode of existence in the psychologist consists of two poles which interact continually. These two poles are dynamic tendencies inherent in the phenomenological quest for the structures and meanings of behavior. This quest is for the understanding of the meaning not only of different behavioral patterns but also of behavior as a whole. The psychotherapist may be interested, for example, in the structure and meaning of depressive language behavior of a patient. We call this type of phenomenological interest differential. However, he may also be interested in the patient's intentional behavior as a whole. This over-all structure colors the differentiated behavior patterns of the patient. The psychotherapist's interest in the over-all structure of behavior tends toward comprehensive phenomenology, the goal of which is the understanding of the whole of intentional behavior.

Differential phenomenology is sometimes simply called phenomenology without any limiting adjective, while comprehensive phenomenology is called existential phenomenology. Anthropological existential phenomenology is both an attitude and a controlled method. It leads to a comprehensive understanding of intentional behavior as a structured whole which is differentiated in many patterns of behavior. One should be careful, however, not to confuse this attitude and method with existentialism, which is something quite different.

Comprehensive and differential understanding of behavior influence each other. Insight into the structure and meaning of a particular behavior pattern of a patient illuminates the understanding of his intentional-behavior as a whole. Insight into the whole of his behavior, on the other hand, deepens the insight into the differentiated patterns of his behavior. Thus there exists a dialectical relationship between the comprehensive and differential components of phenomenological psychology.

OF KNOWLEDGE OF INTENTIONAL BEHAVIOR AS IT
MANIFESTS ITSELF:
"PHENOMENOLOGICAL," "OBJECTIVATING," AND "NAIVE"
KNOWLEDGE OF BEHAVIOR

The phenomenological mode of existence in psychology tends toward a knowledge of intentional behavior as it manifests itself. The phenomena of behavior as they reveal themselves may be contrasted with the data of behavior which are obtained by objectivation. Such data are not spontaneously experienced phenomena as they are uncovered in daily life. The process of objectivation and its resultant data are based on theorizing. Objectivation is a scientific reflection *about* behavioral phenomena instead of a penetration *into* the phenomena that are given. This reflection leads to a planned ordering of behavioral phenomena as objectivated things in a theoretical scheme instead of to an explication of the very structure and meaning of the phenomena themselves. The process of objectivation is not only useful but necessary for science. Science itself is fundamentally theory formation. As we have seen in previous chapters, comprehensive scientific theory in psychology is ultimately theory formation by means of comprehensive and differential constructs which presuppose objectivation of behavioral phenomena. But this objectivation should be preceded by phenomenological explication. The phenomenological approach is the disciplined removal of subjectivistic influences which may distort the phenomena. Such influences are usually present in the naïve experience of intentional behavior in every-day life. But subjectivistic, unrealistic distortions may also be present when behavioral phenomena are objectivated through uncritical theorizing about naïvely experienced behavior.

"OBJECTIVATING" KNOWLEDGE AND THE DANGER OF A SOPHISTICATED SUBJECTIVISM

A special process of knowledge of intentional behavior is thus necessary between the process of naïve knowledge and that of objectivating knowledge. This intermediary function is fulfilled by phenomenological knowledge. Phenomenological insight is the result of a purification of every-day knowledge from subjectivistic influences. The psychologist who listens to naïve descriptions of every-day behavior is clearly aware that these accounts are possibly distorted by subjectivisms.

But if the psychologist is unable to approach the real structure and meaning of behavior with a phenomenological attitude, he may be caught in a sophisticated form of subjectivism. He may unwittingly substitute an artificially devised "scientific" experience of behavior for the real experience of daily life. He may "see" repressions, reinforcements, Oedipus complexes, and sublimations everywhere. This artificial "experience" of behavior is the abortive result of two sources. One is the naïve experience of every-day behavior; the other is the arbitrary interpretation of this behavior by means of an established scientific theory. Such immediate, rash interpretations cannot result from listening respectfully to the unified inner structure and meaning of behavior itself in a specific, unique situation. What really happens is that other established subjectivistic influences are substituted for or added to the subjectivistic distortions which are already present in the naïve experience itself. This impoverished, deformed, made-over subjectivistic experience is then considered to be full, real experience, equated with experience in everyday life. This "scientific" experience is called fact, and this "fact" is regarded as a first, primary, original experience of man. Through the collection of these subjectivistic "facts," one could arrive by induction at the establishment of laws of behavior which could govern the activities of practicing psychologists and their clients. This process could lead to a dogmatic psychology, autonomous and closed within itself; an empty game with empty ideas irrelevant to real intentional behavior of people in real life situations; an unchecked, uncontrolled mythology of behavior claiming to explain everything while it explains nothing. It is obvious that much harm can be done to the development of real human behavior by a practicing psychologist when his perception is distorted by a sophisticated subjectivism.

BEHAVIOR "ITSELF" AND THE NECESSITY OF THEORIES "ABOUT" BEHAVIOR

When the psychologist develops the phenomenological attitude, however, he will first observe and study behavior as it manifests itself. Only afterward will he consider how scientific theory can illuminate this behavior without distorting it; or how theory should be corrected, expanded, or renewed in order to keep it in tune with behavior as it is given in reality. Both processes are necessary. The phenomenological knowledge of behavior is thus insufficient for a psychologist. He must also draw on the rich fund of insight called the science of psychology, which is an accumulation of the intellectual contributions of learned theorists of behavior. The psychologist can select wisely from this treasure-trove of theory. But this selective activity should be guided by real behavior as it reveals itself in his clients or experimental subjects. The phenomenological approach will enable him not only to select the adequate theoretical explanation but also to adapt it to the situation concerned, or even to improve on it on the basis of concrete observation. In the latter case, he will enrich the treasury of psychology so that others coming after him will have greater knowledge available than he himself had.

It should be the desire of the psychologist, however, that those following him will neither abuse his theory through the distortion of data nor substitute his theory for their own phenomenological perception. He should hope that they will listen more to behavior itself than to his expositions about behavior, that their ears will not be deafened by the noise of theories, and that their eyes will not be blinded by explications in manuscripts, journals, and books.

INTENTIONAL BEHAVIOR
THE MULTI-DIMENSIONAL DIRECTEDNESS OF BEHAVIOR
IN SITUATIONS

The phenomenological mode of existence leads to an openness for behavior as intentional, as directed toward reality, as present in a situation which is meaningful for the behaving subject. The subject is always related in his behaving to a meaningful situation within which his behavior evolves. This is true of every dimension of behavior. By dimension of behavior we mean the expression in behavior of such experiences as perception, imagination, feeling, reminiscing, anticipation, or categorical thought. The phenomenological approach aims at the disclosure of the meaningful structures of behavior on all these levels; it proposes to unveil the "lived" behavioral structures which constitute the relationship between the behaving subject and his situation.

In other words, phenomenology is based on the observation that man and his situation are in a dialectical unity. Intentional behavior is always being-in-a-situation. For example, when I perceive a river, play a violin, show a desire for food, or reveal that I recall a humiliating incident in my past, then the river, the violin, the food, the incident, and I are in interaction with one another. They are situated objects of my intentional behavior. Such a meaningful object does not shape me as an imprint molds wax; it does not determine my behavior in an absolute and unchangeable fashion. For both my situated object and I are active participants in a living dialogue. Intentional behavior is the dialectical unity of the person who behaves and the situated object of his behavior.

In a phenomenological explication of intentional behavior, the psychologist can concentrate his attention on one of these two main aspects of intentional behavior. He can investigate either the behaving subject in his "behavioral-tending-towards" or the correlate of this tending behavior, the situated object. For example, when I explicate my intentional behavior as a therapist, I can focus my attention on my own therapeutic behavior. In this case, I make explicit the feelings, experiences, and attitudes which manifest themselves in my behavior toward my patient. On the other hand, I can explore the situated object of my therapeutic behavior. This may be an anxious patient who responds tensely to my posture, the sound of my voice, and even my choice of words. In this case, I attempt to make explicit that which is implicit in the behavior of my client in his life situation.

The behaving subject and the situated object are both necessary constituents of the same whole which is intentional behavior. One cannot exist without the other; they mutually imply each other. Object and subject of behavior are poles of the same "field," not separate but distinct. Intellectual reflection on behavior brings this distinction to light.

OPENNESS FOR INTENTIONAL BEHAVIOR IS NOT INTROSPECTIVE

Openness for the structure and meaning of intentional behavior should not be confused with the characteristic concerns of introspective psychology. Introspective psychology in its classical appearance displayed three characteristics: first, it limited itself to reflexive conscious experiences of man; second, it preferred the phenomena of sensation, perception, and categorical thought to those of feeling and emotion; third and most important, it turned exclusively to the experiencing subject as *detached from* his bodily-behaving-in-a-meaningful-situation.

The phenomenological psychologist does exactly the opposite of the introspectionist. His phenomenological mode of existence is an openness for behavior as a unitary whole, as a "field." This field does not reveal itself initially in consciousness, but in pre-reflexive, pre-conceptual, "lived" behavioral structures. Therefore, phenomenological openness leads to an interest centered more in the behavior—including language behavior—of a person than in the mere intellectual content of his words. The structures and meanings of behavior which are implicit, pre-logical, and unpremeditated are more basic and valid for the phenomenological psychologist than later thoughts or theories *about* behavior, regardless of whether they are offered by unsophisticated people or by philosophers and scientists.

It is evident that man manifests more than conscious intentionality in his behavior. Man is present in his behavior not only as a rationalizing subject, but also as a living, feeling, suffering, loving, hoping, repressing, hating person who always behaves in a situation filled with meanings which he absorbs mainly in a pre-reflexive way.

247

THE COMPLEXITY OF THE "SITUATED" OBJECT-POLE
OF INTENTIONAL BEHAVIOR

The situation in which the object-pole of intentional behavior
is inserted is rich and complex. We share with countless other
human beings, for example, the same worlds of meaning, the
worlds of our culture and subculture. Our very behavior reveals that certain situations mean the same to all of us. We
were inserted very early in these shared worlds of culture which
color the meanings of our individual situations. At home we
learned from the behavior of our family how to eat and dress,
how to use a chair, a spoon, a dish, how to act and speak
properly. We were established by these communications in the
cultural world-of-meaning within which our family was behaving, a world of meaning which was structured without us, long
before we were born. The "lived" behavior of our family introduced us to this common cultural world, inserted us in a behavioral tradition. From that time on, we were able to behave
like other people in the same culture and to encounter our
fellow human beings in many customs and behavioral patterns
which we all experienced as the same in our world. Our initial
insertion into a world of meaning was later expanded by school,
church, and society. They all helped us to be at home in our
world, to share common meanings of particular situations.

The phenomenological mode of existence consequently implies
an openness for structures of behavior which correlate with the
historical and intersubjective cultural aspects of the meaning of
a situation. However, this is not all. Certain structures of behavior correspond with interpersonal meanings developed by
smaller social units, such as husband and wife, close-knit families,
and other intimate associations which share certain functions,
interests, or ideals.

Finally, behavior also expresses a private intentionality corresponding to purely individual meanings of the situation which
arise from one's personal history. No one can communicate easily
the meanings which he does not share with others either culturally or interpersonally. It is obviously important for the

psychotherapist to help his clients to make explicit this private intentionality.

WITH THE LEAST POSSIBLE IMPOSITION OF PSYCHOLOGICAL THEORY OR METHOD, PERSONAL AND CULTURAL PREJUDICE, AND PSYCHOLOGICAL LANGUAGE HABIT

The anthropological psychologist must penetrate into the structure and meaning of behavior itself. But theoretical views, personal bias, and psychological jargon may dim his objective vision. He must therefore avoid these influences in order to be able to observe the phenomena of behavior itself. Consequently, the phenomenological psychologist suspends temporarily all theoretical frames of reference, all statistical, experimental, and symbolical classifications. An absolute suspension of all these influences is impossible, to be sure, but he is aware of the danger of their subtle impact on his perceptions.

We shall briefly consider these distorting influences which are pointed out in our definition. In each case, we shall discuss the temporary elimination, or at least limitation, of these subjectivistic elements by means of phenomenological suspension.

PSYCHOLOGICAL THEORY OR METHOD

Psychological theory uses constructs which, while abstracted from behavior, are definitely not behavior itself. Originally and spontaneously, we do not perceive in behavior such constructs as reinforcement, repression, compulsion, conditioning, feedback, and conditioned reflexes. No psychological construct as such is part of real behavior. Yet these constructs may unwittingly influence our view of behavior. Therefore, the anthropological psychologist attempts to prevent the impact of such constructs on his primary observation. He suspends his theoretical knowledge as far as possible, or at least attempts to be aware of its intrusion. Consequently, the phenomenological psychologist develops an attitude not only of "theoretical suspension" but also of "phenomenological vigilance." He is on guard against a permeation of his perceptions by psychological theories or scientific methods.

Differential psychologists develop their methods in view of limited projects of research. They select those profiles of behavior which are related to their particular research projects. This selective manipulation is legitimate and necessary within the framework of differential research. In phenomenological psychology, however, such manipulation and the categorical view which proceeds from it would obscure the perception of behavior as it manifests itself.

PERSONAL AND CULTURAL PREJUDICE AND NEEDS

By personal and cultural prejudice in psychology, we mean the bias about behavior which is incorporated in the individual views of the psychologist and in the common opinions of his culture. A psychologist has his own implicit appraisal of psychology which may deeply influence his view of behavior. His personal philosophy of life colors and affects his psychological approach. Moreover, not only his personality and temperament but also his culture and subculture nourish and foster his selective perception. Most influential are those cultural trends in his environment and education which are in tune with his own personality structure and private history.

Concerning the needs of the psychologist, we may draw a conclusion similar to what we have said of his prejudices. Every psychologist develops in his personal interaction with his culture certain individual needs which may color his vision of behavior.

LANGUAGE HABIT

Language habit in the present context refers to the embodiment in language of psychological theories. The language concerned may be scientific or pre-scientific; likewise, psychological theories which are embedded in the language may be scientific or pre-scientific. Language is not the experience itself of behavior, but merely an expression of this experience. Words may communicate, moreover, much more than the pure experience of behavior itself. They may express, for example, the pre-scientific view of behavior assumed and fostered in a certain culture. In this case, the language habit implies not only the perception of behavior but also the pre-scientific view which guided this selective and biased perception. By the same token, the language habit conceals other aspects of behavior which fall outside the scope of the pre-scientific theory that dominates the temper of the culture.

A good example of the influence of theory on language is the term "experience." The German word for experience is "Erlebnis," the Dutch "beleving." The German "Erlebnis" is derived from "erleben," which literally means "to live an event," for "erleben" is associated with "leben" which means "to live." The Dutch "beleving" is derived from "beleven," which comes from "leven" and has the same meaning as the German word for experience, "to live." The English "experience," on the other hand, instead of indicating an awareness in the present, points to an awareness in the past. Obviously, language habit may obscure or falsify the perception of the psychologist. He may overlook or misinterpret behavior which embodies an actual "lived" presence of the subject to reality without reflection. An open perception which momentarily suspends language habit, however, may rediscover the reality of behavior which was lost in the language. Such rediscovery may impel the phenomenological psychologist to enrich the language with a new expression which clarifies the lost phenomenon. He may speak, for example, of "lived" experience, of "lived" awareness.

Language is the treasure-trove of accumulated theories, insights, and observations uncovered by a people in the course of its history; the fascinating history of a standing-out-together in certain ways toward reality. This shared involvement in reality reveals itself in ways peculiar to the cultural co-existents. The resulting insights are preserved in the constituted language of a people. This language should be a help, not a hindrance, toward further discovery of reality. Constituted language should

251

not suppress, but support living language; should not fossilize, but foster vision; should not limit, but expand perception.

Constituted *scientific* language presents its own problems. Psychoanalytic, behavioristic, or organismic language should not paralyze, but nurture the openness of observation; should not limit, but expand perception and vision. The phenomenological psychologist may profit fully from the treasure-trove of scientific language if he is able to free himself temporarily from its influence on his perception. Perception unadulterated by theoretical tenets prepares him for a new, fresh appreciation of what other theorists have observed and formulated before him. At the same time, his open perception of behavior as it is, liberates him from the limitations inherent in the position of every theorist.

The phenomenological mode of existence with its attitudes of suspension and vigilance is fundamental for the practicing psychologist who should encounter *people* beyond all theory and classification. Only after encounter may he become aware in what sense and to what degree he may characterize their behavior by constructs *about* behavior. Theoretical psychology then becomes a light that enlightens, not a veil that dims and distorts the perception of the psychologist.

CHAPTER NINE

ANTHROPOLOGICAL PHENOMENOLOGY
AS METHOD

Anthropological phenomenology comprises not only "a mode of existence" but also the method which emerges from this mode of being. Many practicing phenomenological psychologists, however, do not go beyond the phenomenological approach which influences their concrete behavior in encounter with their clients. In other words, they do not validate their phenomenological observations by means of controlling techniques. The extensive demands made on the energy and time of the general practitioner in psychology do not leave him free to carry out research projects. The phenomenological *method*, therefore, is used primarily in empirical, experimental, and theoretical psychology.

We shall first define anthropological phenomenology as method and then analyze the meanings and implications of the elements of this definition.

Anthropological phenomenology as method is a constituent of the scientific psychological mode of existence; it emerges from the phenomenological mode of existence; it is a method which translates the means and ends implicit in the phenomenological mode into well-defined procedures and objectives within concretely delineated projects of research; it develops certain checks and controls which ensure the validity and reliability of the phenomenological procedures used within such projects; its

*purpose is the controlled comprehensive or differential explica-
tion of behavior in order to prevent or correct subjectivistic
distortions in the science of psychology.*

ANTHROPOLOGICAL PHENOMENOLOGY AS METHOD IS A CONSTITUENT OF THE SCIENTIFIC PSYCHOLOGICAL MODE OF EXISTENCE

We have seen that human existence differentiates itself into
various modes-of-existence. Each one of these is a *Gestalt* or
structure whose constituents are unified by a specific interest of
man which orients a particular aspect of his life. Scientific
psychology is a mode of existence which has the specific purpose of the acquisition of scientific knowledge of behavior. The
various scientific attitudes which constitute this mode are
dependent on one another; together they lead to scientific
discovery. The main constituents are: the implicit ontological
attitude; the phenomenological attitude; and the comprehensive,
differential, observational, experimental, and applied attitudes.
Each one of these tends in its own specific way toward scientific knowledge of intentional behavior. All of them refer
ultimately to concrete phenomena of behavior. But only phenomenology is concerned with behavior in its given concreteness.
Consequently, in the hierarchy of attitudes and methods, the
phenomenological is most fundamental, for it is concerned with
that which all other constituents of the scientific mode presuppose and have as their basis. This unique position implies
that very often a phenomenological investigation should be
performed before any other scientific procedures. On the other
hand, phenomenology can never replace other scientific methods
which embody the other necessary constituents of the scientific
psychological mode-of-being, such as experimental and statistical
research.

The fact that phenomenology is a component, and not the
whole, of the scientific psychological mode of existence implies
that it is to some degree dependent on this mode. The unifying
purpose of the science of psychology, which integrates all its
subordinate structures, also regulates its fundamental pheno-

menological component. Thus the demands of psychology as a whole control the particular uses of phenomenological methodology. This is not to say that the phenomenology of a science is structured only by the requirements of the particular science to which it refers; its essential constitution remains dependent also on the mode of being from which it emerges. The phenomenological mode of being should therefore illuminate the methodological attitude. The basic structure of the phenomenological method is safeguarded, in fact, not by the science in which it is integrated but by the phenomenological mode from which it emerges. The concrete purpose which the phenomenological constituent serves within a science is dictated, nevertheless, by the particular science with which it is merged: the science thus determines the concrete direction, not the essential structure, of its phenomenological component.

One might draw an analogy from the position of an executive in a corporation. A company cannot mold the personalities of its directors; it expects their individual endeavors to be in tune, however, with the purpose that structures the association as a whole. The head of a steel company who centered his interest in non-steel products would soon be dismissed as a member of the board of directors. Within the framework of aims and objectives, however, every executive is stimulated to cooperate with the productive team in a creative fashion. Every director may initiate procedures which alter the company's structure in certain dimensions, but not in its essential aim: the efficient production of marketable steel. Moreover, the initiative of each executive must take into account the services of other constituents of the corporation, such as labor, management, and the sales department.

Similarly, the dependency of the phenomenological constituent on the scientific mode of existence in which it participates does not prevent its creative influence on science. Therefore, a human science which fosters the explicit, controlled development of its phenomenological component is different from one which leaves its phenomenological foundation to chance or to the bias of individual scientists. We call the relationship between psychological phenomenology and psychology a dialectical relationship. Dialogue implies a unity in opposition. Opposition means difference; unity indicates the constant mutual inter-action of two dissimilar elements which cooperate closely with-out losing their identity.

ANTHROPOLOGICAL PHENOMENOLOGY AS METHOD EMERGES FROM THE PHENOMENOLOGICAL MODE OF EXISTENCE

This part of our definition implies that the method pre-supposes the phenomenological mode of existence as its matrix; every adaptation, differentiation, or refinement of the method should be influenced by the phenomenological mode of being. The psychologist should not merely repeat a phenomenological procedure which proved to be adequate in a former situation. If his approach is not constantly guided by the phenomenological attitude, he may fall into the trap of blindly applying to a new phenomenon procedures which were satisfactory in a past experiment. Only an attitude of openness will preserve his alertness to the phenomenon as it actually reveals itself. This receptivity for the peculiarity of any appearance whatever implies specific adaptations to be made in method when the psychologist examines a new phenomenon in its unique struc-ture and meaning. In other words, the phenomenological mode and method should always coincide in theoretical, experimental, and empirical psychology, while the mode alone may be suffic-ient during the praxis of psychology or during the creative preparatory phase which precedes theoretical, experimental, and empirical endeavors.

ANTHROPOLOGICAL PHENOMENOLOGY IS A METHOD WHICH TRANSLATES MEANS AND ENDS INTO PROCEDURES AND OBJECTIVES

"Method" is derived from the Greek words *meta* meaning "after, toward", and *hodos* signifying "way". Consequently, the etymological meaning of method is "a way to (something)".

More specifically, method denotes a systematic procedure followed in achieving an objective. Each different objective requires its own method which develops into a set of procedures and purposes that differentiate it from other methods. The basic steps and aims of the phenomenological procedure are implicitly present in the phenomenological mode of existence from which every particular phenomenological *modus operandi* originates. The systematized method makes these implicit means and ends explicit, concrete, and practical by adapting them to a specific object of research. An example of the actual development of such a phenomenological method within a specific research project will be presented in the next chapter.

The Purpose of This Phenomenological Method Is the Controlled Comprehensive or Differential Explication of Behavior

Explication

Anthropological explication is the operation of making explicit that which is implicit in behavior as it manifests itself to the psychologist. This phenomenological operation differs from both explication and explanation as such. *Explication* means a detailed description of behavior. *Explanation* means an interpretation of behavior, usually with recourse to theories, facts, and observations other than the given behavior itself. Anthropological *explication*, on the contrary, connotes an operation of the phenomenologist by which he makes explicit what is already implicitly present in behavior itself. Such explication aims at the discovery of the fundamental psychological structure of a phenomenon of behavior; it attempts to make explicit precisely what a specific behavior is and means, and consequently what distinguishes it from every other phenomenon of behavior. An authentic anthropological explication always starts from behavior itself and not from any theory *about* behavior. Some differential psychologies, such as the Freudian, the Jungian, and the Behavioristic, departing from an *a priori* view of behavior, have formulated certain universal principles concerning behavior. But an authentic phenomenological explication does not start from these theoretical principles. Such a procedure would presuppose that the specific behavior is already included, defined, and explained in the implicit theory of behavior developed by the differential psychology. The uncritical assumption of such *a priorisms* might influence the explication of the data. One might proceed from principles held by a differential psychology and, theorizing from them, arrive at a description of behavior conforming to these principles, but not necessarily to the behavior itself. Yet it is precisely the aim of the explication to determine what the behavior itself is, in order to eliminate subjectivistic influences which may have distorted the implicit philosophies and explanations of differential psychologies. To use the principles of differential psychologies in the above-mentioned deductive way would imply that a full knowledge of the fundamental structure of the behavior is already possessed.

All of us spontaneously understand the behavior of people long before we study the implicit philosophies and explanations of differential psychologies. Perhaps it is difficult for us to verbalize this naïve perception of behavior. Moreover, our natural awareness, so long as it is not subjected to a controlled explication, is influenced by subjectivistic influences. Nevertheless, this primary perception remains our only possible starting point. Every psychologist dealing with behavior starts explicitly or implicitly from his own spontaneous awareness. Otherwise, he could not talk about behavior at all. In natural, naïve perception the psychologist is present to behavior in its confusing complexity. In spontaneous presence to behavior, every detail of the fundamental structure of this behavior is not distinguished precisely as it is. The basic structure of the perceived behavior is obscured both by accidental features arising from the specific situation and by the subjectivistic prejudice of the perceiving person due to his personality, culture, and language habits.

When man speaks about behavior, he attempts to express his spontaneous perceptions, and by this formulation behavior becomes conceptual knowledge. It is simpler to perceive than to express behavior, but the attempt to do so is a necessary preparation for scientific psychology. Only when we have expressed in clear concepts, judgments, and formulations the behavior which we have perceived, can we go further in the science of behavior. For this science requires an exact concept and accurate formulation of what behavior constitutes. The precise formulation of the behavior itself is the aim of the explication which identifies and describes the necessary and sufficient constituents of the behavior concerned. The accurate distinction of the various constitutive moments of a particular type of behavior is necessary in order to prevent confusion with other types. Moreover, psychologists need a proper terminology which will enable them to communicate with other psychological scientists concerning specific behavior. Such explication of behavior provides them with a new, more explicit way of knowing. The behavior which they make explicit is already known to them, to be sure, but only in a vague way. The knowledge contained in daily spontaneous perception is imperfect, disordered, and influenced by subjectivistic bias. Science cannot stop at such knowledge; it clarifies confused knowledge by means of controlled explication. The implicit and obscure perception of a complex phenomenon of behavior changes by this process into an explicit, formulated knowledge of its foundational structure.

The point of departure for explication is therefore the undifferentiated spontaneous perception. Without this initial perception, the explication would lose its validity; the terms produced would not refer to any perceived conduct of man. What is more, perception also constitutes the final aim of the explication. For explication leads to an objective perception in which the constituent elements of behavior itself are clearly represented.

The first endeavor of the psychologist is to change naïve perception implicitly or explicitly into a more detailed conceptual knowledge. Psychologists often differ from one another in their conclusions because they formulate their original perception without first involving themselves in a scientific explication of what they have perceived. This neglect of scientific rigor in the decisive first phase of research—the phase of explication—frequently stands in appalling contrast to subsequent scientific investigations by means of statistical, experimental, and empirical procedures. In the latter, psychologists often use faultless scientific methods which nevertheless cannot correct the inexact or erroneous notions sometimes found at the basis of their investigations. Differences in explication lead to fundamental dissensions among psychologists which cannot be bridged by subsequent scientific endeavors so long as they do not return to the first and decisive operation in their science, the explication of the behavior concerned.

From what has been said, it will be clear that the ultimate norm of any explication can only be behavior itself. Explication must be restricted to the expression of what is actually given in behavior. At this stage of scientific exploration, the psychologist cannot involve himself in any implicit differential theory such as the psychoanalytic, behavioristic, stimulus-response, Jungian, or Adlerian.

Later, when the psychologist attempts to formulate his perception of behavior for fellow scientists, he must necessarily devise a series of psychological statements. This is valid so long as he faithfully follows behavior as it manifests itself and does not go beyond perception as intersubjectively validated. Such explication will be reliable only insofar as it is really an "expression" and nothing more.

CONTROLLED EXPLICATION

The term "controlled" refers to the *validation* of the explication. This validation is of the utmost importance, for explication of behavior forms the basis for the integration of profiles of behavior by the comprehensive psychologist. If this explication is invalid, then the whole structure of comprehensive psychology supported by it will be at least temporarily distorted. Moreover, a false explication would do injustice to the differential psychology which studies the particular profile of behavior explicated by the phenomenologist. It is imperative, therefore, to ensure the validity and reliability of explications by means of adequate controls.

We may distinguish between validation in differential and validation in comprehensive phenomenological psychology.

INTRA-SUBJECTIVE VALIDATION IN DIFFERENTIAL PHENOMENOLOGICAL PSYCHOLOGY

The term *intra*, "within", denotes that the validation is performed by means of a critical comparison of the various phenomenological explications carried out by the same subject. This intra-subjective validation consists of procedures which verify the essential agreement among a sufficient number of explications of the same behavior in a variety of random situations when these explications are performed by the same phenomenologist.

Intra-subjective validation can be performed in a variety of ways. First of all, the psychologist himself can describe his spontaneous perceptions of an identical phenomenon in different situations, and then carry out a phenomenological explication of each one of these perceptions. He can subsequently compare the results of his various explications in order to determine whether they *essentially* agree or disagree with one another. In the case of an essential discrepancy among his explications of the same phenomenon, he must repeat the explications in order to discover the necessary and sufficient constituents of the phenomenon concerned.

Another method of intra-subjective validation is to obtain naïve descriptions of spontaneous perceptions of the phenomenon from samples of untrained subjects. The phenomenological explication begins with these naïve perceptions. Explications of the fundamental structures which appear in the descriptions, systematically compared with one another, may uncover the underlying constants. Untrained subjects usually produce a great number and variety of situations in which they engaged in the behavior under study. This fact facilitates scientific treatment, for it implies a natural variation of the independent variables. The variety of situations enables us to distinguish that which is constant from that which varies in the different situations. In this manner we may discover the foundational structure which appears in all behavior of the same kind. An added advantage is the fact that other scientists may control our procedure and repeat it, because the naïve descriptions of the original subjects can be made available to them. This validation is called *intra-subjective* because only the naïve descriptions—and not the subsequent phenomenological analyses—are provided by subjects other than the phenomenological scientist who performs the validation.

INTER-SUBJECTIVE VALIDATION OF THE EXPLICATION

The term *inter*, which means *between* or *among*, implies that the phenomenological explications are both performed and critically compared by different phenomenological scientists. Inter-subjective validation is the result of operations which are analogous to those performed in the intra-subjective approach; the principle difference is that they are performed by several instead of by only one phenomenologist. Like the intra-subjective, the inter-subjective validation can be achieved in various ways. A number of phenomenological scientists may independently describe their spontaneous perception of the phenomenon. After this procedure, they may make critical comparisons of their descriptions and explications.

Another possible method is to collect naïve descriptions of the phenomenon under varying conditions from random samples of unsophisticated subjects. After various phenomenologists explicate these reports independently, they may make critical comparisons.

EXPERIMENTAL VALIDATION OF THE EXPLICATION

The phenomenological explication may also be validated indirectly by means of scientific experiments. Such validation is called indirect because it does not directly verify the phenomenological description itself; rather, it tests certain hypotheses which can be deduced from the description. These hypotheses show a typical "if . . . . then" relationship: if this phenomenological description is true, then this or that must happen when this specific experimental situation is set up. Thus the results of the subsequent experiment can affirm or deny the precision of the phenomenological explication. In the case of non-affirmation, the experiment will result in a new attempt at phenomenological explication. Phenomenology maintains, for example, that man on the proper level of his existence is always in some kind of dialogue with reality. From this phenomenological statement, we may deduce the testable hypothesis that *if* we expose man experimentally to conditions of sensory deprivation, *then* he will maintain some kind of dialogue with reality by means of imagination, emotionality, or even dreamlike, illusory, or hallucinatory activities.

Ideally, the psychological phenomenologist should make use of as many validating procedures as possible so that he can provide the theoretical comprehensive psychologist with observations which have reached the highest possible degree of validity and reliability.

VALIDATION IN COMPREHENSIVE PHENOMENOLOGICAL PSYCHOLOGY

Comprehensive phenomenological psychology attempts to make implicit perception of behavior-as-a-whole explicit in order to create a comprehensive frame of reference. This structure must be capable of integrating the particular profiles of behavior which are studied in differential psychologies and which are explicated by differential phenomenological psychologists.

Comprehensive psychology, therefore, must provide the science of psychology with evidences so fundamental that they cannot be proved by more evident demonstrations. It is clear that statements which are truly self-evident cannot be proved, because every demonstration of a statement is necessarily based on other evidence. Self-evident assertions provide original and direct insight; hence their compelling impact of immediate conviction. The fact that I exist, for example, needs no demonstration; the negation of this fact would immediately lead to absurd consequences. On the other hand, the avowal that all my "higher" attitudes and activities are mere sublimations of my libido is not self-evident. I can deny this without immediately falling into absurdities. The latter claim, therefore, must be proved. The psychologist who believes it will attempt to demonstrate its validity by reducing this non-evident statement to an absolutely evident assertion.

The comprehensive psychologist must be absolutely sure that his fundamental constructs manifest this compelling character of inescapable evidence. This crucial validation is existential. Consequently, we call such existentially validated statements existential evidences. In order to understand the nature of existential validation and evidence, we must consider carefully the various types of evidence that are possible.

We shall, therefore, adapt to our specific topic of evidence in comprehensive psychology the doctrine of evidences which has been developed by the Dutch phenomenologist, Stefan Strasser. We may distinguish the types of evidence as spontaneous self-evidence, differential-scientific evidence, and comprehensive-scientific evidence. We propose that the last-named type of evidence should always be an existential evidence.

Spontaneous Self-Evidence

Certain ways of behaving appear to us in daily life as clear and obvious; their nature and meaning are so unmistakable that we feel compelled to say: "This is what it is." We do not have to reason, to explain, to theorize about it; we simply report what we spontaneously perceive. Much of the pre-scientific psychology of everyday life is based on such spontaneous evidence. In daily life it seems self-evident that a crying child is sad, pained, or angry; that the girl friend is lovely; and that the wall of the room is white. These and other naïve perceptions are the inescapable starting points not only of pre-scientific but also of scientific psychology. If psychologists themselves had not somehow perceived, for example, the behavior of crying, they could never have reflected scientifically on the conditions of this behavior. Again, psychologists would have been unable even to begin experiments on color perception if they had never experienced a naïve color perception such as that of the whiteness of the wall.

We shall see that these spontaneous self-evidences of daily life are more reliable than the differential-scientific evidences of the differential psychologies. On the other hand, spontaneous self-evidences will prove to be less reliable than existential self-evidences. For this reason, comprehensive-scientific psychology must produce only fundamental constructs which have the character of existential self-evidence.

DIFFERENTIAL-SCIENTIFIC EVIDENCE

This type of evidence plays an important role in differential psychologies and in their empirical hypotheses. For example, the hypothesis that learning is based on a process of conditioning can be verified only by differential-scientific evidence; it cannot be validated directly by either spontaneous or comprehensive-scientific evidence. The evidences of differential psychologies are only indirect evidences. They do not make behavior itself manifest; they are deduced from spontaneous evidences by means of abstract scientific methods. The latter may consist of logical, mathematical deductions or of empirical inductions, the methods of which may differ in each differential psychology. To be sure, the conclusions of differential psychology possess their own type of evidence. Yet such scientific-differential evidences are always less reliable than naïve self-evidences.

Let us illustrate this statement with an example. When we observe the behavior of a perceiving person who looks at a white wall and reports to us what he spontaneously perceives, we may make two different statements concerning his behavior. We may simply say: "He perceives that the wall is white." As physiological psychologists, however, we may state that his behavior manifests that his sensory and nervous system is affected by light of a certain wave length which is reflected by the wall. Differential-scientific psychologists will be inclined to consider this latter statement as more scientific than the former. To the comprehensive theoretical psychologist, however, the first spontaneous report is more basic and reliable. The comparative historical study of scientific theories has made the theorist aware of the possibility that one day a second Einstein may prove the one-sidedness or incompleteness of present theory concerning the wave lengths of light. But the spontaneous report of the perceiving subject will not change fundamentally regardless of the continual change in theories.

The history of differential psychology teaches us that all differential-empirical theories are only provisional. And the comprehensive theorist also knows that, no matter what differential psychologists in the coming centuries may assert concerning color perception, they will always be obliged to start from the fact that the behavior of human subjects manifests that they spontaneously perceive color. In other words, every psychologist must start from such spontaneous pre-scientific self-evidence. The contrary is unthinkable. Moreover, differential scientists always presuppose pre-scientific knowledge when they conduct experiments in their laboratories. Therefore, pre-scientific self-evidences appear to be more basic, necessary, and reliable than indirect differential-scientific evidences.

COMPREHENSIVE-SCIENTIFIC EXISTENTIAL EVIDENCE

The comprehensive psychologist, while aware that the spontaneous self-evidences of daily life are more fundamental and reliable than the evidences of differential psychologies, also knows that these naïve self-evidences may be erroneous. Therefore, he cannot use them as fundamental constructs in his comprehensive frame of reference. He knows experimentally that man's perceptions and judgments and therefore his self-evidences in daily life may be influenced by such factors as optical illusion, emotion, mood, prejudice, temperament, or past experience. It is impossible, therefore, to develop a trustworthy comprehensive-scientific theory based on spontaneous self-evidences alone. This is not to deny that it is of crucial importance for a practicing psychologist, such as the psychotherapist, to develop an understanding of the spontaneous psychology of his client, which may be based on mistaken evidence which is "self-evident" only to this patient. Such a private response, while valuable in explaining the distorted universe of meaning of an individual, obviously cannot be used as a foundation for a comprehensive psychology which aims to be true for all human beings. It may be used by the comprehensive psychologist as one descriptive example of the general possibility that human behavior may develop in such or such a direction when influenced by a specific type of mistaken self-evidence. But comprehensive psychology is not merely the expression of universal possibilities of individual human development in either healthy or unhealthy directions. It is the conquest of a universal frame of reference which applies to all human behavior, and which forms the descriptive and explanatory ground for those very qualities present in every human being which make possible the development of individual deviations. An animal could never develop typically human perversions.

The comprehensive psychologist, therefore, requires a method in order to validate pre-scientific self-evidences in such a way that he may reduce them to foundational, comprehensive-scientific ones. We call these existential self-evidences. As formulated by the phenomenologist Strasser, they have the distinguishing mark that whoever would attempt to deny them would be compelled to reaffirm them, at least implicitly, in his very denial. We call these self-evidences *existential* because our very existence affirms them. Our very behavior demonstrates inescapably what we may attempt to deny intellectually. For this reason we may also call these evidences behavioral self-evidences. Even our language behavior negates the intellectual denial which may form the content of our spoken language. Let us illustrate with a few examples.

The fact that man can reflect is an existential or behavioral self-evidence. If someone were to tell us that man cannot reflect, he would contradict by his very statement the intellectual content of this communication. The very fact that he makes the statement necessarily implies that he reflects; otherwise, he could say nothing about man's ability to reflect or not to reflect. The actuality of his attempt to communicate his idea to us implies, moreover, that he believes in the possibility of our reflecting on his statement so that we may agree or disagree with him. Moreover, his concomitant behavior—his posture, his thoughtful utterance, his divorcing himself temporarily from involvement in a world of pragmatic tasks—demonstrates that he reflects. To be sure, man's ability to reflect can never be proved as such. It can only be perceived in his behavior, which communicates it in such an unmistakable way that its denial would necessarily lead to absurd consequences.

Let us take another example. The fact that we are beings who enjoy some form and some degree of freedom is an existential or behavioral self-evidence. A differential psychologist may concentrate in his particular type of research on the non-free or determined aspects of behavior. He quite rightly abstracts from the aspect of freedom as long as he stays within the limits of his differential research. He may be tempted, however, to generalize from this necessary condition for his particular type of research to all types. He may even go further and say that all human behavior, observed under all possible perspectives, reveals no evidence of freedom. He may attempt to convince us that we are never free but, on the contrary, are entirely determined by physical, physiological, and social conditions. If he does this, he denies an existential self-evidence. For the very fact that he attempts to persuade us implies a fundamental evidence. Obviously, when he speaks with us he takes into account the two possibilities that we will or will not agree with him. Otherwise he would not even try to win us over to his viewpoint. It is not a mere accident that such a differential psychologist enters into discussion with other psychologists and not with vegetables, rats, or monkeys. Only men can be converted; the differential psychologist himself is aware of this fact and *behaves* in accordance with it. This is a *behavioral* or existential way of saying that only men are free beings. This truth is thus implicitly affirmed by his behavioral attempt to deny it. Thus existential or behavioral self-evidence emerges whenever a differential psychologist attempts to deny it.

This implicit recognition of an evidence which one attempts to deny is the distinguishing mark of only existential evidences, and not of other types of evidences. For example, we can deny the fact that we perceive the wall as white without contradicting ourselves in any way. Existential evidences are more fundamental, however, than spontaneous self-evidences, for they are intimately connected with our very existence or behavior. They are characteristic features of our being. When we deny them, we contradict ourselves, not in a formal way as in logic or mathematics, but in a behavioral way. We never pretend intellectually that A is not A. But we may contradict ourselves by what we do, say, and think. Our very way of existing and behaving may reveal an implicit repudiation of our intellectual doubt. Therefore, existential or behavioral self-evidences can be critically examined and validated. They are valid for the comprehensive foundational psychologist when they are in accord with the characteristic marks of our observable behavior. If they do not conform with our characteristic modes of behavior, they are not really existential or behavioral.

It is clear that a comprehensive scientific psychology should be based essentially on existential self-evidences. Thus it will assume the character of a comprehensive phenomenological psychology. We may conclude that the method of building a comprehensive frame of reference which can integrate all the contributions of psychology consists in choosing naïve spontaneous self-evidences as a starting-point, in validating them, and in advancing from them to behavioral self-evidences.

THE DIFFERENT BUT MUTUALLY COMPLEMENTARY FUNCTIONS OF COMPREHENSIVE AND DIFFERENTIAL EXPLICATIONS OF BEHAVIOR

Phenomenological explication aims at disclosing structures of behavior; it reveals the "lived" structures which constitute the relationship between behaving man and the world. When explication attempts to discover the most basic, holistic structures of human behavior, we call it a comprehensive, foundational, or radical explication; for it aims at revealing those structures which comprehend in the root (*radix*) all differentiated structures peculiar to human behavior in specified situations.

We may attempt, however, to explicate a specific type of behavior not in its foundational character but merely in its "specificity" or particularity. In this case, we engage not in a comprehensive but in a differential explication. However, such situated structures of behavior, even when considered merely in their particularity, maintain their underlying universal structures. The fundamental structures of behavior appear in particular manifestations even when we abstract our attention from them temporarily in order to focus on the situational character of the behavior. We must even say that these fundamental structures of human behavior constitute the precise condition for the possibility of any personalized or situated structure of behavior whatsoever. For example, the homosexual structure of human behavior implies the fundamental sexual structure; the structure of neurotic guilt implies the universal possibility of guilt; neurotic anxiety points to the structure of human anxiety; reinforcement by rewards in specific laboratory situations reveals the general receptivity for reinforcing experiences. On the other hand, we can never observe universal structures of human behavior as such; they always appear as particularized in concrete life situations. For example, we can never observe in its pure form the basic sexuality of man; we are always faced with actual forms of sexual behavior in man's typical cultural, social, and personal situations.

Consequently, two types of controlled explication are required in psychology. One is the differential explication of situated structures of behavior insofar as they are situated. The other is the comprehensive explication of those universal structures which are implicitly present in every particular structure of behavior. Both explications start from the same data: behavior as given in concrete situations. Only the focus is different.

The differential explication is by its very nature linked to differential psychologies since they deal operationally with "situated" and "differentiated" structures of behavior. The comprehensive explication is related to comprehensive psychology since it seeks to discover those fundamental structures of behavior which comprehend all sub-structures or cultural and personal particularizations of universal structures.

DIFFERENTIAL EXPLICATION OF BEHAVIOR

The situated structures of behavior are studied empirically and experimentally by differential psychologists. One may ask, is it necessary to add to empirical research the difficult task of a controlled differential explication of the behavior under study?

The differential scientist is necessarily guided by a differential theory. In fact, operational theory is the essence of a differential science and sets it apart, on the one hand, from mere description and, on the other, from comprehensive scientific theory. However, theory is not an aim in itself; it is merely a tool—indispensable but nevertheless a tool—which helps us to understand the phenomena of behavior. Theory should be guided by phenomena, not vice versa. The phenomena themselves should be our ultimate criteria, not the implicit philosophies and abstract constructs of individual psychologists. Consequently, it is necessary that we constantly rediscover phenomena in their pure appearances, unadulterated by any theory.

Every scientific judgment of a differential psychologist ultimately refers to a phenomenon of behavior to which he is immediately present; his judgment is an abstract "mediation" of something immediate, namely the direct perception of the phenomenon. His immediate presence to an appearance of behavior may be termed his "lived" perception. Behavior as directly perceived is not the behavior the psychologist theorizes about, for his judgments *about* behavior always necessarily presuppose his perception of the behavior itself.

Perceived behavior is thus the starting point, the presupposition, the occasion of all psychological reflection and

271

experimentation *on* behavior. For example, when a psychologist declares that a person in a certain phase of psychotherapy becomes dependent on the psychotherapist, his judgment presupposes, first of all, a perception of a structure of behavior that may be labeled "dependent"; second, the perception of a situation which may be termed therapeutic; finally, the perception of a structure of behavior that may be called therapeutic. If it were not for these perceptions, the psychologist would be unable to make his judgment concerning dependency.

The scientific views of differential psychologists about perceived behavior are always expressed in theoretical judgments. Such judgments, which are necessarily removed from perception, may contain more than what was given in the direct perception of the psychologist; they usually imply certain theoretical conceptions which may or may not be in accord with reality-perception itself. The danger of contamination of perception by prejudice necessitates the explication of the phenomena to which the constructs refer. The differential-phenomenological psychologist, therefore, will ask such questions as: In the statement of the psychologist, what is reality perception and what is merely hypothetical explanation? How far do theoretical models unconsciously influence this judgment? Is there some impact of wishful thinking, imagination, or unchecked theoretical prejudice? Has an implicit philosophical position colored the statement of fact?

Any judgment of behavior by a differential psychologist, no matter how abstract and theoretical, is ultimately a distillate from a more primary "lived" perception of the behavior. Every differential psychology is a constellation of objectivations and judgments concerning a particular aspect of behavior. This "ideal" world of judgments necessarily rests on the foundation of certain perceptions. For example, a differential psychologist may posit that learning behavior is a function of reinforcement, and he may verify this statement by experimentation. Yet his psychology of learning necessarily presupposes a perception of what he is experimenting *on* and theorizing *about*, namely a phenomenon of behavior called "learning." Without this perception, he cannot even begin to experiment. Moreover, the differential psychologist who is a learning theorist perceives learning behavior from *one* psychological viewpoint, that of the theory of conditioning. Physiological or cultural-social psychologists may take other viewpoints when observing this same type of behavior, for their psychologies are based on different positions. Other features of the behavior called learning may thus reveal themselves in the light of other perspectives which are just as real as that of conditioning. The point to note here is that none of these differential psychologists directly perceives "conditioning by reinforcement" or "neuro-physiological concomitants of the learning process" or "cultural-motivational aspects of learning behavior"; each perceives only the learning behavior of every-day life and a certain aspect of this behavior which may be labeled with one of these scientific constructs.

One might argue that the differential psychologist uses a pure theoretical knowledge which is not based on any perception when he deals with behavior statistically. However, statistics are meaningless if they do not point to something perceived which they symbolize. We must even say that statistical operations in themselves are somehow rooted in perception. For example, mathematical calculations would be meaningless to us if they did not appeal implicitly to our lived perception of reality. A percentage, for example. would mean little if we had not at some time perceived a certain quantity of concrete objects in daily life and a certain number subtracted from it and viewed in comparison to it. For this reason, the teaching of elementary mathematics to school children or primitive tribes begins with the addition and subtraction of concrete objects such as marbles or apples.

Thus, no judgment of a differential psychologist represents his "first" knowledge; it always presupposes his perception in immediate encounter with behavior. Therefore the integrational theorist must always be alert for possible non-perceptual elements in a differential judgment which might obscure or even falsify the perception of the behavior itself.

This phenomenological purification of differential judgments should be performed by specialized differential phenomenologists of each field of psychology, and not by the comprehensive phenomenologist, who performs a different function in psychology. His work is the integration of differential judgments about behavior. His final aim is to insert the differential profiles presented by phenomenologists in each field of psychology into a universal structure of systematically organized profiles of human behavior. Such profiles reveal implicitly the fundamental structures of intentional-functional behavior as a whole; in other words, they make it possible for the comprehensive psychologist to examine the elucidated phenomena further and to uncover even more fundamental structures which root these phenomena in human behavior as such.

We may conclude that differential phenomenology searches for the structure of the empirical phenomena of behavior which are discovered and named by differential psychologies. Among these are the structures of phenomena such as the Oedipal constellation, reinforcement, repression, fixation, rote-learning, the process of problem-solution, color perception, neurotic guilt, and paranoid behavior. Differential psychologists study these phenomena in so far as they appear in observable behavior under certain empirical or experimental conditions. To date, there is a deplorable scarcity of differential phenomenologists in the various fields of psychology. There is need for behaviorist, psychoanalytic, learning, perceptual, social, and psycho-physiological phenomenologists who are specialists in their fields. Because of this lack, the anthropological psychologist himself must frequently perform a phenomenological elucidation which could be done more effectively by specialized differential phenomenologists.

A concrete example of a differential phenomenological elucidation is more clarifying than an abstract discussion. Therefore, we shall present in the following chapter an outline of a specific study which illustrates a differential phenomenological procedure.

Anthropological Phenomenology as Method

THE RELATIONSHIP BETWEEN COMPREHENSIVE PHENOMENOLOGY AND COMPREHENSIVE THEORY IN PSYCHOLOGY

The phenomenological elucidation of differential psychologies leads to the discovery of phenomena which await re-integration by the comprehensive phenomenologist into the holistic structure of man's behavior. This reconstruction will never be accomplished completely, for we shall never have at our disposal an exhaustive elucidation of all possible phenomena or perspectives of human behavior. At this point, comprehensive scientific *theory* emerges to complete the work of phenomenology. It provides the constructs that point most effectively to the holistic structure of behavior uncovered by comprehensive phenomenology. Comprehensive theory also creates the explanatory links that bind together within an understandable synthesis the phenomena discovered to date in the history of psychology. If we were to create an imaginary scale for the development of psychology from the lowest to the highest degree of integration, we might devise the following sequence: spontaneous perceptions; scientific-differential theory and data-gathering in an increasing number of differential psychologies; differential-phenomenological elucidation of the data and judgments found in different psychologies; comprehensive-phenomenological elucidation of the differentially elucidated phenomena of the differential psychologies; integration of the comprehensively elucidated phenomena into the holistic structure of human behavior already developed by comprehensive phenomenology; and finally, comprehensive theory construction on the basis of the available holistic phenomenological structure of human behavior.

The comprehensive theorist, in his attempt to provide explanatory links for human behavior-as-a-whole, will be enlightened by similar theoretical attempts in differential theories. The main difference between the two is that differential theorists attempt to explain the whole of human behavior only *insofar as* it appears in the light of their *differential* perspective. Psychoanalysts, for example, may create a differential-comprehensive theory of human behavior insofar as it appears in the perspective of

275

dynamic motivation; learning theorists, insofar as it reveals itself under the aspect of conditioning; certain cultural-social psychologists, insofar as it is uncovered in the light of acculturation. The comprehensive theorist, however, has the task of integrating all these perspectives in an over-all explanatory construct. This synthesizing structure should not destroy valid explanations of behavior under its various differential aspects as given by differential theorists; at the same time, it should point most effectively to the elucidation of differential data by the comprehensive phenomenologist. In other words, the holistic phenomenological structure of behavior is the criterion of the comprehensive theorist in his use and evaluation of differential theories.

As we have already seen, however, even the comprehensive theorist keeps his constructs hypothetical, for he realizes that the holistic structure of behavior uncovered by the comprehensive phenomenologist may be influenced by the culture in which both the comprehensive and the differential phenomenologist are living. Therefore he continually searches in the history of both explicit and implicit psychologies of his own and of other cultures for possible evidence that his constructs are still too narrow, influenced as they may be by his own cultural frame of reference.

Comprehensive Phenomenology and Three Types of Differential Psychologies

Comprehensive phenomenology as foundational must elucidate the differential phenomena of the various fields of psychology. This elucidation clarifies the basic structure of the differential phenomenon. It manifests how and where this particular human phenomenon is rooted by its very nature in the fundamental holistic structure of human behavior as such. Comprehensive phenomenology does not elucidate the concrete situational components of the differential phenomenon, such as its cultural and individual constituents; this task has already been performed by the differential phenomenologist. Foundational phenomenology, on the contrary, places these components temporarily in the background in order to concentrate on the basic structure of behavior which transcends its situational appearances.

This foundational phenomenological elucidation is concerned with three types of differential psychology, namely differential-personal, differential-functional, and mixed personal-functional.

DIFFERENTIAL-PERSONAL PSYCHOLOGIES

Differential-personal psychologies are concerned with human behavior under one particular aspect, for example, the motivational or the perceptual profile of human behavior. Moreover, they usually limit themselves to the appearance of that behavior under certain cultural or experimental conditions. The psychology of emotionality, for instance, limits itself to the emotional aspect of human behavior; it may point to other aspects—for every perspective refers implicitly to all other perspectives—but it does not elaborate them. Nor does it attempt to point out how and where this emotionality is rooted in the holistic structure of human behavior in comparison with all other phenomena studied by all other differential psychologies. Furthermore, the psychology of emotionality usually studies emotions as they are revealed within a particular culture. The differential phenomenologist in the field of emotional psychology elucidates the concrete data of emotional behavior presented by differential psychologists, but he does not clarify the phenomenon in its fundamental rootedness in the structure of human behavior as such.

An illustration of a differential elucidation of an emotional phenomenon will be presented in the next chapter, in which we shall take as our example the experience of feeling understood by someone. The foundational phenomenologist accepts the phenomena presented by the differential field of study. The fact that, in the case cited, they are already *human* phenomena (already elucidated by the differential phenomenologist) enables the comprehensive phenomenologist to clarify their most fundamental structure, and subsequently to integrate them directly into a comprehensive phenomenology of human behavior.

Existential Foundations of Psychology

DIFFERENTIAL-FUNCTIONAL PSYCHOLOGIES

The same cannot be said of differential-functional psychologies which study isolated functions of behavior under the perspective of their similarity to measurable aspects of infra-human processes. The de-humanized function studied in artificial isolation has first to be re-humanized before it can be reintegrated in human behavior as a whole. This re-humanization implies that the psychologist must first of all investigate how this phenomenon changes when perceived as an integral part of an aspect of human behavior within a meaningful human life situation. For example, the differential phenomenologist of the psychology of conditioned learning must analyze how the laws of conditioning—discovered in animals—change in characteristically human social-cultural situations. Only when this is done will the comprehensive phenomenologist be able to seek for the most fundamental structure and meaning of the phenomenon of human learning presented to him by the differential phenomenologist. His foundation elucidation of this particular phenomenon will help him to articulate the full phenomenon of human behavior.

MIXED PERSONAL-FUNTIONAL PSYCHOLOGIES

Some differential psychologies show a mixed personal-functional character. Freud's psychoanalytic psychology may serve as an example. Part of his differential theory takes the form of mechanistic descriptions of de-humanized isolated functions, while another part presents human behavior as an existential and intentional whole in living human relationships in meaningful situations; it is a mixture of process-theory and existential theory. Psychoanalytic psychology as a process-theory makes behavior an abstraction or a bundle of abstractions not directly related to the human person in his very humanity. Psychoanalysis as an existential theory studies behavior as rooted in living human existence; it is concerned with existential experience and motivation as they appear in behavior. This typical blend of functional and personal terminology in psychoanalytic theory is due to the struggle of its founder, Sigmund Freud, to make the transition

278

from the natural science of neurophysiology to a human existential approach to the behavior of man. In his writing on the "Project", he uses the language of physics and cerebral physiology, while in his ego-psychology he uses human existential formulations. He does the latter reluctantly, forced by his spontaneous perceptions of the human predicament. In fact, he never quite decided to move in one direction or the other. The comprehensive psychologist who desires to integrate the contributions of this particular differential psychology into a comprehensive anthropological psychology is thus faced with a double task. The aspects of man's behavior which have been functionalized and dehumanized by psychoanalytic theory must first be rehumanized by differential phenomenology. Psychoanalytic theory which stresses the human quality of behavior, on the other hand, can be integrated in the same manner as the contributions of other personalized differential psychologies.

COMPREHENSIVE PHENOMENOLOGY AS FOUNDATIONAL AND AS INTEGRATIONAL

In a former chapter on the theoretical mode of existence, we distinguished between comprehensive theory as foundational and as integrational. Similar distinctions can be made concerning comprehensive phenomenology. In the preceding section we considered comprehensive phenomenology mainly in its integrational aspect, or the manner in which it deals with the phenomena presented by the differential phenomenologists. We stressed two features: first, comprehensive phenomenology has already uncovered a fundamental holistic structure of human behavior which remains open, however, to change and differentiation; second, comprehensive phenomenology elucidates differential phenomena to such a depth that it reveals how and where they insert themselves into the holistic structure of man's behavior. This continuous insertion of differential phenomena increasingly differentiates the foundational structure.

Comprehensive phenomenology *as integration* is thus the continual differentiation of the holistic structure of behavior by means of a foundational elucidation of differential phenomena.

Comprehensive phenomenology *as foundational* is the continual uncovering of the fundamental holistic features themselves. The comprehensive phenomenologist reveals this holistic structure through elucidation not only of differential psychologies, but also of phenomena not yet offered by differential psychologies but found, for example, in philosophical anthropology, in art, in literature, in the daily life of people, or even in his own experience.

In other words, while foundational and integrational endeavors are aspects of the same comprehensive phenomenological activity which mutually penetrate and sustain each other, they are not fully identical and therefore they can be distinguished intellectually.

With this conclusion in mind, we may now describe somewhat more concretely the nature of phenomenological explication in psychology. Comprehensive phenomenological explication aims at the disclosure of the "lived" structure of behavior as a whole, which constitutes the relationship between behaving man and the world. It is a fundamental method of research which leads to the discovery of that foundational structure of observable behavior which constitutes the possibility of any human behavior whatsoever. It concentrates by its very nature on behavior as a dynamic, unified interrelation with the world whose primary characteristic is intentionality. This differentiated "lived" structure of behavior is originally pre-conceptual and pre-reflexive, and it is the basis of all possible patterns of behavior. If it were not pre-reflexive, we would not need a comprehensive phenomenology to bare its structure by reflective knowledge. The pre-reflectively perceived world is the always present correlate of intentional behavior. Therefore, all phenomenology, both comprehensive and differential, implies the explication of the situation-pole, object-pole, or world-pole of behavior. Differential phenomenology explicates the particular situation, the specific world which is the counterpart of a specific pattern of behavior. Comprehensive phenomenology, on the other hand, clarifies the foundational structure of the world-pole, which is the correlate of the foundational structure of human behavior as such.

Briefly, comprehensive phenomenology in psychology is the uncovering of the primary structure of human behavior and its correlative, the primary world. Comprehensive phenomenology as *foundational* studies differential phenomena insofar as they implicitly reveal the fundamental structures of intentional-functional-situational behavior as a whole. Comprehensive phenomenology as *integrational* inserts differential phenomena into the holistic structure of human behavior. The final outcome of comprehensive phenomenology as both foundational *and* integrational is a differentiated holistic structure of human behavior. Because this outcome is never completely achieved, comprehensive theory is required to complete this unfinished structure by means of hypothetical links and explanatory constructs. The latter are developed in cooperation with the differential theories, but always in tune with the phenomenological holistic structure, which is perceived and not "thought out" as a theoretical structure is.

Comprehensive phenomenology is therefore the touchstone, the criterion for the development of comprehensive scientific theory. The dialogue between comprehensive theory and comprehensive phenomenology in psychology leads to the fusion of thought and perception, theory and reality, construct and concept. This fusion may lead to confusion if we are not aware that the fused elements retain their own origin and identity and should be so distinguished. As a result of this osmosis, foundational constructs in comprehensive theory point to the phenomenological structure of the pre-predicative, pre-conceptual, prelogical, psychological, behavioral relationship between man and world. They thus point to the necessary condition for all the phenomena of behavior discovered and investigated in the differential psychologies. For the pre-reflexive, pre-conceptual, prelogical structures of behavior are at the origin of human behavior, prior to any theory, construct, or experiment *about* behavior. Comprehensive phenomenology expresses human behavior as it is perceived at the present historical moment of our perceptual knowledge of behavior. Comprehensive theory completes by means of hypothetical constructs that which is not yet perceived or may never be perceived. Comprehensive phenomenology as foundational limits itself to the revelation of those structures of observable behavior which are universally necessary. Thus comprehensive theory is able to devise foundational constructs which are sufficiently comprehensive to integrate the findings of all differential psychologies.

Comprehensive psychology—both phenomenological and theoretical, foundational and integrational—is concerned with the fullness of human behavior in its total, concrete, "lived" density as it is found in real life situations. The latter are encountered in the clinic, hospital, therapy room, playground, theater, church, home, laboratory, bedroom, army barracks, school, or industrial plant. Each one of these sectors of behavior represents a different world of meaning and its correlate, a different style and structure of behavior. The ultimate aim of comprehensive scientific psychology is therefore not the foundations of human behavior, but the *practical* understanding of full human behavior in its "lived" density within concrete life situations. Practical understanding is that type of concrete insight which can lead to methodical psychological procedures conducive to concrete, observable changes in the behavior of individuals and groups. Comprehensive phenomenology alone would be insufficient for the formation of a comprehensive scientific psychology relevant to the methodical change of behavior. Only the union of comprehensive phenomenology and theory on the basis of differential phenomenology and theory, can lead to a comprehensive scientific psychology relevant to change in man's behavior.

The very nature of comprehensive scientific psychology suggests three cardinal rules for research. First of all, no new hypothetical link or explanatory construct should be devised unless phenomenological research proves to be as yet incapable of uncovering in behavior itself the integrating link which is not yet perceptible. Second, established hypothetical links and explanatory constructs should be altered when phenomenological research leads to a change or expansion of the perceptible phenomenological structure which negates these theoretical constructs. Finally, the theoretical expression of the perceived phenomenological structure should be considered as subject to change, for this theoretical "shorthand" may be an imperfect or even distorted representation of the structure.

The preceding considerations on phenomenology may lead us to a deeper understanding of the terms of the expression, "existential comprehensive scientific theory". It is called existential precisely because it attempts to keep foundational theory in tune with the results of foundational and differential phenomenology. It is called comprehensive because it attempts to integrate the contributions of differential psychologies within an increasingly differentiated holistic structure of behavior. It is called scientific because its results are checked by the differential psychologies through deduction of testable hypotheses; because its holistic-differential search is guided by the findings of differential scientific psychologies and by the needs of applied scientific psychology; and because its main integrational structure is checked directly (as far as this is possible) by means of deduction of those testable hypotheses not yet proved by differential psychologies. Existential comprehensive scientific theory, finally, is called theory insofar as its final over-all structure always has a theoretical character because, on the one hand, the outcome of phenomenological research will always be limited and requires the completion of theoretical explanatory links and, on the other hand, it requires a translation into theoretical constructs which are apt to interact with other constructs.

THE MUTUAL INTERACTION BETWEEN COMPREHENSIVE AND DIFFERENTIAL PHENOMENOLOGY

Differential phenomenology does not carry on its many-faceted function in complete isolation from comprehensive phenomenology. On the contrary, the differential and the comprehensive poles of psychological phenomenology complement each other in constant mutual interaction. Findings of differential phenomenology illuminate the foundations of anthropological psychology which the comprehensive phenomenologist continually attempts to elucidate. When, for example, various differential psychologists explicate different phenomena of "situated" behavior, they provide the comprehensive phenomenologist with a variety of explicated situations within which this behavior appears. Thus he is enabled to distinguish what is universal and necessary in this intentional behavior from what is due to incidental circumstances.

On the other hand, comprehensive phenomenology—in disclosing and thematizing universal structures which are at the root of human behavior—provides the differential phenomenologist with clues to the particularized presence of these structures in the situated phenomena of behavior which he explores. His perception of the universal structure facilitates that of the situated behavioral structure. Comprehensive and differential phenomenology in psychology thus maintain a dialectical relationship, stimulating each other's development. It is this dialogue which will establish the sphere for a truly existential behaviorism which will gradually integrate the divergent streams of thought in the divided world of psychology.

Without comprehensive phenomenology, psychology can never achieve synthesis and comprehensive understanding. On the other hand, comprehensive phenomenology and theory would be irrelevant and incomplete if they did not illuminate and were not illuminated by the concrete cultural, subcultural, and individual particularizations of the universal structures which they describe. This dialogue, furthermore, makes comprehensive psychology relevant for the concrete situations with which the psychologist has to cope in every-day existence.

The comprehensive scientific theorist develops a frame of constructs in accord with the structure presented by the comprehensive phenomenologist. This skeleton of constructs requires the meat of concrete data. Such data are provided by the differential psychologist and clarified in their relationship to human behavior as a whole by the differential phenomenologist. As a matter of fact, the comprehensive phenomenologist and theorist will usually illustrate the relevance of the explication of the whole structure of behavior by means of the phenomenologically elucidated data of the differential psychologies. Otherwise, their work would provide merely an abstract outline which would lose contact with the concrete ground of the differential psychologies. Hence, psychological phenomenology is a dynamic field that consists of two interdependent poles, the comprehensive and the differential.

Anthropological psychology as a differentiated whole is thus far more than an explication of the fundamental structures of behavior. We may even say that the foundational constructs would remain useless, psychologically speaking, if they could not be applied increasingly to the data of the differential psychologies. It is true that some empirical data provided by differential psychologies may prove to be incomplete or even false. This is one reason why comprehensive psychology always remains an open system, constantly in flux according to the progress of the differential psychologies. This situation implies the necessity of an unceasing dialogue, on the one hand, between comprehensive and differential phenomenology and, on the other hand, between differential phenomenology and the data of the differential psychology in which it specializes.

Such a dialogue keeps the foundational phenomenologist in constant touch with concrete profiles of situated behavior as explored by differential psychologists; it ensures the continual test of empirical applicability of his foundational constructs.

THE METHOD OF FOUNDATIONAL EXPLICATION

Having discussed the place and function of foundational and differential phenomenology in anthropological psychology, we may now consider the main characteristics of methodological explication as carried out respectively by foundational and differential phenomenology.

The two main phases of a phenomenological explication in psychology are that of temporary elimination of aspects of behavior and that of integration of all perspectives available after this elimination. Both procedures are necessary in foundational as

285

well as in differential phenomenology. These two phenomenologies differ in regard to both the aspects which they temporarily eliminate from consideration and the number and type of perspectives which they must integrate. While foundational phenomenology eliminates all those particular aspects which are due to the situation in which a phenomenon appears, differential phenomenology implies at least certain selected aspects due to the cultural or developmental situation in which the phenomenon manifests itself.

We shall first consider the methodological explication which is characteristic of the foundational pole of comprehensive phenomenology. Afterwards we shall discuss the method typical of the differential pole.

THE TEMPORARY ELIMINATION FROM CONSIDERATION OF ALL INDIVIDUAL AND PARTICULAR ASPECTS OF BEHAVIOR

A foundational explication of behavior deals with the necessary universal structure of the behavior under study. The latter may be defined as that which remains identical in all possible variations in the subjects and situations of the behavior concerned, and which combines all necessary structural constituents discovered by differential psychologists in their varied exploration of this behavior. The fundamental structure thus admits only those constituents which remain unchanged in all possible variations of the original phenomenon of behavior. Therefore, the foundational psychologist must distance himself from all particular aspects manifested in the behavior so that he may discover only that which is universal, fundamental, and necessary for that type of behavior regardless of the situation in which it appears.

When I search for the fundamental structure of all possible dependency behavior, for example, I may explicate the behavior of a dependent child, a dependent client, a dependent student, a dependent minority group within a culture, or a dependent member of a gang of adolescents. I must eliminate, however, all reference to that in their behavior which colors their personal, developmental, cultural, or subcultural case of dependency. This act of temporary distancing from these aspects is not an act of isolating abstraction or selective attention. Such an abstraction could never provide me with an insight into the universal structure of the behavior. For this fundamental structure actually appears in those aspects which I eliminate from consideration. What I really do is to consider them insofar as they reveal the basic structure, and to distance myself from them insofar as they manifest merely situational aspects of behavior. This approach leads to a real perception of the fundamental structure of the behavior. Such perception reveals at once the necessary and sufficient constituents of, in this case, dependency-behavior. Foundational phenomenology is thus a gradual penetration into the purified primary structure of behavior which culminates in a revealing perception of this structure.

The temporary elimination of individual and particular aspects of behavior in order to perceive its universal, necessary, and sufficient constituents is not always easy. The foundational phenomenologist in psychology may therefore collect random samples of a variety of dependent behaviors among various individuals and populations. This sample enables him to observe dependent behavior from many different aspects. He may perceive what is identical in many appearances of dependent behavior and also what is different because of individual and particular aspects of the situation. He may then attempt to make explicit the underlying structure which unifies these various apearances of dependent behavior.

INTEGRATION OF ALL AVAILABLE PERSPECTIVES FOLLOWING THE ELIMINATION OF INDIVIDUAL ASPECTS

The foundational structure of behavior combines all necessary and sufficient structural constituents which are discovered in the light of the various perspectives assumed by differential psychologists. Therefore, foundational phenomenology in psychology is not merely a matter of eliminating all the individual and particular aspects of the behaving subject and his situation. The comprehensive phenomenologist knows that behavior presents itself in a certain perspective, which is dependent on the attitude which the psychologist assumes toward behavior. He may look at dependency behavior, for example, from the viewpoint of a psychotherapist or of a social psychologist. Each of these attitudes reveals an aspect of dependency behavior which can be explicated by the foundational phenomenologist, who may then uncover a basic and necessary constituent of all dependency behavior.

Each of these aspects, however, refers implicitly to all other aspects of behavior which may be revealed by other attitudes on the part of the perceiving psychologist. Moreover, the specific attitude adopted by the psychologist also refers to other possible attitudes which he can assume. For example, the psychologist who observes dependency behavior from the viewpoint of its emotional meaning for the subject is implicitly aware that this behavior also has physiological, social, and learning aspects. The same may be said of the phenomenologist who uncovers a basic constituent of dependency behavior by explicating any one of these other aspects. If he eliminates all individual and cultural aspects of dependency behavior as described by the social psychologist, for example, he may uncover the basic social characteristic of all dependency behavior. But he is aware, at the same time, that this characteristic is not the only constituent of dependency behavior.

Behavior as it is discovered and described by a psychologist is always a correlate of his observations, which are in turn a correlate of his specific attitude. In other words, the object of his observation is a structure of his systematically organized perspectives of the behavior, which are in accord with the various attitudes on which his observation depends.

The foundational phenomenological psychologist who searches for the universal structure of a behavior must carefully explicate the various attitudes which have been taken by psychologists toward this phenomenon of behavior. He must also analyze the different profiles of behavior which form the correlates of these observational attitudes. He therefore explores the views of all differential psychologies on this particular type of behavior and the perspectives which these views have opened up in order to assess the various profiles. He explicates each perspective in order to discover as many basic constituents as possible which together may present the total foundational structure of the behavior. This type of research will enable him to structure the behavioral phenomenon in question as a *gestalt* of systematically organized aspects discovered by the differential psychologies. Because the number of possible perspectives is virtually inexhaustible, the foundational psychologist can never claim certainty that his phenomenological explication of the universal structure of a type of behavior is exhaustive, final, and complete. Hence the description of the foundational phenomenologist always remains open to change and development in accordance with the possibility of both new findings in existing differential psychologies and the emergence of new differential psychologies, which implies the opening up of totally new perspectives and correspondingly new profiles.

Foundational phenomenology insofar as it serves comprehensive psychology never stops with the explication of only one fundamental constituent of behavior; it aims at a holistic view of man and his structures so broad that comprehensive psychology can devise constructs to integrate the findings of all differential psychologies. For this reason, foundational phenomenology in psychology should not only eliminate all individual and particular characteristics of a behavior, but also integrate the "explicated" profiles of that behavior opened up by the perspectives of all differential psychologies.

THE METHOD OF DIFFERENTIAL EXPLICATION

Like foundational explication, differential phenomenology also entails a procedure of elimination and of integration. This activity does not aim to uncover the most fundamental structures which appear in behavior, however, but the structure of the phenomenon as it appears in certain situations and includes certain aspects of these situations. Consequently, the differential explication distinguishes itself from the foundational one by the

deliberate limitation of its eliminating and integrating procedures.

The Temporary Limited Elimination from Consideration of Certain Individual and Particular Aspects of Behavior

The differential pole of comprehensive phenomenology differs
from the foundational one in various ways. First of all, differential phenomenology does not abstract from all particular aspects
of a behavior. The phenomenologist may, for example, be interested in the behavior of people who feel really understood in a
situation. He may decide to study this behavior as it manifests
itself in American teenagers who belong to a city population or
in people who are in psychotherapy. He may not be interested,
however, in the differences between males and females in this
situation. Thus he defines the object of his phenomenology as
the behavior of feeling understood as it manifests itself in urban
teenagers or in therapy patients, and he temporarily eliminates
from this object their being male or female.

The scope of his differential-phenomenological study obviously
differs from that of a foundational phenomenologist who is interested in the universal structure of the behavior of feeling understood. Such a structure would manifest itself in all people of all
times and cultures who have this experience. The foundational
phenomenologist, therefore, would eliminate *all* particular cultural characteristics from his object of study. Among them would
be being a teenager in a city or a client in psychotherapy.

The fact that the differential phenomenologist does not eliminate *all* individual and particular aspects from a behavior does
not imply that he removes none of them. When he explores the
behavior of feeling understood in teenagers, for example, he
may collect samples of behavior of city teenagers in a variety
of situations in which they feel understood. These samples will
enable him to perceive what is identical in all situations of feeling understood in teenagers, and what is different because of
those individual aspects which are not the particular developmental aspect of being a teenager. In this way, he can make

explicit the structure of behavior which essentially unifies these various appearances of the behavior of teenagers who feel understood.

INTEGRATION OF A SET OF PERSPECTIVES LIMITED IN PRINCIPLE

A second difference between the foundational and the differential poles of anthropological phenomenology can be found in the operation of integration of perspectives.

The foundational phenomenologist aims at the integration of all perspectives opened up by all differential psychologies. The differential phenomenologist, however, is interested in the integration of only those profiles which appear in studies of psychologists who have limited themselves to a specific phenomenon. The phenomenologist who studies the behavior of feeling understood in teenagers, for example, will integrate only those perspectives which are revealed by psychologists who have studied the same behavior in the same developmental situation.

A behavior can be studied on a virtually inexhaustible number of levels, depending on what the differential phenomenologist eliminates or does not eliminate from its concretely situated structure. Thus we can imagine a continuum of degrees of elimination and a consequent continuum of differential phenomenologists in psychology, beginning with those who consider the structure of individual behavior in its peculiarities and ending with those who eliminate all particularizing factors except one. The more extensive the elimination of particulars, the greater the number of perspectives that can be integrated. Ideally, a behavior should be studied by differential phenomenologists on as many relevant levels of elimination as possible, and finally on the level of foundational elimination by comprehensive phenomenologists. The different levels of elucidation will clarify one another and lead to as perfect a grasp of the behavior in question as possible. Such a presentation of a widely and deeply elucidated phenomenon of behavior will facilitate the task of the comprehensive scientific theorist.

We have already discussed the task of the differential phenomenologist who specializes in one field, school, or area of psychology. His integration of perspectives is typically limited to those opened up by the particular psychology which is his concern. Each differential psychology is the implementation of a certain attitude toward behavior. This special viewpoint opens up a certain horizon within which behavior can appear only under certain perspectives. The differential phenomenologist who is committed to such a field of specialization is thus interested only in the integration of those perspectives which have been revealed by the attitude which defines and structures this field as a whole. For example, a differential phenomenologist in the area of dynamic-analytical psychology will integrate all *motivational* aspects of behavior which have been opened up by different psychoanalytic observers and theoreticians of this behavior, such as Freud, Jung, Adler, Horney, Fromm, Alexander, Melanie Klein, and Fairbarn. He will not integrate, for example, the perspectives of dependency behavior which have been explored by physiological and social psychologists. This task he will leave to the differential phenomenologists who specialize in these areas.

We have outlined only the two main operations of the foundational and differential poles of anthropological phenomenology. These two operations differentiate themselves in many more concrete operations, according to the rich variety of phenomena of the behavior under study. Furthermore, the phenomenologist must validate the outcomes of his research by empirical or experimental operations and create a system of checks and controls, which may differ in every specific situation.

We shall demonstrate some of these possible operations and controls in a concrete differential phenomenology of "The Experience of Really Feeling Understood by Somebody" in the following chapter.

CONCLUSION

Empirical observation, experimentation, measurement, and accumulation of data should be fostered in all differential psychologies. From the viewpoint of comprehensive psychology, however, much of this admirable effort is wasted if there is no phenomenological explication of *what* it is that is being observed, experimented upon, measured, correlated, and applied. In this sense, anthropological phenomenology becomes the foundation or ground of comprehensive scientific psychology, its only secure basis, and its instrument for a methodical revision of differential psychologies when necessary. Anthropological phenomenology provides comprehensive psychology with a necessary method for the solution of seemingly insolvable contradictions between statements of "fact" made by differential psychologists. It provides a return to the experienced behavioral phenomena from which these contradictory "facts" were originally derived and to which they refer. Such a return will ordinarily solve the apparent incompatibility of "facts" and enable the comprehensive psychologist to clarify what is really experienced and observed and what is theoretical, philosophical, cultural, personal, emotional, or linguistic contamination in these seemingly incompatible statements.

In our explanation of anthropological phenomenology as used in empirical psychology, we have restricted our discussion to the foundational and differential explications of intentional behavior.

As we have seen earlier, anthropological psychology also requires the explication of its ontological assumptions and of those of the differential psychologies. This task belongs primarily to philosophical anthropology. Therefore, the anthropological phenomenologist in psychology requires at this point the close collaboration of those philosophical phenomenologists who specialize in philosophical anthropology. He applies their conclusions to his own field so long as they are compatible with the evidences provided by differential psychologies. If they are incompatible, he fosters a prolonged dialogue between philosophical anthropology and the contradictory evidences of his own field until a sufficient clarification has been attained by both.

CHAPTER TEN

APPLICATION OF THE PHENOMENOLOGICAL METHOD

Existential psychology is not a special school or a specific method. It is an approach to the study of intentional - functional behavior. Therefore, a research scientist of any school or area of psychology can adopt the existential attitude without having to give up anything essential to his own differential psychology. This attitude implies continual vigilance; it guards against any form of subjectivism, which might distort research, interpretation, the formulation of conclusions, or the application of these findings to psychological practice. Subjectivism is the one-sided attempt by an investigator to impose man-made categories, methods, and schemata upon objectively-given data.

Subjectivism may take any of four forms in my work as a psychologist. In the first form, I approach my object of study, man, exclusively with the methods of physical science, even though many actual and observable aspects of man, in their objective givenness, cannot be circumscribed by such methods. Second, I may use exclusively intuitive methods in my study of man, even though the aspects of behavior under investigation lend themselves more readily to empirical and statistical methods. Third, I may consider as valid only a few of the many effective research methods developed by psychologists, even though objective aspects of my investigation require other approaches. Finally, I may fall into subjectivism by the dogmatic assertion that positive science, as a theory of man, is capable of providing all possible insights into human existence.

I call such approaches subjectivistic because they arise not from my observations of objective reality but from an *a priori* concept which I, the subject, hold about reality.

·The main source of my subjectivism is my refusal to open myself first to the phenomena as they are given to me, and only then to decide which methods, categories, and statistical approaches should be developed in order to investigate these phenomena. Existential psychology demands that my potential data be observed as they exist before I attempt to interpret them.

I can open myself to the phenomena themselves in either a critical or an uncritical way. The critical method of observation implies the use of the phenomenological method. This method leads, ideally, to the type of description and classification of phenomena which can be affirmed by experts in the same field of psychology. Research performed in this way is pre-empirical, pre-experimental, and pre-statistical; it is experiential and qualitative. It sets the stage for more accurate empirical investigations by lessening the risk of a premature selection of methods and categories; it is object-centered rather than method-centered. Such preliminary exploration does not supplant but complements the traditional methods of research available to me.

I shall consider briefly the phenomenological method in relation to research in psychotherapy. Such research clearly implies scientific investigation of the *human* process of psychotherapy by means of empirical methods. The qualification "human" is crucial here. The process of human psychotherapy is not merely a bio-chemical, physiological, or gross motor process. Therefore, research in psychotherapy must take into account—at least implicitly—the specifically *human* character of the process. I wish to emphasize by the use of the term "human" that the process of therapy manifests features that are true only of human relationships. In addition, I use the term "human" to refer to man as a concrete unity, manifesting himself in concrete human behavior. This use of the word "human" implies that I reject the artificial split, introduced by Descartes, which separates man into an "internal (thinking) substance" and an "external (objective) substance." This dualism of Descartes has led to a dualism in modern psychology. There are schools of psychology which claim one-sidedly that the internal substance can be used to explain the whole man; the interior substance for them takes the form of an interior self, with drives, dynamics, needs, or complexes. Other psychologists attempt to explain the whole man in terms of the external substance; for them, man's reactive organism, artificially isolated from his intentionality and purposiveness, is his essential nature.

The anti-dualistic, or existential, viewpoint is significant for the development of research in psychotherapy. It enables me as a psychologist to perceive the behavior of man as a concrete unity of orientation and of the embodiment of this orientation in observable behavior. Thus I can use empirical methods in the study of man without fearing that I may have hidden some crucial aspect of his behavior behind a methodological screen. I can reach conclusions about him as a whole person which are susceptible to intersubjective affirmation by other observers in my field. In my research, I am no longer dependent on perceptions and insights which are accessible only to me as one single psychotherapist, or to one exclusive group of psychotherapists.

At this point I should perhaps ask myself, what is the specifically human character of my object of research? How does it differ from the object of the physical sciences? The latter study man as an organism dependent on an environment and defined biologically. Physical science can, therefore, provide me with valuable information regarding physical, physiological, and biological foundations of psychotherapy. As a human scientist, however, I study man as the originator and cultivator of his world. I do not focus my attention exclusively on biological conditions, therefore, but on all of the observable interactions between two or more persons. It would be an intrusion of subjectivism into the realm of psychotherapy were I to eliminate on principle the human interpersonal aspect of therapy from the field of scientific investigation. This aspect appears objectively and undeniably in my perception.

To be sure, my methods of study must lead to scientific propositions. However, I would hold a subjectivistic, *a priori* concept of science if I should dogmatically declare: Only those propositions are scientific which have been established by the methods of mathematics and of the natural sciences. It would be more complete to say: Only those propositions are scientific which have been proved valid according to certain rules and which can be verified by many independent observers who are experienced in this particular area of observation. Research in psychotherapy as a human science can thus be defined as the investigation of the objective aspects of therapeutic interaction by means of an objectifying approach. This approach will necessarily lead to the establishment of useful constructs, such as libido, Oedipus complex, resistance, transference, reinforcement, client-centeredness. Here again, the existential attitude will protect me from the danger of subjectivism which threatens my objectivity in every phase of my research. I must remind myself constantly of the fact that such constructs, while closely connected with my perceptions in psychotherapy, nevertheless transcend the level of perception.

The study and practice of psychotherapy, from one or another viewpoint, provide an opportunity to form these constructs. A language or framework of these constructs might even be devised on the basis of their interconnection. This frame would then permit therapists not only to organize their observations, but also to communicate with those who study psychotherapy from the same standpoint. This possibility of organization and communication by means of interconnected constructs has led to the development of various useful frames of references such as the Behaviorist, the Client-centered, and the Psychoanalytic. However, to prevent the intrusion of subjectivism, I should constantly be aware that no framework used for research and practice in psychotherapy will possess an absolutely binding character. It represents an attempt to understand, systematically and from one specific viewpoint, the potentially inexhaustible wealth of interactions which constitute the total process of psychotherapy. Such frameworks are not themselves the total possible interactions of psychotherapy, they are merely models which enable us to grasp *something* of this complete reality. The existential position in psychology implies that all such scientific frames of reference are not "true" nor "false", but only "useful" or "useless", "effective" or "ineffective". The sole criterion which the existential view demands for each frame of reference is: Does it increase our knowledge of the objective process of psychotherapy? A frame may be "effective" for the understanding of one objectified aspect of behavior while quite "ineffective" for the understanding of another. For example, the scientific model of Behavorism is useful for the exploration of the behavior of animals in artificial surroundings, but it is inadequate for the understanding of certain specifically human aspects of the therapeutic interaction. I should become the victim of subjectivism, therefore, if I were willfully to force the objectively-given phenomena of human interaction into such a frame merely because it has been successfully used in another type of research.

I may use any methods only provisionally, always being ready to change them when they do not lead me to better understanding of the objective phenomenon under study. I should always drop methods devised by investigators, who are the *subjects* of research, if the *object* being investigated seems to expose aspects of behavior for which the methods are inadequate. Therefore it is most helpful for me to make my first approach that of a phenomenological method, which does not confine or restrict the phenomenon under study to a structure of established theoretical constructs.

To illustrate the process of such preliminary phenomenological research, I have selected one relatively simple concrete phenomenon that appears in psychotherapy. The patient at times "feels really understood" by the therapist. What is the fundamental structure and meaning of this experience of "feeling understood?" I shall answer this by outlining at least the main steps which I followed in my explication of this phenomenon.

Application of the Phenomenological Method

PRELIMINARY CONSIDERATIONS*

"Feeling understood" is a human experience. When one reflects on the character of human experience, one becomes increasingly impressed by its complexity. It seems to be continually moving; it suggests an appearing and disappearing of perceptions, needs, emotions, which interact in various ways. New moments come continually to the fore, changing the total picture; a dynamic picture that would seem to forbid the rigid isolation of a perception or a feeling. These changes appear only as moments, as mutually-dependent parts of a process.

On the other hand, these mutually-dependent moments do not appear as identical with one another, nor with the process of human experience as a whole. The feeling of love for a girl-friend is quite obviously different from the feeling of being bored with a teacher. The experience of disappointment over bad weather is nothing like the feeling of delight at being understood by a sympathetic listener. In everyday life the experiences of feeling understood, feeling rejected, feeling fascinated, and feeling threatened are experienced as different from one another. Even when they are present at the same time, they are not experienced as intrinsically identical. One might feel delighted, for example, that somebody really understands him, and at the same time experience a surge of admiration for the kind person who understands. Thus people distinguish one experiential phenomenon from another. They do not seem able, however, to isolate them as rigidly as they do physical entities.

Complexity and fluidity are characteristic not only of the experiential process as a whole, but also of each specific moment of experience. "Feeling understood" is conceived of in everyday life as distinct from other moments of experience, though even a superficial observation makes it clear that this

*This part of the chapter is based on my Ph.D. dissertation submitted to the department of psychology, Western Reserve University. I wish to express my gratitude to Dwight W. Miles and George W. Albee for their encouragement and advice, and to Carl Rogers, A. H. Maslow, and Kurt Goldstein for many stimulating discussions.

299

specific experience also displays a complexity and fluidity of its own.

Some of the subjects whom we questioned experienced this feeling globally, as being understood in their whole person. They specified no distinct problem or specific emotion that had been grasped by the person doing the understanding. Other subjects, on the contrary, emphasized that a specific problem or a peculiar feeling had been understood by the person. Thus there was a definite distinction in emphasis. Nevertheless, in both descriptions the experience of really feeling understood was always present. And in both, mention of the emotions that seem most often to accompany this experience appears in the reports of the subjects.

Another example of the complexity and fluidity of this specific experience may be seen in the feeling of relief reported by many of the subjects. It seems to relate, in one way or another, to their experience of being understood. But we also know that relief can be found outside this specific experience, for example, after successfully passing a test. Relief, therefore, is probably not a feature that in and by itself distinguishes the experience of being understood from all other experiences.

Still another sign of complexity may be found in the differences of intensity of feeling. A subject who talks about the precious moment in a love relationship in which she felt really understood for the first time in her life, shows a deeper relief, a more overwhelming joy, than a highschool girl who tells about a teacher who understood her inferiority feeling about her lack of accomplishment in mathematics. In the former case, the elation led to gross somatic phenomena such as a pounding heart and a quivering body, while in the latter, the more moderate feelings of relief were accompanied by somatic changes so slight that the subject did not mention them.

Thus the moment of experience labeled "feeling understood" does not appear at first glance to be clearly delineated in the totality of the experience. It does not seem possible to isolate this phenomenon as one would a chemical element. Nevertheless, there must be something in the experience itself that makes us label it as "feeling understood." For feeling understood is certainly not experienced as feeling bored or feeling rejected. It must be possible to discover that which is characteristic of the feeling of being understood, that which constitutes this specific moment of experience.

RESEARCH QUESTION EVOKED BY THE PHENOMENON

The average person is probably not pained by any problem concerning the feeling of being understood so long as his life develops smoothly. The problem poses itself only when he is in acute need of giving or receiving understanding. Then it may take such forms as: "How can I understand my wife? my girl friend? my teenage son or daughter? my employee? my boss?" Or, "How can I make myself really understood by people who do not understand me, and who misinterpret my behavior?" Many times the person works out a successful response to his question; a concrete response that helps him to find understanding in a specific situation and to respond to a certain type of person in a special way. At other times, he does not discover a satisfactory response.

For the psychologist, the phenomenon of feeling understood is thought-provoking. He becomes aware daily that this feeling may be very important in the life of an individual. He observes changes in other feelings, attitudes, and behavior that accompany or follow this emotional experience. It appears to him that the lack of this experience might hinder the full development of certain aspects of the personality. He observes this situation more dramatically when he is a clinical psychologist treating daily, in institutional or private practice, a number of clients. His considerations may make him curious about the inner structure of the phenomenon he observes. Therefore he may decide to make it an object of scientific research.

The question he will ask himself is: What is this phenomenon? What exactly is this feeling of being understood and what distinguishes it from every other subjective experience? Or, to formulate the question more exactly: *What are the necessary and sufficient constituents of this feeling?*

Another aspect of the problem of feeling understood is still to be considered—not a psychological but a philosophical-anthropological one. Approaching the feeling of being understood in a philosophical way, one would ask: "What does the existence of this feeling tell me concerning the nature of man, or how can I conceive this feeling in the light of my view of the nature of man?" To be sure, it is impossible to approach human nature directly. One can understand it only through its expression. But there are innumerably more expressions of human nature than that of feeling understood. These other expressions, at least some of them, have already provided us with philosophies of man. Therefore, conclusions concerning human nature, as they are expressed in the phenomenon of the feeling of being understood, already presuppose a more or less developed, explicit or implicit, view of man on the part of the psychologist. This presupposed specific view of man will make for different conclusions held in accordance with respectively different philosophies of man. It will vary in the light of the implicit philosophical views of man developed by various psychological scientists, for example, the Freudians, the Jungians, the Adlerians, and the Behaviorists. It would be interesting to determine what "feeling understood" would mean in the light of these various implicit philosophies.

It would also be a fascinating and challenging task to build a philosophy of man on the phenomenon being studied, as has been done by so many psychological scientists on the phenomena with which they were especially concerned. But, without denying the intellectual delight of projecting a philosophy of man from the vantage point of one or another psychological phenomenon, the existential psychologist still prefers not to transcend the limits of his empirical observation and will not do so in this study.

METHOD OF APPROACH TO THE PHENOMENON

The deductive method in science attempts to discover particular validities by beginning with universal ones. The particular validities are then assumed to be contained within the universal law. But such a method does not seem useful for the discovery of the necessary and sufficient constituents of the experience of feeling understood as introduced above.

Some psychologies, like the Freudian, the Jungian, and the Behavioristic, departing from an accepted view of man, formulated certain universal principles or laws concerning the human personality. But it does not seem desirable to start from any of these laws in order to identify the experience that is called "feeling understood." For such a procedure would presuppose that this experience is encompassed in the general implicit philosophy of man developed by the school chosen. Assuming this philosophy *a priori* might influence the explication of the data. One would proceed from certain general principles held by the school, and then, theorizing from these, might develop conclusions concerning a situation to which these principles are applicable. This situation would then be said to be the experience which people call "feeling understood."

But to determine what kind of experience is called "feeling understood" and how it is experienced is precisely the problem of our research. By using the deductive method in the way indicated, we would suppose that we already have a concept of "feeling understood," whose content and applicability are already defined. We would be assuming an answer before even exploring our problem. Therefore, in this phase of our research, the method used must necessarily be inductive. We must start from the various data of experience in order to formulate a valid description covering the various data of the sample.

We shall begin by examining man's awareness. Long before we studied psychology, even when we were children, we were aware of people, of their actions, of how they felt. We were also aware of ourselves, of our own feelings, thoughts, and desires. At that time, it was perhaps difficult for us to formulate a concept of this natural awareness. But we were sure that we experienced this way of knowing. Every human being possesses an elementary awareness of his experiences, though he may not be able to translate his awareness into clear psychological statements. This primordial human awareness encompasses an extensive field. One knows in this way all subjective experiences, such as feeling rejected, feeling thankful, feeling sorry, or feeling understood.

Every psychologist who deals with experience begins, consciously or unconsciously, with awareness. Otherwise, it would even be impossible for him to experience what people are talking about when they say that they "feel understood." He would also be unable to understand in an experiential way the external signs of the experiences of relaxation, joy, and relief in a person who feels understood. Precisely because a person himself has been aware of a particular feeling at one time or another, he is able to experience what his fellowman attempts to communicate when he says, "I feel understood."

This primary awareness of experience brings man into immediate contact with his own loving, hoping, suffering, experiencing self. Man's experience may be complex, but it is present to his awareness in its complex totality. On the other hand, although it is true that his experience is immediately present to him in all its complexity, this does not mean that every moment that is contained in a specific experience is distinguished by him exactly and distinctly as it is.

Awareness cannot be proved; no more than one can prove that red is red or that perceiving is perceiving. But everyone observes experience in himself. In others words, experience is a primary datum that in itself cannot be proved.

EXPLICATION OF AWARENESS

When man begins to think or to speak about his experiences, he is attempting to express his awareness. It is by this formulation that awareness becomes conceptual knowledge. Only when we have expressed our experience in clear statements, concepts, and judgments can we proceed in a scientific manner. The scientific discussion of a phenomenon requires first of all an exact idea of what it contains and an accurate formulation of this idea. Such a precise formulation is our aim in attempting to identify and describe the necessary and sufficient constituents of the feeling of "being understood". The accurate distinction of the various moments in this feeling syndrome is necessary in order to prevent confusion with other subjective phenomena. We need to find appropriate terms that will enable us to communicate with other scientists concerning the phenomenon under discussion.

This formulation will provide us with a new and more explicit way of knowing the experience of feeling understood. What we wish to express is already known to us, but we know it only in a vague way. The knowledge is imperfect, confused, and disordered. Science makes clear a knowledge of experience which is vague and imprecise. In other words, science formulates explicitly what was experienced implicitly in awareness. We label this process *explication*. By explication, implicit awareness of a complex phenomenon becomes explicit, formulated knowledge of its components. The process is loosely analogous to therapy, in which the patient gradually learns to express his implicit, vague, painful self-experience in an explicitly labeled description of what is going on in his subjective life.

Explication always starts from awareness, without which it would lose its validity. One would only be expressing terms unrelated to a known reality. Moreover, awareness also constitutes the final aim of the explication. Explication produces an *enlightened* awareness in which the constituent elements of experience are precisely represented. Here again the process of psychotherapy offers an analogy. The labeling of the experience by the patient results in a sharper, enlightened awareness, for example, of his feeling of hostility.

The first endeavor of the psychologist is to change vague awareness into a more detailed conceptual knowledge. Often psychologists deviate from one another in their conclusions only because they formulate their original awareness without a scientific observation of it as it is actually present in sufficiently varied samples of subjects. This neglect of scientific rigor in the decisive first phase of research often forms a striking contrast to the following scientific build-up by means of deductive and inductive procedures. Many scientists use faultless scientific designs which are nevertheless powerless to compensate for the inexact, popular, or introspective notions which initiated their research. Thus differences in explication of awareness, the most important step in every research concerning experience, cause unnecessary but fundamental dissensions among psychologists.

The present study of the phenomenon of feeling understood will be primarily an explication of awareness. In other words, this research will deal predominantly with the first and decisive phase of the scientific objectivation of experiential phenomena.

From what has been said, it will be obvious that the norm can only be awareness itself. The psychologist must restrict himself in his explication to the expression of what is given in awareness. During the process of explication he ought not to involve himself in any implicit philosophizing, be he of a Freudian, a Behavioristic, a Stimulus-Response, a Jungian, or any other school.

When the psychologist has finally expressed awareness, he translates it necessarily into a series of psychological statements. But, in doing this, he must follow the data of awareness. He must not go beyond the content of his data in his attempt to express it. His explication is valid and reliable only insofar as it is really an "expression," uncolored by the flavor of a typical school.

PROBLEMS OF METHOD INVOLVED IN THE EXPLICATION

The possibility that the psychologist may express more than is given in the awareness, especially if he attempts to base his explication on his limited personal experience, has been indicated as a major problem. We shall deal with this problem at length.

Another factor that hinders the process of explication is the lack of descriptive concepts in psychology. This lack may be explained as follows. Phenomena of experience are different from the pure physical kind which man is aware of by means of his sensory equipment. Joy, hate, hope, guilt, love, feeling understood are never met with as such in the physical universe. The extent to which they differ from physical phenomena determines the degree of difficulty of expressing them in concepts and statements. This is so because concept-formation is very dependent on our sense-knowledge of the physical universe. This fact makes it difficult to explicate the non-physical phenomena of experience by means of concepts that find their origin in the knowledge of physical phenomena.

Many subjects, for example, describe a feeling of relief when being understood. The term "relief" seems to be an apt expression for a certain feeling. But it is by no means an original psychological label. It was first used to describe the action of someone's lifting-up of a physical object that exercised pressure on someone else's body. This lifting-up resulted in measurable changes in physical and physiological characteristics. At the same time, the subject experienced an emotion accompanying these changes. Soon the label of the physical experience, "Lifting up," "Relief," was applied to the experience itself. Gradually all experiences of becoming free of guilt, anxiety, worries, were labeled as feelings of relief. The sudden unburdening of one's bent, tired back, when somebody removes a heavy load became a striking image of what is felt when another frees us of our conflicts, anxieties, or sickly suspicions.

It is sometimes impossible to express directly certain forms of experience. The subject feels forced to use comparisons and metaphors borrowed from the world of sensible physical events and objects. By means of these indirect media he attempts to convey his inner experience. The explication of the feeling of being understood is no exception. The person who explicates has to use comparisons, metaphors and terms, as for instance, "relief," that cannot be understood in a literal way. This fact obliges us to use special safeguards because an indirect description may easily lead to inexactness.

In awareness one experiences the living, concrete, dynamic totality of feeling understood. But the explication violates this reality by breaking down its natural unity. This is so because the explication necessarily expresses itself in a series of psychological statements. Each statement expresses only a part of the concrete experience. The explication fixates that which in reality is process. The expression becomes a sum of separate formulae expressing the necessary and sufficient components of this process. It comprehends that which is concrete and individual in universal statements. It exteriorizes that which is interior. But the whole series of psychological statements, however perfect, will never express fully the living process of the experience itself.

Anyone who has never had the experience himself cannot know what it is like from its description alone. Nevertheless, the attempt to give expression to it is necessary for psychology, for the purpose of explication is not the explication itself. It aims at a new, more clear and detailed definition of an awareness, which will enable the psychologist to understand human experience more distinctly. The implications of this objectivation for personality-theory, therapy, education, test-construction, cultural and social psychology are evident.

EXPLICATION OF THE SELF-AWARENESS OF THE SCIENTIST

One method of explication of the experience of feeling understood is to observe one's own experience of this phenomenon and to express it as faithfully as possible. After this self-explication, one might ask a sampling of subjects whether their experiences have been similar. But this method has disadvantages and pitfalls.

The scientist who begins with his own analyzed experience may be prejudiced from the very beginning. It is far from easy to determine precisely what feeling understood is. The experience is mixed with other emotions which are dependent on a variety of conditions in the particular situation in which feeling understood is experienced. Between boy and girl, the experience of mutual understanding might be blended with the onset of love; in the therapist-patient relationship, it might be influenced by a feeling of belief in some occult power in the therapist.

Similarly, the personal experience of the scientist himself may be colored by elements that are not a part of feeling understood in its pure form. It is possible that he may not perceive that his explication is contaminated by features of the type of situation which he himself has predominantly in mind when concentrating on feeling understood. When he tries, after explicating his one-sided experience, to find out how other people feel, he may be prejudiced in his way of questioning them or of devising tests to find out whether they have had a similar experience, for he is the one who determines the classifications of his tests or questionnaires. And classifications operate as suggestive limitations for the subjects who are submitted to them.

Another disadvantage of the primary explication of one's own experience is the possibility of carrying out the process under the influence of theoretical prejudice. One might be trained, for example, in a certain personality theory. It might be that feeling understood is defined in this theory in a prescientific way, based on the impressions and feelings of the persons who represent these theories. It might even be that the psychologist is no longer aware that this vaguely defined concept of feeling understood is only an interesting "hunch" not empirically validated. In this case, the personal explication of the feeling might follow the line of the subjectivistic notion that one is trained to believe in. The result will again be slanted questionnaires, or distorted tests, always proving that the researcher is right. Other deviating experiences cannot be expressed because no provision is made in the categories for their spontaneous expression.

A further disadvantage is that the explication of one's personal experience is not open to scientific control. The expert may be prejudiced while explicating his own experience of feeling understood, but there is no way for other scientists to control the correlation between the explication and the awareness of the psychologist.

Some psychologists aim at objectivity by communicating their explication to cooperators who are expected to produce compensatory views. But the extreme complexity of the experience itself, its quality as process, its combination with many other elements in the situation render this method inadequate. The communication of what is experienced when feeling understood is easily influenced by elements of the communication-situation itself. Implicit, slight, mutual suggestions might modify in the participants, in a subtle way, the experience itself and the direction of the process of explication. Moreover, the cooperators would almost all be experts in the field of psychology. This situation could lead to a compounding of professional prejudices. For these reasons, it does not seem scientifically desirable to begin with an explication by the psychologist of his own experience of feeling understood.

PRESCIENTIFIC EXPLICATION BY OTHERS

Another method of explication would begin, not with one's own experience, but with the accumulation of explications obtained from samples of untrained subjects. Then the scientist would begin with his own explication of the raw observable data of the objectified experiences written down in these descriptions. In explicating these data of behavior, systematically comparing them with one another, he would attempt to find the underlying constants. Untrained subjects would probably produce a greater number and variety of situations in which they felt understood. This advantage would increase the scientific value of the method, for it would mean a natural variation of the independent variables. It would enable the psychologist to distinguish that which is constant from that which varies in the different situations. Thus he would have an increased probability of discovering the factors common to all experiences of feeling understood. Finally, the scientist would be better able to control the explication of the common human awareness objectified in the various descriptions.

The justification of this procedure rests on the following suppositions:

1. Feeling understood is a relatively common human experience.
2. Common human experience is basically identical.
3. This basically identical human experience is expressed under the same label.

Let us consider the validity of these suppositions.

310

The feeling of being understood is obviously a reality not only in the clinic or in the office of the therapist; it happens in daily life. People tell us that they have felt really understood at one time or another, by one person or another, in certain situations. Therefore, we may suppose that most people have at least a vague notion of what it is to feel understood.

There are people, however, who contend that they do not know what it means to feel understood. It seems to be true that a certain number of them really do not know what this feeling means because they have never had the experience. It appears, however, that most people who contend that they do not know this experience really mean that they do not know how to express it. That they do know the feeling is evident from the fact that they distinguish feeling understood from other feelings in the same way as other people do who also contend that they do know the experience. When questioned about it, they distinguish feeling understood from feelings of being hated, of being hurt, of being praised, and so on, just as the majority of people do. Therefore, they must be aware of this specific experience, at least basically and vaguely. Since a significant majority of people make this distinction regularly and in the same way, we assume that feeling understood is a relatively common human experience, in spite of the fact that not everyone is able to express it.

There are many and different circumstances in which people experience this phenomenon. Some subjects, when asked about feeling understood, will think immediately of the quiet moments of love in their lives. Others are reminded of the difficult hours in which they felt compelled to seek advice from an understanding representative of their religion. Others, again, remember a good friend who knew how to listen in a deeply interested way when a worry was confided to him. Still others cherish the moment in which they were able to communicate their elated feeling about a musical performance and were filled with joy when their companion felt the same elation, and communicated in an understanding glance and smile.

311

If we collect descriptions of the feeling of being understood, then we have to assume that others are focusing their attention on basically the same kind of feeling that we are when we describe our experience. This statement is founded on the supposition that experience, with all its phenomena, is basically the same in various subjects. It presupposes that other people experience basically the same sensations, perceptions, images, needs, desires, feelings, and intellectual acts that the scientist experiences.

This basic identity of experience is an axiom in psychology. The building of experimental psychology rests on this foundation. This general working hypothesis can never be proved, but it is accepted as long as, and to the extent that, it is not refuted by contrary facts. When an experimenter has the experience of seeing a rat in a maze, for example, then he presupposes that other observers have had the same experience, and that they therefore understand what he means when he expresses his experience, "rat," which follows the physical exposure of his sensory equipment to waves coming from the grey object, and imping-ing on the nerve ends in his sense organs. It does not seem un-reasonable then to accept this axiom of the experimental psy-chologist, when one deals with what could be called normal individuals belonging to similar groups.

This axiom seems to be confirmed by daily experience. If there were not a basic identity of experience, then it would be impossible for us to communicate with one another. This un-derlying identity seems to be, in fact, the basis of the cultural uniformity represented in the labels attached to various phe-nomena. This is why people understand what the experimenter means when he says "rat" or "this color on the color wheel is red." Similarly, we say that other people do understand what is basically meant when somebody says, "I am happy," or "I am bored," or "I feel sad." In other words, by understanding one another regularly and continually in daily life, people feel sure that they are referring to basically the same feelings when they use the same term.

We cannot deal here with the genetic history of this uniformity. It is clear, however, that growing up in a certain culture is the common way to learn the language symbols that are used to communicate the common experiences in that culture.

The uniform cultural label helps people to understand one another in general outlines, when expressing certain experiences. The labeled experience represents, at least basically, the same feeling. It might be true that a few members of the culture deviate from the common pattern, even in general outlines. But one perceives this deviation immediately. If a person says that he feels really understood by somebody, and the other answers: "Congratulations! And when are you getting married?", then it is clear that the person responding in this manner does not understand the specific experience that is expressed. He labels with "feeling understood" an experience which, by the significant majority of people in his culture, is called "love." The deviation from the socially accepted code of labeling is evident. But it is not always so clear, especially if one is dealing with experiences that are closely related to one another, or that regularly manifest themselves at the same time.

It is improbable, for example, that the label "feeling understood" comprehends, in an absolute sense, the same elements for everyone in every situation. Our data reveals immediately that feeling relaxed, feeling "loosened up" inside, feeling relieved, feeling wanted and respected, feeling important, and feeling that one is taken seriously, approach very closely the feeling of being understood. There is also a relationship between this experience and one of insight into personal problems, or a new perception of the world.

In other words, one can only be certain that the *significant majority* of people label that experience as feeling understood which basically contains the necessary and sufficient constituents of the feeling. One cannot be certain that common people, or even scientists when dealing with this phenomenon in a philosophical or introspective way, really describe the pure feeling of being understood without blending with it other phenomena or characteristics of the specific situation in which it is experienced.

The blending of absolute and relative elements in the prescientific descriptions necessitates a second explication. The scientist now has at his disposal a number of crude, spontaneous, or prescientific explications made by untrained subjects. As we have seen, their being untrained made it probable that they would produce the data of their awareness without undue interference from implicit philosophies of schools of psychology. At the same time, the number and variety of their descriptions increase the probability that, when combined, they will touch on the underlying necessary and sufficient constituents of the experience.

These factors make it possible for the psychologist to begin the second phase of explication in a manner that is more subject to scientific control. He bases his explication on the raw data instead of on his own personal experience of feeling understood. Briefly, instead of analyzing and comparing the elements of the explicit awareness of his own experience, he analyzes and compares the written expressions of the explicit awareness of his subjects.

SCIENTIFIC PHASE OF THE EXPLICATION

The scientific explication is performed in six operations: listing and preliminary grouping, reduction, elimination, hypothetical identification, application, and final identification.

These operations do not always follow the indicated order, and tend to overlap one another. They form a set of ordered abstractions partly describing the complicated mental process that the phenomenological scientist experiences as a natural totality.

The first operation of the scientist is to classify his data into categories. These categories must be the result of what the subjects themselves are explicating. Therefore, the scientist makes his initial categories from empirical data, in this case, a sufficiently large random sample of cases taken from the total pool of descriptions. To insure the validity of this procedure, he must strive for intersubjective concurrence with other experts concerning the agreement of these initial selections with the data taken from the random sample. After this, the researcher analyzes every descriptive expression found in the samples and lists them. When necessary, the initial lists and groups are supplemented by others in order to encompass every basically different statement made by the subjects. Finally, in order to be recognized as objectively valid, the actual listing must be agreed upon by expert judges.

The final listing presents a review of the various moments of the feeling of being understood as described by various subjects. It also presents the percentages of these various elements in this particular population, a possible clue to the predominant features of the phenomenon.

Now that the elements are laid out for him in a quantitative and qualitative fashion, the researcher can proceed with the second operation of the scientific explication. He reduces the concrete, vague, intricate, and overlapping expressions of the subjects to more precisely descriptive terms. When, for example, a subject writes, "I feel a hundred pounds less heavy," or "A load is off my chest," the psychologist may reduce this statement to "a feeling of relief." To a certain extent, this operation of reduction was already active in the initial listing and preliminary grouping. It brings the necessary clearness and organization into the wealth of vivid and picturesque descriptions used by the subjects. Here also an intersubjective agreement among expert judges is necessary in order to prevent subjectivism in the selection of reduction terms. By comparing the different elements and the different descriptions in which they are used, the researcher attempts to determine those elements that might probably be said to be constituents of the experience of feeling understood.

By means of the same operation, he now attempts to eliminate those elements that probably are not inherent in the feeling of being understood as such, but rather are complexes which include being understood in a particular situation, or which represent a blending of the feeling of being understood with other phenomena that most often accompany it.

The operations of classification, reduction, and element-elimination result in the first hypothetical identification and description of the feeling of being understood. The identification is called hypothetical because it was hardly possible to take into account at once all the details of all the descriptions during the element-elimination.

Therefore, a fifth operation of the scientific explication is required, namely, the application of the hypothetical description to randomly selected cases of the sample. This tentative application may possibly result in a number of cases of feeling understood that do not correspond to the hypothetical formula. It may be that the formula contains something more than the necessary and sufficient constituents of feeling understood. In this case, the formula must be revised in order to correspond with the evidence of the cases used in the application. It may also be that some descriptions still contain elements that probably are not inherent in the experience of feeling understood as such, but rather characterize either the experience of feeling understood in a particular situation, or an experience other than the phenomenon under study. After careful analysis, the researcher again applies the operation of elimination. After such changes, the new hypothetical formula must be tested again on a new random sample of cases.

When the operations described have been carried out successfully, the formerly hypothetical identification of the phenomenon of feeling understood may be considered to be a valid identification and description. It is evidently valid only for the population represented by the samples. The validity lasts until other cases are presented which can be proved to be cases of really feeling understood, and which do not correspond to the necessary and sufficient constituents contained in the formula. The facts and only the facts remain the final criterion for the empirical scientist.

Application of the Phenomenological Method

CHOICE OF THE SAMPLE

As we have said, the subjects who write down their prescientific explications ought not to be specialists in psychology. Nevertheless, their difficult task requires certain abilities and the fulfillment of certain conditions. The chief ones are:

a. The ability to express themselves with relative ease in the English language.
b. The ability to sense and to express inner feelings and emotions without shame and inhibition.
c. The ability to sense and to express the organic experiences that accompany these feelings.
d. The experience of situations in which the subject felt really understood, preferably at a relatively recent date.
e. A spontaneous interest in his experience on the part of the subject.
f. An atmosphere in which the subject can find the necessary relaxation to enable him to put sufficient time and orderly thought into writing out carefully what was going on within him.

Which group of the population in our contemporary American culture would best fulfill these requirements? We arrived at the hypothesis that the group best suited for the prescientific explication of the experience of really feeling understood would most probably be a group of female high school seniors from an institute of learning recognized for its scholastic standards.

The high school senior, just at the end of her teen-age period, is on the threshold of adult life. Inner experience is beginning to take form more and more for her. She is in a stage of finding herself after the turbulence of the years of transition and assimilation, of meeting the new and the unexpected. This process leads her to spontaneous interest in her present and past emotional experiences that are for her as so many revelations of herself, the "self" that fascinates her in this period of synthesis. This spontaneous interest is especially true of her experience of really feeling understood. Many studies in adolescent psychology reveal that the period of her life that is now for the most part

317

behind her was characterized by loneliness, insecurity, and be-wilderment. Therefore, "really feeling understood by somebody" was a sometimes impressive experience for the lonely high school girl during this strange state of sudden self-discovery.

In order to discover the necessary and sufficient constituents of the phenomenon under study, moreover, the researcher should have at his disposal explications that cover a sufficiently wide range of situations that facilitates the isolation of that which is necessary and sufficient from that which is incidental or pecul-iar to specific kinds of situations.

The range of situations in which the average high school sen-ior experiences the feeling of being understood is probably wider than it is for the average adult. The period of adolescence is replete with discoveries, emotional conflicts, new patterns of be-havior, and seemingly daring adventures. These are the source of numerous anxious moments in which the teen-ager wonders whether anybody else could possibly understand her. The same situations are consequently occasions of finding understanding and enjoying this experience. In average adult life, the need for understanding is not spread over such a variety of situa-tions as in adolescence. The average adult has found his way in life. He experiences in a culturally identical way many com-mon life situations that are no longer new and strange to him. His need for, and his experience of, understanding seems to be more concentrated in certain areas, such as the experience of love.

Consequently, in order to obtain a sufficiently wide range of situations, a population of high school seniors seems to be pref-erable. A high school girl is still not absorbed, moreover, by the often hectic and disturbing influence of factory, office, or col-lege life that might later lessen her sensitivity to experience. At the same time, since she has had a reasonably good training in English, she may now, as a senior, be skillful enough to ex-press her inner experiences. And the school can provide the time, order, and well-organized surroundings necessary for se-rious concentration during the subtle enterprise of really ex-pressing herself.

Application of the Phenomenological Method

It is also recognized, at least in our culture, that the average female senses and expresses her inner feelings more easily and completely, when she really wants to, than males usually do. On the other hand, it seems probable that an increasing number of older, "adult" females in our culture, under the influence of certain vocational adjustments and social cultural variables, lose this quality to a certain degree. For all these reasons, it seemed to us that the best group of subjects available in our culture for the prescientific explication of the human experience of really feeling understood would be a group of female high school seniors who enjoy the qualities already described.

The basis of our sample is a group of 150 female high school seniors taken from five different senior classes of an all-girl Academy in Chicago, Illinois.

In accordance with our hypothesis, the average paper written by this group showed a livelier interest in self-experience and a more carefully elaborated description of it than the average papers presented by the subjects of other samples. The 150 papers represented a wide variety of situations and personalities with corresponding variety in descriptions. It was therefore relatively easy to isolate the consistent necessary and sufficient pattern. In spite of this, we made sure that a few samples, taken from a different population, presented us with the same basic picture. If analysis of these samples yielded the same necessary and sufficient constituents, it would contribute nothing to our investigation to make them as wide as our basic group, originally chosen for their supposed ease and spontaneity in sensing and expressing feelings. If the necessary and sufficient constituents had proved to be radically different, however, from those presented in the sample of the girls, we would have been obliged to expand these new samples.

In the latter samples, however, in spite of accidental differences and less spontaneous expression of feelings, we were confronted again with the same necessary and sufficient constituents. Therefore, we found no scientific necessity to increase the number of samples. They proved that the "average" self-expression of the "average" female high school senior in this specific

Academy was reliable in the essentials of its message, when given under the special conditions set up by the researcher. We combined the later samples with that of the high school seniors and formed one collection of empirical material on which to build our scientific explication.

The samples thus combined with that of the 150 female high school seniors were those of 95 male school seniors from another high school in Chicago and those of 60 female and 60 male students from a college in Pittsburgh.

Hence our total sample contained:

> 150 Female High School Seniors
> 95 Male High School Seniors
> 60 Female College Students
> 60 Male College Students
> ———

Total   365 Subjects

FORMULATION OF THE PAPER PRESENTED TO THE SUBJECTS

The subjects were asked to write down their experience of really feeling understood. In every school concerned, a class hour was set apart for this task. During this hour, the subjects were free to spend as much time as they wished on this project.

Each subject received a blank paper, on top of which was the following information:

Age_____ Sex_____

1. Do *not* write your name or any other personal identification at the top of this paper.
2. Write *only* your age and sex on the top of this paper.
3. Describe how you feel when you feel that you are really being understood by somebody.
   a. Recall some situation or situations when you felt you were being understood by somebody; for instance, by mother, father, clergyman, wife, husband, girl friend, boy friend, teacher, etc.
   b. Try to describe how you felt in that situation (not the situation itself).

    c. Try to describe your feelings just as they were.

    d. Please do not stop until you feel that you have described your feelings as completely as possible.

This formulation was agreed upon by two other independent judges, Gene Gendlin and Anthony Barton, at that time psychologist-therapists at the Counseling Center of the University of Chicago.

LISTING OF THE DATA

A 20% random sample of 80 subjects was taken from the pool of 365 descriptions. The expressions contained in the sample were listed by three judges: Anthony Barton and Leonard Gottesman, psychologists at the Counseling Center of the University of Chicago, and the author.

A phenomenological explication bases itself on the data as presented by the subjects. This faithfulness to "the things as they appear" (phenomenon— that which appears) results in a wide range of listed expressions. Every expression revealing a moment of experience not manifested in formulations of other subjects must be written down, whether or not the researcher believes it to be worthwhile. Thus some formulations are included which are somewhat superfluous for a scientific explication aiming at the necessary and sufficient constituents of the phenomenon. Nevertheless empirical phenomenology, which is a return to the existential data, adheres to this procedure in order to exclude the influence of any implicit philosophy and to keep open for scientific control the process of explication on the basis of the prescientific data.

One advantage of this process is that disagreement among judges presents no problem. Independent listing and categorizing may reveal that one judge listed an expression of a subject that was not covered by the other judges; or it may show that one judge was not convinced that a particular expression of a subject was really covered in experience content by the formulation under which it was listed by his colleagues. The solution of the first case is to add the expression overlooked; of the second, to supplement the formulation which was doubted. In empirical phenomenology, the original expression of the subject is preferred, in principle, when an insoluble doubt arises as to whether or not a moment of experience is adequately expressed in analogous formulations.

A disadvantage is that some expressions will seem to express the same experience in overlapping ways. Nevertheless, the researcher will reduce them further only in the later process of scientific explication, so that every scientist reviewing his study may be able to control their elimination. In our case, the readjustment of the established list required the addition of a few original expressions overlooked by one or other of the judges.

With the initial list of expressions and the tentative groupings of different expressions made by the three judges as a first orientation, the author, with two other independent assistants, began the identification and classification into these broad initial classes of each expression in the 365 descriptions. Every original expression, when it represented some moment of experience not covered in the initial list, was added. The expressions were listed on the margins of graph sheets. When the analysis of a certain description yielded an expression closely similar to an expression on the margin, the index number of this description was placed in the next open square of the horizontal row corresponding to the expression listed. Hence the horizontal rows indicated both the number of subjects who used the same or analogous expressions and the index numbers of these subjects who used them. This latter information would be useful later for understanding those expressions which might be in contradiction to the formula that would be applied tentatively to the significant majority of the descriptions as a hypothetical identification of the necessary and sufficient constituents of the phenomenon described. (See "The Six Operations of the Scientific Explication.")

To insure objectivity, this further listing of the expressions in the 365 descriptions was done by three persons, two of them different from the judges who did the initial listing, namely Miss Kylikki Raitasuo, a Finnish student at the Counseling Center of the University of Chicago, Miss Sonia Eberhardt, and the author. New expressions or doubtful expressions were again brought to the attention of the other two judges of the initial listing and resolved in the manner indicated above. A similar procedure was carried out with some descriptions which on the whole did not apply to the question under study. Many subjects described not only the experience of really feeling understood, but also how they felt "when not understood," "when looking for understanding," "when trying to express themselves," and so on. The determination to categorize all data, and the awareness that in these descriptions the experience of really feeling understood might be revealed in negative or indirect ways, impelled us to list these expressions as carefully as the others.

Finally we arrived at a total of 157 different expressions listed under 16 different headings. The scope of this chapter does not make it desirable to publish the tables concerned.

PHENOMENOLOGICAL EXPLICATION OF THE DATA

Having listed the data quantitatively and qualitatively, we may now progress to the other operations of the phenomenological explication already described. The wealth of material could have been a source for a variety of investigations. Therefore the researcher had to be careful to remain faithful to his original objective, "the necessary and sufficient constituents of the experience of really feeling understood." Every operation of the scientific explication had to be performed in the light of this objective alone.

In the operation of further "Reduction," each one of the 157 expressions had to be tested on two dimensions:

1. Does this concrete, colorful formulation by the subject contain a moment of experience that might be a necessary and sufficient constituent of the experience of really feeling understood?

2. If so, it is possible to abstract this moment of experience and to label the abstraction briefly and precisely without violating the formulation presented by the subject?

After testing all the expressions on these two dimensions and ascertaining the moments of experience contained in them which were relevant to his objective, the researcher was able to take a second step. He now tested whether many of these seemingly different expressions really had in common the same relevant moments of experience which had just been discovered in each of them separately, by means of the former procedure.

Next, all expressions discovered in this way, as either direct or indirect representatives of a common relevant moment of experience, were brought together in a cluster. This was labeled with the more abstract formula expressing the moment common to all.

The reduction resulted in nine probably necessary and sufficient constituents, each of them heading a certain number of expressions in which they were originally contained, and each of these expressions accompanied by the percentage of descriptions in which it was present.

Next, the researcher began the final identification of each one of these moments of experience which, so far, were only "hypothetically" identified as necessary and sufficient constituents of the phenomenon of feeling understood. As indicated in the introduction, arriving at this final identification required a trying-out of the hypothetical experience-moment on random samples of cases.

The constituents which were identified in this way as being together necessary and sufficient for the experience under study had to be synthesized into one description, which then identified the total experience of really feeling understood.

RESULTS OF THE PHENOMENOLOGICAL STUDY

In this way, we arrived at the necessary constituents of the experience under study, with the following general operational definition: A necessary constituent of a certain experience is a moment of the experience which, while explicitly or implicitly expressed in the significant majority of explications by a random sample of subjects, is also compatible with those descriptions

324

which do not express it. Nine constituents were finally identified as being together necessary and sufficient for the experience of "really feeling understood." These are condensed in the following table.

Table. Constituents of the Experience of "Really Feeling Understood" as Finally Identified, with Percentages of 365 Subjects Expressing Each Constituent, Explicitly or Implicitly.

Constituents of the Experience of "Really Feeling Understood"	Percentages Expressing the Constituents
Perceiving signs of understanding from a person	87
Perceiving that a person co-experiences what things mean to subject	91
Perceiving that the person accepts the subject	86
Feeling satisfaction	99
Feeling initially relief	93
Feeling initially relief from experiential loneliness	89
Feeling safe in the relationship with the person understanding	91
Feeling safe experiential communion with the person understanding	86
Feeling safe experiential communion with that which the person understanding is perceived to represent	64

The synthetic description of the experience of really feeling understood, containing these constituents, is given below, followed by a justification and explanation of each phrase of the description.

The experience of / "really / feeling understood" / is a perceptual-emotional Gestalt: / A subject, perceiving / that a person / co-experiences / what things mean to the subject / and accepts him, / feels, initially, relief from experiential loneliness, / and, gradually, safe experiential communion / with that person

/ and with that which the subject perceives this person to represent.

The experience of: The term "experience" is preferred to "feeling" because the data show that this phenomenon, commonly called feeling, contains perceptual moments too.

really: The adverb "really" added to "feeling understood" emphasizes the distinction between objective and subjective understanding. The latter includes the "what it means to me" element and the emotional involvement of the subject.

feeling understood: This popular expression is maintained because it is used by most people when they express this experience spontaneously.

is a perceptual-emotional Gestalt: The data compel us to distinguish between perceptions and feelings (emotions), the former being predominantly object-directed, the latter subject-directed. But the perceptions and emotions are interwoven in experience; the term "Gestalt" implies that the distinction we make between perceptual and emotional moments does not correspond to a separation in reality.

A subject, perceiving: The perceptual moment is mentioned first because of its priority in the explications obtained. The feeling of really being understood presupposes the perception of understanding as it is evidenced by various behavioral signs of understanding.

that a person: The subject perceives that a "person," a fellow human being, understands him in a personal way. The understanding person is not experienced only as an official, a teacher, an adult, or so on, but as being-a-person.

co-experiences: The understanding person shares at an emotional level the experiences of the subject understood. The prefix "co-" represents the awareness of the subject that the person understanding still remains another.

what things mean to the subject: The subject perceives that the person understanding experiences the events, situations, and behavior affecting the subject in the way in which they affect him, and not as they might affect others.

and accepts him: Even, while sharing experiences of the subject which the person understanding does not accept personally, he manifests exclusively and consistently genuine interest, care, and basic trust toward the subject, whether or not the subject intends to change his views, feelings, or behavior.

feels, initially, relief from experiential loneliness: The initial feeling of relief is the joyous feeling that experiential loneliness, a disagreeable perceptual-emotional Gestalt, is receding to the degree that real understanding is experienced. The adjective "experiential" specifies that it is not primarily a physical loneliness, but a being-alone in certain psychological experiences.

and, gradually, safe experiential communion: This expresses that the subject gradually experiences that the self is in the relieved, joyful condition of sharing its experience with the person understanding. "Safe" emphasizes that the subject does not feel threatened by the experience of sharing himself.

with that person: The deep personal relationship between the subject and the person understanding is prevalent not only in the perceptual, but also, and still more fundamentally, in the emotional area. Therefore our synthetic description not only opens, but also closes with a reference to this person-to-person relationship.

and with that which the subject perceives this person to represent: When the person understanding typifies for the subject a certain segment of mankind, or perhaps all humans, or all beings, i.e., humanity and nature, or the all-pervading source of being, God, then the subject will experience communion with all those beings which are exemplified for him by the person understanding, and do this to the degree that this person is perceived as their representative.

COMPARISON WITH OTHER APPROACHES

As I have pointed out in an earlier article in the *Journal of Individual Psychology*, phenomenal analysis yields descriptive definitions of certain experiences which people in a given culture or subculture have in common. The experimental psychologist who works with the phenomenal method need not, however, stop here; he may deduce a number of testable hypotheses from the descriptive definition and submit these to experimental test. An example of such a study is that by Ex and Bruyn on the influence of mental set upon perception of identity and substitution. They found that paired subjects who have an intimate relationship with each other tend in their judgment to shift less toward the direction of the deviating judgment of their partner, than paired subjects who do not have such an intimate relationship. From a study such as this it becomes clear that there is no difference whatsoever in the technique of experimentation itself, with its functional-operational-statistical mechanics, as employed in phenomenological and in other psychologies.

Regarding the operations in the phenomenal analysis itself, a certain similarity to the usual analysis of an open-end question in an opinion survey will have been noted. The difference between the two methods is essentially one of objective. The phenomenal analyst restricts himself to one question, carefully aimed at obtaining spontaneous descriptions of subjective experience, and it is formulated so that the subjects are able to relate freely a wide variety of situations. The purpose is to discover the moments common to all individual experiences of the same kind. The survey analyst, on the other hand, typically uses a number of questions, which are formulated so as to obtain the specific reactions of certain populations to definite objects, persons, or events. His purpose is to understand a human experience not as such, but as an indicator of the way in which people are related to certain objects in a certain social environment. From this main difference follow certain differences in analyzing the data, which will not, however, be presented here.

In general, the differences between the phenomenological approach and other approaches lie not so much in the method as in philosophic assumptions, the nature of the hypotheses, the application of the results, and the areas of fundamental concern. While the old introspectionism was based on rationalism, and behaviorism is based on positivism, phenomenal-existential psychology is rooted in an original synthesis of certain tenets of positivism and rationalism, and of phenomenology and existential philosophy. A synthetic system of intelligible constructs, based on philosophical assumptions and tested out gradually, is still in its early phase in phenomenal-existential psychology. It is developing differently from that of other systems insofar as it is mainly concerned with the laws which govern human experience.

In forming hypotheses, phenomenal psychology tends to start from an overall analysis of the human situation in its immediate givenness; whereas introspectionism started from "objects" which were supposed to be inside the mind, isolated from the total existential situation; and behaviorism starts from the external aspects of behavior, isolated from their experiential content. The overall analysis by the phenomenologist of the concrete human situation in its givenness leads to a complex qualitative description of experiences in those situations, as we have seen above, from which further testable hypotheses may be deduced. The older psychologies tend to reduce the givenness of the situation to testable hypotheses much earlier. The result is that their hypotheses appear quite different and—at least in the opinion of the phenomenal psychologist—have less bearing on the concrete condition of human existence.

Regarding the application, the results of phenomenal psychology seem to be of greater use in reaching the deeper layers of common human existence, which is the concern of the present study. To the extent that phenomenal psychology is also and primarily interested in the explication of an experience in its individual givenness, its results are useful in problems of therapy and counseling, interpretation of personality tests, development of personality, creativity, and human relationships. The results of traditional academic psychologies seem to be of greater use in the construction of intelligence and aptitude tests, in problems of sensory perception, human engineering, mechanical learning, and industrial psychology. It is apparent, then, that the results of both kinds of psychology do not exclude but complement each other.

329

CHAPTER ELEVEN

ANTHROPOLOGICAL PSYCHOLOGY AND BEHAVIORISTIC ANIMAL EXPERIMENTATION

The aim of the present chapter is to make clear how the findings of animal experimentation can be integrated within a comprehensive psychology of human behavior. In other words, we shall look at the relevance of animal experimentation from the viewpoint of a comprehensive psychology of man. This does not mean that we deny that such experiments are relevant in many other important ways, even if they are not a contribution to the understanding of human psychology. Neither should the purpose of this chapter be confused with the question of the relevance of phenomenology to experimental psychology.[1]

Since the early part of the present century, experimentation in American psychology has almost exclusively used animals as subjects, and as a consequence many theories of behavior have been

---

[1]At Duquesne University one of my colleagues in experimental psychology, Dr. Amedeo Giorgi, is preparing a book on the relationship between phenomenological psychology and experimentation.

One of my students, Larry V. Pacoe, wrote a dissertation on the topic of this Chapter, which is based on my discussions with him while guiding his dissertation and on the final text of his unpublished M.A. thesis, *Anthropological Psychology and Behavioristic Animal Experimentation*, Duquesne University, June, 1963. The author graciously allowed the use in this Chapter of his final formulations on which we agreed during my guidance of his studies.

constructed on the basis of data collected from the study of subhuman organisms and the subsequent generalization of these findings and theories to human behavior. The entire process, involving experimentation, theory construction, and generalization to human behavior has been done within the behavioristic frame of reference. As we know, behaviorism approaches behavior with the methods of the physical sciences which lead to an interest in only the objectively defined and quantifiable aspects of behavior. The behaviorist aims at the construction of fully quantified theories of behavior, which implies that as he generalizes to human behavior, he is limited to dealing with only those human behaviors which can be quantified and for which he can establish some principle of similarity with the findings of animal behavior. As we have seen in earlier chapters, a comprehensive personality theory attempts to integrate all the substantiated insights of psychology insofar as they are relevant to the understanding of human behavior. Such an absorption of behaviorism's findings is only possible if the data collected by the behaviorist are clearly relevant to the understanding of human behavior.

The data collected by the behaviorist does not initially fulfill this requirement of evident relevance to the understanding of human behavior. Therefore, something further is needed. It is just this later demand with which this chapter is vitally concerned. We shall see that it is the phenomenological approach which eventually enables a comprehensive theory of personality to incorporate in a special way some of the findings of animal experimentation by means of a process of extrapolation which meets the particular needs of anthropological psychology. Our primary concern will be with a presentation and clarification of the principle of similarity as used by the behaviorists. The solution of our problem will be found in a special dimension of similarity, namely whether or not the similarity is seen at the concrete behavioral level or at the level of abstract scientific constructs. Anthropological psychology can only integrate those findings of animal experimentation which show unmistakably a correspondence between the *concrete* behavior of animal and man and not merely a correspondence on the level of abstract theoretical constructs. From our discussion it will become evident that a comprehensive theory of human behavior and the differential psychology of behaviorism require different kinds of data. Therefore, we shall at the end suggest a method of animal experimentation and a process of extrapolation which will be more directly relevant for anthropological psychology.

Most animal experimentation has been influenced by a particular differential theoretical position: behaviorism. The tenets of this differential scientific viewpoint have influenced experimental methodology, problems, selection of data, and the theoretical interpretation and extrapolation of results. To be sure, behavioristic psychology, like any other differential psychology, has differentiated itself into many divergent positions. Nevertheless, all psychologists who approach behavior from this specific differential viewpoint have certain attitudes and approaches in common that enable us to identify a psychologist as a behaviorist and not, for example, as a psychoanalyst or a self psychologist. For our aim, it is sufficient to realize that a behaviorist psychologist persistently attempts to meet the criterion of the physical sciences, that he strives after the complete quantification of all psychological variables in his experiments, and that these aims have led to a situation where the methodology dictates and necessarily limits the areas to be studied. The integrative theorist of human behavior must be aware that the data offered by the behaviorist captures only those aspects of the phenomenon which can be studied by quantitative methods, and that there may be other vitally important aspects of the phenomenon which have been ignored because they were not amenable to the available techniques.

Anthropological psychology focuses on the uniquely human aspects of man's psychological functioning and their physiological and other conditions, as well as those functions which man has in common with animals, such as conditioning. The chief concern of the behaviorist is learning, which is only one aspect of man's behavior, and touches on areas such as emotions, motivation, and anxiety only as variables associated with learning. The other possible approaches that can be taken on these phenomena are developed in other differential psychologies. Up to this point, the procedure is legitimate, but a problem emerges when the differential learning theorist wants to shift to a comprehensive psychology of human behavior and shows an inclination to explain all of human behavior in terms of learning only. Since the behaviorist has used animal experimentation as the basis for his theories, any attempt to explain human behavior must be founded on an extrapolation of animal findings. Extrapolation is defined: "To project by inference into an unexplored situation (some sequent) from observation in an explored field, on the assumption of continuity or correspondence."[2] The behaviorists are extrapolating from an area of animal behavior, which has been thoroughly explored, to the realm of human behavior in which very little experimentation has been done. The validity of this or any method of extrapolation lies on the basis of the assumption of continuity or correspondence between the two areas. In fact, the key to comprehending any method of extrapolation is to understand the principle of similarity that the scientist uses to provide a transition from one area to another.

There are different methods of extrapolation. We shall be concerned here with two main methods of extrapolation, namely, that used by the behaviorists and a method of extrapolation based on the approach of anthropological psychology. We shall compare these two methods of extrapolation on the basis of one dimension of similarity. This dimension is whether the similarity is seen at the concrete behavioral level or at the level of abstract scientific constructs. Similarity at the behavioral level demands that the scientist see correspondence between the concrete behaviors of animal and man. Similarity at the abstract, theoretical, conceptual level, however, demands only that the two behaviors meet the criteria of the scientific concepts, and there is no necessity that the observable behaviors be comparable.

---

[2]*Webster's New Collegiate Dictionary*, Springfield, Mass., G&C Merriam Company, 1960, p. 294.

The key to understanding the behavioristic approach to the study of behavior is to see clearly the behaviorist's attempt to attain objectivity, the hallmark of a natural science. Objectivity in the sense of high intrasubjective and intersubjective reliability could be attained best by using only pointer readings or physical measurements to record data.[3] The insistence on pointer readings implies another aspect of the behavioristic approach to behavior: abstraction.

Any pointer reading, any physical measurement is designed to measure only certain isolated parts of behavior such as a bar press, a change in electrical conductivity of the skin, etc. This means that only certain isolated parts of the total behavior or situation are included in the data. A Skinnerian, for example, is interested only in the bar press responses of the rat, and any other behavior is irrelevant insofar as his data is concerned. Whether the rat attempted to escape, chewed the side of the box, moved rapidly or slowly around the box is not recorded in the data, and consequently does not enter into his theory of behavior. Essentially the scientist is abstracting those aspects of the behavioral situation which fit the available methods of measurement and which are considered relevant by the theoretical system.

The behaviorist imposes the S-R paradigm on all behavior. He is interested in establishing functional relationships between the stimulating situation and the organism's response.[4] In essence, the behaviorist is assuming that all the relevant variables for understanding, predicting, and controlling behavior are implied in the S-R paradigm. Further, he assumes that by abstracting those variables from the total situation, he has the scientific essence of the organism's behavior;[5] he possesses those elemental atoms of behavior which transform the chaos, mystery, and seem-

---

[3]Leo Postman and Edward C. Tolman, "Brunswik's Probabilistic Functionalism," *Psychology: A Study of a Science*, Vol. I, Sigmund Koch, editor (New York: McGraw-Hill Book Company, Inc., 1959), p. 505.

[4]B. F. Skinner, *Science and Human Behavior* (New York: The Macmillan Company, 1953), p. 35.

[5]*Ibid.*

ing spontaneity of behavior into orderliness, clarity, and deter-minedness. This *a priori* S-R paradigm is partially the result of the standpoint that the behaviorist takes in relation to behavior.

In regard to the behavior he is studying, the behaviorist is an external observer who can see only the physical movements of the organism.[6] He sees the rat drink, the pigeon peck, or the human being raise his arm so many degrees. For the behaviorist, a shrug of disgust is simply an unreliable inference of the in-ternal state of the organism, which is behind the behavior and not in it. This fixed viewpoint enables the behaviorist to group the mathematical orderliness of an organism's physically meas-urable behavior, but equally, it blinds him to the expressivity of behavior and to the experiential aspect of behavior.

In summary, the behaviorist's approach to the study of be-havior is an adoption of the natural scientific methodology, in which the cornerstone is objectivity. This demand for objectivity is best met by physical measurement or pointer readings, which necessitate abstracting certain measurable aspects of the situa-tion. These abstracted aspects are chosen *a priori* on the basis of the S-R paradigm, which points to the stimulating situation and the organism's response as the relevant variables which will enable the psychologist to understand, predict, and control be-havior. Finally, in keeping with the traditional approach of the natural sciences, the psychologist takes the stand of an external observer who can see, scientifically speaking, only the external behavior of the organism and record his observations only in terms of physical measurement. It is from a position such as this that Skinner approaches the scientific study of behavior.

Skinner's Approach to Behavior

Skinner describes his approach in terms of a "functional an-alysis which specifies behavior as a dependent variable and proposes to account for it in terms of observable and manipu-lable physical conditions. . . ."[7] He is seeking to establish rela-

---

[6]*Ibid.*, pp. 35-36.
[7]*Ibid.*, p. 41.

tionships between the stimulating situation and behavior and thus to formulate scientific laws. Finally, "a synthesis of these laws expressed in quantitative terms yields a comprehensive picture of the organism as a behaving system."[8] This, in a few words, is Skinner's approach to psychology.

Skinner's method of extrapolation is based on the applicability of his abstract concepts to both animal and human behavior. From his experimentation with animals, Skinner has constructed a number of abstract concepts which he uses to explain behavior. Some of these constructs are operant conditioning, reinforcement, extinction, punishment, reinforcing schedules, etc. Each is defined in very abstract terms, such as reinforcement, which is any condition which tends to increase the probability of the response's occurring in the future.[9] On the basis of this definition, such widely divergent behaviors as a hungry rat eating a pellet and a worker getting incentive pay are considered as reinforcement. Thus, such an abstract definition can be applied to a wide variety of behaviors, regardless of the differences from one another in terms of the concrete, observable behavior. By defining his concepts abstractly in terms of probability and by not referring to the concrete behavior which is the basis of the concept, Skinner has built into his system a principle of similarity between the behaviors of all organisms. If the functional relationship as defined by his concept is the same for any two behaviors, he considers them as being subject to the same laws regardless of the difference between the concrete behaviors. This can be illustrated by returning to the previous example of the hungry rat getting a pellet for pressing a bar and the worker getting incentive pay for producing articles. It is obvious that there is no similarity in the concrete behavior of the rat and the man. However, Skinner sees a similarity in terms of his definition of reinforcement. Just as the food pellet increases the probability of the rat's pressing the bar in the future, the incentive pay increases the probability that the worker will produce

---

[8]*Ibid.*
[9]*Ibid.*, p. 65.

more articles. This similarity is the basis for Skinner's extrapolating the laws of behavior to man which he has created from his animal data.

In *Science and Human Behavior*, Skinner attempts to apply his concepts to such human behavior as self control, thinking, social behavior, group control, and social institutions. Skinner's discussion of self control will illustrate his method of extrapolation. Skinner begins with the assumption that man ". . . . controls himself precisely as he would control the behavior of anyone else—through the manipulation of variables of which behavior is a function."[10]

According to Skinner, an individual controls his behavior when it has both positive and negative results.[11] For example, drinking alcoholic beverages leads to confidence and sociability, which is reinforcing, and thus increases the probability of future drinking. However, a hang-over and irresponsible behavior are negatively reinforcing and have the effect of punishment—suppression of the response. The result is not a compromise between the positive reinforcing and punishment factors in which the person would drink only half as much as usual. Instead "when a similar occasion arises, the same or an increased tendency to drink will prevail, but the occasion as well as the early stages of drinking will generate conditioned adversive stimuli and emotional responses to them which we speak of as shame and guilt. The emotional response may have some deterrent effect in weakening behavior—as by 'spoiling the mood'."[12] More crucial, however, to the issue of self control, is that anything which reduces the drinking behavior is positively reinforced because it decreases the adversive stimuli such as guilt and shame. In Skinner's words, "The organism may make the punished response less probably by altering the variables of which it is a function. Any behavior which succeeds in doing this will automatically be reinforced. We call such behavior self control."[13]

---

[10]*Ibid.*, p. 228.
[11]*Ibid.*, p. 230.
[12]*Ibid.*
[13]*Ibid.*

337

Skinner continues the chapter with a list of the techniques of self control which point to parallels in the control of others. In his survey he enumerates physical restraint and physical aid, changing the stimulus, depriving and satisfying, manipulating emotional conditions, using adversive stimulation, drugs, operant conditioning, punishment, and doing something else.[14]

Skinner is quite aware that his survey does not explain why the individual uses these techniques. He solves this by stating that society is responsible for self control and the individual himself has little ultimate control. All self control can be accounted for by the variables in the environment and the person's history and, according to Skinner, "it is these variables which provide the ultimate control."[15]

One can see from this example of Skinner's extrapolation, that he is lifting his abstract conceptual system, which seems adequate for his animals, and placing it intact, without any modification, upon human behavior.

Skinner's first assumption that a person controls his behavior by manipulating the conditions of which the behavior is a function, is necessary for two reasons. First, in order for him to be able to apply his paradigm, both the dependent and independent variables must be observable; the observable response must be functionally related to an observable physical condition. Secondly, all of Skinner's experiments have followed a paradigm in which the experimenter manipulates the environmental situation and observes the changes in behavior. Consequently, all of his concepts are in the form: if this change is made in the stimulating situation, then the behavior will have such and such characteristics. Therefore, if he is to be able to apply his system of generalizations, he must assume that all human behavior is a function of the stimulating environment.

Also, Skinner's examination of self control illustrates the way that he uses his concept to explain both animal and human behavior. He states that the feeling of confidence which accom-

---

[14]*Ibid.*, pp. 231-240.
[15]*Ibid.*, p. 240.

panies drinking is a positive reinforcement; the confidence increases the probability that drinking will occur in the future.[16] This concept of positive reinforcement was created from such behaviors as a deprived rat's pressing a bar and receiving a pellet of food immediately afterwards. Naturally, Skinner found that the bar press response increased in frequency and that when food no longer followed the bar press, the frequency decreased. From experimental situations such as these, he created his definition of positive reinforcement, which is any stimulating condition which increases the probability of a response's occurring in the future. Skinner's extrapolation is based on the similarity between the rat and man in that they both have identifiable events which increase the probability of a given response's occurring in the future. In essence, Skinner's method of defining his concepts is in terms of the functional relationships between environmental conditions and behavior. It is important to note that there is nothing in his definition which specifies the kind of condition or behavior; he specifies only the relationship between the two variables. Thus, on this basis the bar press response of the rat and its relation to food pellets is equivalent to the drinking behavior and the feeling of confidence in man because the same concepts of behavior apply. Skinner's principle of similarity is the functional relationship between physical conditions and behavior.

One can see that Skinner's principle of similarity is abstract, in the sense that there need be no comparability between the concrete observable behaviors. It is also possible to base extrapolation on a principle of similarity in which the concrete observable behaviors of both the animal and man are comparable. Such a process, based on the phenomenological approach to psychology, may prove to be another fruitful method of seeing the similarities between animal and human behaviors.

While Skinner's method of extrapolation may prove to be productive, the anthropological psychologist is interested in a concrete phenomenological approach to studying behavior that is

---

[16]*Ibid.*, p. 230.

quite different from Skinner's abstract system. In Skinner's system, one is not able to see any comparability in the animal and human behaviors, because they are similar only in terms of the functional relationship between an unspecified stimulus and an unspecified response. Since the anthropological psychologist is interested in concrete situated behavior, another method of extrapolating animal findings to human beings must be proposed. In other words, a method of extrapolation must be found which incorporates the comparability of concrete behaviors. In order to arrive at such a proposal, this chapter initially will be concerned with the requirements of a system of extrapolation that meets the needs of anthropological psychology and phenomenology. Secondly, it will examine past and present work which points to a method of extrapolation consistent with the needs of anthropological psychology. Finally, an outline of a method of establishing similarity between the behavior of animals and man which incorporates the anthropological and phenomenological approach will be proposed.

PHENOMENOLOGY AND EXTRAPOLATION

One of the anthropological psychologist's main requirements for a system of extrapolation is implied in three tenets of phenomenology; namely, that all of man's knowledge is founded in the lived world of immediate experience, that man's knowledge is in the appearances of a thing or process, not behind it, and finally, that all of man's knowledge is perspective. Since these tenets are so closely related, it is practically impossible to show the implications that each has for a principle of similarity, but it is only possible to show the criterion which follows from all three as a unit.

The main requirement of relevance for anthropological psychology is that the principle of similarity in extrapolation must be built on an observable comparability between animal and human behavior. For example, if one is interested in the implications of mother-offspring relations in the monkey for the human mother-child relations, he must be able to establish comparability on the level of observable behavior. In other words, the behavioral interactions between the mother and offspring of both organisms must appear similar to a human observer. One can see that this requirement flows from the first two basic tenets of phenomenology, by the fact that it relies on the experience of a human observer to see the similarity between behaviors, and that it insists that the similarity must be in the observable behavior and not in the abstract scientific constructs.

One can immediately see that this principle of similarity differs from Skinner's in that he is interested in the concrete behavior only insofar as it can be used to establish the dependent and independent variables and the functional relation between them. In fact, the concrete behaviors and the aspects of the situation are defined as relevant on the basis of the scientist's being able to demonstrate a functional relationship between the two. So in Skinner's system there is the priority of the functional relationships between situation and behavior, and the concrete behaviors are of secondary importance. In the phenomenological system of extrapolation, the priority is quite different. The situated behaviors are the central focus and the abstract, conceptual constructs are subservient to the observable behavior. So the anthropological psychologist is seeking animal and human behaviors which appear to be observably comparable, rather than comparable in the abstract, ideal world of the scientific concept. However, this demand for concreteness does not sufficiently describe the principle of similarity, for the question remains: In what relevant dimension of behavior is the anthropological psychologist interested in finding comparable behaviors between animals and man?

Just as Skinner is interested in behavior which is a function of environmental conditions, the anthropological psychologist studies behavior from a particular standpoint. He focuses his attention on intentional behavior, which can be defined tentatively as purpose, or the orientation or directedness of the organism in its behavioral field. This definition can be concretely illustrated by placing a food-deprived rat in a variety of situations in which the food can be reached by various paths. For example, if a rat is placed in an open field situation with a variety of objects scattered throughout the box and food at one end, the rat moves through the box sniffing the different objects, and when he discovers the food, his behavior changes from sniffing to eating; if a relatively short barrier is placed between the rat and the food, he will climb over or go around it. If it is impossible for the rat to get past the barrier, he may attempt to burrow under it or chew through it, and once he is past the barrier he goes straight to the food and eats. The consistency of the rat's movements toward the food, even by long circular routes, indicates the intention or the purpose of the various behaviors.

Most psychologists deny that purpose is a legitimate area of empirical study because it violates the fundamental principle of science which rejects final causes.[17] In this view, all behaviors must be understood in terms of past events in order to fit the causal S-R paradigm. In spite of this widespread and emphatic rejection of purpose as part of behavior, there have been several psychologists who have attempted to develop a concept of purpose which is consistent with empirical psychology. The two outstanding men are E. C. Tolman and D. O. Hebb, who use purpose as an important construct in their systems.

PURPOSE IN TOLMAN AND HEBB

Tolman began writing about purpose as an important construct in 1925. Tolman was in the behavioristic movement from its beginning, and while he strongly believed in the basic behavioristic orientation, his writings were proposing ways of reincorporating many psychological phenomena which had been rejected by behaviorists. He wanted to reinstate purpose, cognition, ideas, and emotion as vital areas in the objective study of behavior.

In his article, *Behaviorism and Purpose*, Tolman proposes that purpose is an observable, objective, and descriptive property of

---

[17]B. F. Skinner, *Science and Human Behavior* (New York; The Macmillan Company, 1953), pp. 87-90.

behavior. Tolman defines purpose as the "persistence until character" of behavior and shows that it is present whenever, in order to adequately describe the behavior, it is necessary to give the behaviors reference objects.[18] For example, trial and error responses in a rat running a maze "are only completely describable as responses which persist until a specific 'end object,' food, is reached."[19] An error is defined as a turn in the maze that will not lead to food, and a correct response is a turn that leads to food; so that the experimenter is defining his variables in terms of purposeful behavior, whether he is aware of it or not. Tolman continues by saying, ". . . . whenever, in merely describing a behavior, it is found necessary to include a statement of something either *toward which* or *from which* the behavior is directed, there we have purpose."[20] One can see that any description of purposeful behavior cannot be a description of the organism's movement without any reference to the environmental situation, but it must communicate the relationship between the behavior and goal objects or situation. Tolman concludes:

> In short, purpose is present, descriptively, whenever a statement of the goal object is necessary to indicate (1) consistency of goal object in spite of variations in adjustment to intervening obstacles, or (2) variations in final direction corresponding to differing positions of the goal object or (3) cessation of activity when a given goal object is entirely removed.[21]

In his article, Tolman has opened a way to identify and describe purposeful behavior in organisms. One can see that Tolman's concept of purposeful behavior is similar to the anthropological psychologist's concept of intentionality. Thus with purpose or intentionality being a practical descriptive property of behav-

---

[18]Edward C. Tolman, "Behaviorism and Purpose," *Behavior and Psychological Man* (Los Angeles: University of California Press, 1961), pp. 33-35.
[19]*Ibid.,* p. 34.
[20]*Ibid.*
[21]*Ibid.,* p. 35.

ior, it opens the possibility of establishing a dimension of similarity between purposeful animal and human behavior. However, before examining the possibilities of such an approach in extrapolation, it is helpful to look briefly at a contemporary psychologist who is using the concept of purpose as an important part of his system.

D. O. Hebb is one of the few psychologists who advocate purpose as a vital aspect of the scientific study of behavior. According to Hebb:

> Behavior is classed as purposive when it shows modifiability with circumstances in such a way as to tend to produce a constant end effect; it is behavior which is free of sensory dominance, controlled jointly by the present sensory input and by the expectancy of producing the effect which is its goal. When the situation changes, the behavior changes accordingly.[22]

An example of this definition is the traditional situation in which a monkey has to get food suspended out of his reach. If boxes are available, he will pile them on top of one another to reach the food. If the boxes are absent, he may put the poles together to knock the food down. If neither the box nor pole is available, the monkey may pull the experimenter near the food and climb him to reach it. The chimp performs a wide variety of behaviors, all with the same result: obtaining the food.[23]

Both Tolman and Hebb affirm purpose as a legitimate descriptive property of behavior. The important aspect is that purpose can be determined from observation. Hebb points out one practical aspect of observation: "In principle, a number of examples of a given kind of behavior have to be observed before we can conclude that purpose is involved, since it is only in this way that we can demonstrate that the behavior adjusts itself to circumstance. In practice, however, one may know enough about the species—or about a particular animal—to be able to identify

---

[22]Donald O. Hebb, *A Textbook of Psychology* (Philadelphia: W. B. Saunders Company, 1958), p. 206.
[23]*Ibid.*

purpose in a single trial."[24] With the insights of Tolman and Hebb, it is becoming evident that a comparability of human and animal behavior along the dimension of purpose or intentionality is a possible basis for a principle of similarity.

It has been shown previously that anthropological psychology is centrally focused on intentional or purposeful behavior, and that any extrapolation based on phenomenology must have a principle of similarity which insists that the comparability of behavior must be evident on the concrete observable level and readily apparent to a human observer. Tolman's and Hebb's development of purpose as an observable, identifiable, and descriptive property of behavior has opened the possibility of establishing intentionality or purpose as a dimension of extrapolation which meets the requirements of phenomenology. Consequently, it is now possible to discuss more concretely some of the issues of such an extrapolating process.

A PHENOMENOLOGICAL APPROACH TO EXTRAPOLATION

In many ways a phenomenological approach to behavior is similar to naturalistic observation because both are a description of an event or process. While naturalistic observation implies reporting a unique, natural situation, the phenomenological observer is interested in repeatable events as well as unique ones. The phenomenological observer is mainly interested in discriminating the relevant and fundamental structural aspects of a situation. In order to accomplish this task, it is often necessary for him to observe a situation repeatedly and to create a formal category system which describes and records the purposeful behavior of the organism. This category system is the key to any formal scientific observation, and an examination of its properties and purpose will give insight into the concept and process of phenomenal similarity.

The category system is essentially a delineation of the observer's experience of a behavioral situation. As he begins to dif-

---

[24]*Ibid.*

ferentiate the relevant aspects of the situation, he can attempt to formally describe the behaviors as distinguishable behavioral units. Once he has the category system, he can then record the frequency and sequence of the behaviors in which he is interested.

In keeping with the demands of phenomenology, the category system must be constructed of descriptive language rather than inferential language. The categories must represent what appears to the observer, not what is inferred about the organism. For example, one can observe a young child being afraid of his father, but he cannot observe and describe the Oedipus complex because it is an inferential and conceptual system to explain the child's fear. Since anthropological psychology is interested in intentional behavior, the category system will focus on describing purposeful behavior of the organisms.

Tolman states that if it is necessary to refer to the objects toward which and from which an organism is moving, then the behavior is purposeful.[25] This statement points to the relevant aspect of a situation which must be referred to in order to adequately describe the purpose of an organism. One cannot describe the organism as if it were totally isolated from a situation, but the behavior must be described in reference to the goal objects in the environment. In other words, the behavior must describe the organism's movements toward or away from the significant objects in the environment. Also, the quality of the movement must be included—whether the behavior is fearful, cautious, etc.—because the quality of behavior often indicates a vital aspect of the purpose of the organism's movements.

Since the aim of this process is to establish a comparability between certain areas of human and animal behavior, the category system must be designed to reveal any existing similarity. In other words, the behavioral category systems used for both sets of behavior must have an almost point-to-point or category-to-category correspondence. For every class of animal behavior there should be a comparable class of human behavior, because

---

[25]Tolman, *loc. cit.*

such a system not only reflects the similarity the observer sees and incorporates into the categories, but it permits the possibility of comparing both frequency and patterning of human and animal behaviors. It is evident that a demand for a close relationship between the descriptive categories narrows the range of animals which can be used.

The animals which seem most likely to fit the demands of the category system are the primates. Not only is their anatomy most similar to man's which opens up the possibility of comparable behaviors, but also the association areas in the brain are proportionally closest to man's.[26] So while the range of possible animals is severely limited, the closeness of the primates and man increases the probability that the animal studies can make a contribution to the psychologist's understanding of human behavior.

While what has been presented is speculative, it points to the possibilities for establishing empirical dimensions of similarity between human and animal behavior. Our example has concentrated on purposeful behavior because it is of special interest to the anthropological psychologist, but it is also possible to establish emotional and cognitive dimensions of similarity as well as many other behavior patterns that are common to animals and man. Such an approach is particularly useful to anthropological psychology because it finds the similarity on the concrete behavioral level rather than the level of scientific abstraction. This is a useful approach because, as phenomenology has pointed out, the basis of all our knowledge, even our scientific knowledge, is in our experience of the way things appear to a human being. Consequently, the construction of the categories of behaviors is based on the relevant discriminations of a human observer, rather than on the basis of measurability. The categories are designed to capture the purposeful behavior of the organism by describing the relationship of the behavior

---

[26]Ester Milner, "Differing Observational Perspectives as a Barrier to Communication among Behavioral Scientists," *Review of Existential Psychology and Psychiatry*, Adrian van Kaam, editor (Pittsburgh: Duquesne University Press, Fall, 1962), p. 251.

to the goal objects in the situation. And finally, both the comparability of the descriptive behaviors and their patterns of occurrence point to the similarity of behaving.

The logical question is that once the similarity has been established, then how can the animal findings aid the scientist in understanding human behavior? The next section will outline the possible ways of applying the animal data to human behavior.

THE APPLICATION OF ANIMAL FINDINGS TO HUMAN BEHAVIOR

A most important consideration for the science of psychology in general is the manner in which the findings of animal experimentation are subsequently related to the study of human behavior. It is possible, for example, to attempt to use the findings to *explain* human behavior in the manner of B. F. Skinner's method of extrapolation. Or it is possible to use the animal findings to stimulate thinking in certain areas of behavior which man and animal might share as possible behaviors-in-common— to consider what may be learned from the results of animal experimentations which may have implications for broadening the scope of possible ways of understanding human behavior. It is in the latter spirit that the anthropological psychologist approaches the findings of animal experimentation.

SKINNER'S APPROACH TO APPLICATION OF ANIMAL FINDINGS TO HUMAN BEHAVIOR

Skinner's method of applying animal findings to human beings can be described briefly as an attempt to explain human behavior parsimoniously. Consistent with the methods of the natural sciences, he is attempting to explain the variety and complexity of human behavior with as small a number of concepts as possible. For example, he attempts to explain self control when drinking alcoholic beverages in terms of concepts like positive reinforcement and punishment.[27] Positive reinforcement,

---

[27] B. F. Skinner, *Science and Human Behavior* (New York: The Macmillan Company, 1953), p. 230.

in the sense of confidence, tends to increase the frequency and amount of drinking; while punishment, in terms of the possibility of irresponsible behavior, tends to suppress the drinking response. Furthermore, anything which tends to reduce the adversive stimulation of the guilt or shame associated with drinking is reinforced and, consequently, since less drinking reduces guilt and shame, it is reinforced. This reinforced decrease in drinking is what Skinner calls self control.[28] In this example, Skinner attempts to explain an already observed phenomenon in terms of positive reinforcement, punishment, and negative reinforcement. He is taking a complex event and reducing it to a limited number of concepts which he establishes on the basis of animal experimentation. Skinner is explaining behavior because he is focusing on an already observed behavior and attempting to apply his concepts to the situation in order to understand it in terms of a functional analysis. While this is what Skinner does, there is also another consideration which is important for understanding his extrapolation of animal to human behavior: his attitudes toward the validity of his applications.

Skinner's attitude toward the validity of his application of animal findings to human behavior is ambiguous because of discrepancies in his writings. In some of his statements he seems to be cautious and consistent with the empirical and tentative character of science. This attitude is epitomized in the following quotation in which he is discussing the availability of extensive animal research to be applied to human behavior:

> The use of this material often meets with the objections that there is an essential gap between man and the other animals, and that the results of one cannot be extrapolated to the other. To insist upon this discontinuity at the beginning of a scientific investigation is to beg the question. Human behavior is distinguished by its complexity, its variety, and its greater accomplishments, but the basic processes are not therefore necessarily different. Science advances from the simple to the complex; it is constantly concerned with whether the processes and laws discovered at one stage are adequate for the next. It would be rash to assert at this point

---

[28]*Ibid.*

that there is no essential difference between human behavior and the behavior of lower species; but until an attempt has been made to deal with both in the same terms, it would be equally rash to assert that there is.[29]

The tentative quality of Skinner's attitude makes it a scientifically sound statement that most psychologists could agree with. However, Skinner makes other statements which implicitly contradict this attitude.

An example of Skinner's contradiction is contained in his discussion of self control. He explains self control in terms of a person controlling his behavior by manipulating the external stimuli of which behavior is a function. In other words, the person knows which environmental stimuli elicit a particular response; so he manipulates the situation so that the appropriate stimulus is presented which elicits the desired response. In concluding his chapter, Skinner states that his view is in conflict with the traditional concept of self control and personal responsibility. In this context he makes the following statement:

> It must be remembered that formulae expressed in terms of personal responsibility underlie many of our present techniques of control and cannot be abruptly dropped. To arrange a smooth transition is in itself a major problem. But the point has been reached where a sweeping revision of the concept of responsibility is required, not only in a theoretical analysis of behavior, but in the practical consequences as well.[30]

Skinner is implying that social institutions such as government and religion should be modified so that they can incorporate theoretical and practical attitudes which are consistent with Skinner's analysis of behavior. In the initial quote, Skinner says he is attempting to discover whether animal findings and his approach are adequate for human behavior; yet, in the latter quote he seems to assume that his approach is not only adequate, but true, to the extent that he proposes changing social institu-

---

[29]*Ibid.*, p. 38.
[30]*Ibid.*, p. 241.

tions to see behavior in terms of his analysis. Thus, it would seem that Skinner believes his extrapolation of constructs to human behavior to be valid, even though its validity has not been demonstrated. In contrast to Skinner's systems and attitudes in regard to the application of animal findings to human beings is anthropological psychology, which uses animal findings to clarify human behavior by pointing to relevant issues and implicit assumptions.

ANTHROPOLOGICAL PSYCHOLOGY'S APPLICATION OF ANIMAL FINDINGS TO HUMAN BEHAVIOR

In applying animal experimentation to man's psychological existence, anthropological psychology follows the lead of D. O. Hebb, who uses animal experiments to illuminate human behavior, rather than to explain human behavior.[31] Hebb's most basic principle is that animal experiments do not prove anything about human behavior. Instead, they may serve as a 'pointing to' which enables the psychologist to focus on facets of human behavior which he would not have noticed without the aid of animal experimentation. Secondly, animal experiments may point to assumptions that the psychologist has not made explicit. And finally, animal experimentations may suggest a new principle of human behavior.[32] These three ways of applying animal experimentation to the human situation summarize the possible ways that anthropological psychology hopes to use animal experimentation in constructing a theory of human behavior.

The first contribution of animal experimentation—drawing attention to important areas of human psychological functioning which previously have not been noticed—can be illustrated by Harlow's study of affection in baby monkeys.[33] He studied the

---

[31]Donald O. Hebb and W. R. Thompson, "The Social Significance of Animal Studies," *Handbook of Social Psychology*, Gardner Linzey, editor (Cambridge, Mass.: Addison-Wesley Publishing Company, Inc., 1954), p. 533.

[32]*Ibid.*

[33]Harry F. Harlow, "The Nature of Love," *The American Psychologist*, XIII (December, 1958), pp. 673-685.

variable of comfort contact or tactility in the relationship between the young monkey and mother surrogates. There were two types of mother surrogates: one made of terry cloth and the other made of wire. The mother surrogates were constructed to supply the monkeys with milk, and as soon as they were strong enough, all of the baby monkeys' food came from one of the mother surrogates. In the initial experiment, the monkeys had free access to both types of mother surrogates, but half of the population was fed solely by the wire mother and the other half was fed only by the cloth mother. However, all of the monkeys were almost exclusively with the terry cloth mothers. This was true of the monkeys who were fed by the wire mother surrogates as well.[34] Thus, it was demonstrated that physiological satisfaction may not play as important a role in the baby monkey's attachment for the mother as previously speculated. Further, the experiment has shown that comfort contact is an important variable in the baby monkey's attachment to its mother. While this experiment *proves nothing* about the role of comfort contact in the relationship between human babies and mothers, it does *suggest* this as a possible relevant variable which should be investigated on the human level. One can see from this illustration that animal experiments can bring into figure areas of human behavior which previously were ground.

Hebb has demonstrated that animal experiments can reveal implicit assumptions that the psychologist has made about man's psychological functioning.[35] A review of the literature concerning the relation of environment and heredity to the development of intelligence reveals confusion and contradiction. This, according to Hebb, stems from an implicit assumption concerning human learning. In other words, psychologists have been assuming something about human learning which they have never made explicit. They have concluded that if special experiences do not affect a child's intelligence at the age of seven or twelve, then

---

[34]*Ibid*, pp. 675-676.
[35]Hebb, *loc. cit.*

special experiences do not affect intelligence at any time in a child's life. Implicit in this reasoning is the assumption that the learning process and the generality of transfer learning is the same for all ages. However, this assumption is brought to light and challenged by animal experiments which indicate that in the rat early experiences have widespread and long-lasting influences on behavior. While the rat experimentation proves nothing about human behavior, it does help the psychologist to see clearly the assumptions that he has made about human behavior.[36]

Besides pointing to implicit assumptions, animal experiments can also suggest new principles for understanding human behavior.[37] Perhaps the most obvious example of a principle which has been established on a basis of animal experiments and then applied to human behavior is the principle of conditioning. While there is wide disagreement on the range of human functioning to which conditioning properly applies, it would be very difficult to construct a valid theory of human behavior which did not contain some construct comparable to conditioning. For example, Dollard and Miller[38] constructed a theory of behavior which is built entirely on the process of conditioning, while the anthropological psychologist is attempting to integrate conditioning into a theory of total human psychological functioning. Despite the disagreement concerning the range of application of conditioning as a principle of learning, it is making a valuable contribution to understanding human behavior. The three possible ways of using animal findings just illustrated demonstrate the variety of applications to human behavior. Underlying each application is the principle of similarity that the psychologist uses to make a transition from animals to man.

---

[36]*Ibid.*

[37]*Ibid.*

[38]J. Dollard and N. E. Miller, *Personality and Psychotherapy: An Analysis in Terms of Learning, Thinking, and Culture* (New York: McGraw-Hill Book Company, Inc., 1950), *passim*.

CONCLUSION

Two different methods of extrapolation have been compared according to the different principles of similarity. Skinner's method is basically an abstract conceptual similarity which focuses on the functional relationship between the stimulating situation and the organism's response. Contrary to the method most useful to the anthropological psychologist, Skinner is not interested in the similarity of concrete behavior. The needs of the anthropological psychologist are best met by a method of extrapolation which focuses on the comparability of concrete behaviors. Further, since anthropological psychology is interested in intentional behavior, the behavior of the animal and man must be comparable in their purposeful relations to goal objects. Also, it should be noted that while the method of comparing purposeful behavior was presented as a formal system, it is not always necessary to generate formal category systems with a category-to-category correspondence. Generally, a formal system is required only when one plans a long involved research project on animals to illuminate some aspect of human behavior. In many cases of extrapolation, where the psychologist is attempting to use animal experiments which already have been done, only an informal, intuitive comparability of the animal and human behaviors is required. However, to avoid confusion, the psychologist should be aware of the principle of similarity he is using.

There are more principles of similarity than the two discussed in this chapter. In fact, they represent two extreme points on a continuum, with one emphasizing the abstract conceptual similarity and the other, the concrete behavioral similarity. No one. of these methods can be thought of as absolutely better than any other. Each serves a different function in a particular theoretical system. If one is seeking to explain human behavior in a minimal number of abstract scientific terms which apply to all organisms, then Skinner's method is most appropriate. However, if one is attempting to understand concrete, situated, intentional behavior, then the proposed method of anthropological psychology best meets this need. Thus, the goal of the psychologist doing the extrapolation determines the adequacy of any particular method.

And finally, the criterion for evaluating the validity of any single extrapolation must be stated in terms of the goal of psychology: the clarification and understanding of human behavior.[39] If the extrapolation clarifies some small area of human behavior, then it is relevant. However, if a psychologist is attempting to extrapolate a whole theory of behavior, then a further question must be asked: Does it adequately account for all relevant behavior? Since animal behavior lacks the range and amplitude of man's functioning in such areas as language and association, the answer is usually negative. This limitation does not negate extrapolation, because it has been demonstrated that animal studies can contribute to the psychologist's understanding of human psychological existence.

---

[39]Hebb, *loc. cit.*

CHAPTER TWELVE

EXISTENTIAL AND HUMANISTIC PSYCHOLOGY

A clarification of the relationships of existential and humanistic psychology demands first of all a discussion of the function of implicit views of life in the development of science, art, and culture. We shall then consider more specifically the existential image of man in its relation to existential and humanistic psychology. Finally, the introduction of the concept of anthropological psychology is relevant to the understanding of our discussion.

An at least implicit view of human nature continually directs man's social and personal endeavors. Initially, such a view influences cultural development pre-reflectively; we "live" the anthropological orientation that is ours without thinking about its structure and its subtle, continual influence. Nevertheless, this submerged evidence of life is a decisive power in the dynamic evolvement of our culture, of religion, science, art, and education. The intimate structure of this guiding image of man alters in the course of human history, which is a story of humanization despite prolonged periods of regression and decline. All progress in humanization presupposes the enlightenment of man, first in certain areas of life, then in the global view of reality. We realize, therefore, that new insights in the arts and sciences gradually lead to striking transformations in the outlook of man and concomitantly in the pattern of his culture. The partial light of each one of these areas of insight does not alter our view of man significantly, for each of them is too specialized to effect a metamorphosis of the fundamental light that orients the unfolding of man's civilization. Many innovations in the limited areas of cultural specialization, however, carry implications for the wisdom of living; these implications—far transcending their limited fields of origin—filter down into the pre-reflective realm of consciousness where they collide and fuse, erode former convictions, and insert a new awareness that leads to a rebirth of central vision. We live such a new image in attitude and action before we know it rationally. Sooner or later, however, we feel compelled to reflect on it, to make it explicit so that we may know what propels us so powerfully, to scrutinize it critically, and to utilize it as a principle of renewal within various reflective fields of thought and performance. In this attempt we are not alone, for a similar transformation of vision emerges simultaneously all over the globe in sensitive men who participate in the evolution that marks the historic period in which we live.

When a pre-reflective view of man's nature has been raised to the level of reflective thought and action, it tends to give rise to a corresponding humanism or a project of improvement of the human condition in the light of the newly explicated vision. This innate humanistic tendency explains the appearance of successive humanisms such as positivistic, atheistic, Christian, Marxist, romantic, technical, rationalistic, and behavioristic humanisms. Each newly emerging humanism may find a reverberation in a corresponding humanistic psychology which studies certain psychological aspects of man as relevant in the light of the parallel humanistic movement and of the specific view of man from which the latter emerged.

If the history of humanization is nourished by an implicit vision of man, we may ask ourselves which view orients contemporary humanization? It is not simple to answer this question, since various visions are simultaneously present in a society which is fluid and pluralistic. The purpose of the present chapter limits us to the consideration of one contemporary view of man emerging in this century: the existential vision. We are concerned here not with a philosophical or psychological view of man, but with a "lived" pre-philosophical and pre-psychological image which can be explicated in a psychological, philosophical, theological, sociological, or any other reflective direction. As a corollary of contemporary development, an existential image of man seems to be present in sensitive people of almost all Western nations, cultures, and religions, and in the representatives of the most diverse professions and disciplines. We are already moving beyond this stage of the unknown "lived" image that emerged almost unnoticed as a result of the forces of evolution. We can already find reflective expressions and elaborations of this implicit view in many arts and sciences, one of which is the science of psychology. When we study these various expressions, we realize at once that each specific mode of knowledge makes explicit only that aspect of the implicit contemporary image of man that is relevant to the specificity of the mode of knowledge concerned. For example, philosophy may make explicit the ontological, whereas psychology would stress the psychological aspect of such an implicit view. Moreover, each art or science re-evaluates in a unique way its own structure, methodology, content, applications, and problems in the light of this explicated aspect of the contemporary image of man. In the elaboration of the explicated aspect, the art or science concerned increasingly transcends and expands this initial explication by means of its own traditions and methods of exploration, experimentation, and theory construction. An existential psychology, for example, should be fundamentally different in these respects from existential physics, philosophy, sociology, or physiology.

We may ask why it is that the various explications of aspects of the existential image are fundamentally distinct. These elaborations are different because of the uniqueness of the aspect on which each one of them concentrates, and because of the basic difference of methodology by means of which each of them explores its unique perspective and incorporates it within the traditional dialogue of its own field of competence. In spite of these differences, some restricted dialogue and mutual enrichment is possible among, for example, existential physiology, philosophy, psychology, and physics. The different aspects which each one of these disciplines develops in its own way are rooted in the same image of man. Moreover, a variety of developments of the same original vision is possible even within one discipline concerned with one specific aspect of the pre-reflective image. This diversity of development is especially observable in philosophy, where the explication and elaboration of the same philosophical aspect can lead to diverse developments in accordance with the personal or cultural orientation of the philosopher concerned. No existential philosophy, therefore, can set itself up as "the" authoritative explication of the contemporary existential image of man. Each existential philosophy is a different *philosophical* explication of this pre-philosophical image. Each one of these philosophical explications is influenced by the cultural or personal orientation of the philosopher concerned.

Consequently, existential psychology should never be a simplistic application of any specific existential philosophy. Existential psychology is a unique explication and elaboration of the psychologically relevant aspects of the implicit existential image of man, just as theoretical physics is a unique assimilation of the dimensions that are relevant to physics.

As soon as psychology has discovered and totally assimilated this relevant aspect—partly by means of existential psychology —the prefix *existential* should be dropped, for psychology as such will then be existential, which simply means that psychology will have assimilated this relevant perspective and will be in tune with the latest phase of the evolution of human insight. After this assimilation, psychology will again await its further fundamental enrichment by its assimilation of the next development of our view of man, which will emerge as a result of the next phase of the human evolution. Physics, being an earlier established science, has already gone through the phase of assimilation of contemporary insight. Theoretical physics has already assimilated the insights implied in the existential view, for example, that of perspectivity. Gradually, the field of physics adopted this view under the influence of theoretical physics.

Therefore, the prefix *existential* would now be superfluous in this field. We may add that assimilation is a two-way process in which both the assimilating field and the assimilated aspect are progressively transformed.

Existential psychology is thus a temporary attempt to assimilate into the science of psychology those aspects of the contemporary existential image of man which are directly relevant for the evolvement of empirical, clinical, and theoretical psychology. This movement of reconstruction by assimilation will tend to become superfluous as soon as psychology has fundamentally restructured, deepened, and expanded itself by the integration of insights which have recently emerged in Western humanity as an inescapable result of its cultural and historical evolution.

Evidently, such a new impetus in psychology may give rise to a new type of humanistic psychology, namely an existential humanistic psychology which is fundamentally different from a rationalistic or a behavioristic humanistic psychology, related respectively to the humanism of the eighteenth century enlightenment and nineteenth century scientism. This fundamental difference does not imply that an existential humanistic psychology discards the contributions made by a rationalistic and a behavioristic humanism. On the contrary, existential psychology fosters respect for these contributions insofar as they remain relevant within the light of contemporary insight. Existential psychology is a leaven of positive reconstruction which gives rise to re-evaluation, not elimination of positions of prevalence among the theories, methods, and data with which the field of psychology was enriched in the past as a result of implicit or explicit former views of man and reality. A humanistic psychology which is existential will share in this respectful attitude of the movement of reconstruction from which it sprang.

A discussion of the meaning of anthropological psychology is relevant here. In current usage, the meaning of "anthropology" is restricted to "the science of man in relation to physical character, origin, and distribution—or races, environmental and social relations, and culture." (*Webster's New Collegiate Dictionary,* Springfield, Mass., G and C Merriam Company, 1960, p. 38.) This restriction of the term "anthropology" stresses only one of the three main dimenions of "anthropos" or man, namely the cultural-social one. Etymologically, the term "anthropology" does not have this restricted meaning, for it is derived from the Greek words *anthropos,* which means man, and *logos,* which means word or science. Therefore, every concept, construct, word, or science which refers to man as a whole may be properly called anthropological. Man in his entirety, however, appears to us under many aspects. For example, we may perceive man insofar as he appears physically, racially, socially, or culturally. In the latter case, we speak of cultural anthropology. We also perceive man in the light of other sciences or disciplines, such as medicine, history, sociology, philosophy, or theology. In these cases, we may rightly speak of a medical, historical, social, philosophical, or theological anthropology. The psychologist too may study man insofar as he appears in the entirety of his behavior. Such a study may be called anthropological psychology.

It presupposes, however, the development of many differential psychologies through the gradual uncovering of different abstracted aspects of behavior by observation and experimentation. Consequently, an anthropological psychology is possible only after this differential revelation. The main method of such a psychology is the dialectical integration of the results of these differential approaches. In other words, anthropological psychology is a comprehensive theoretical psychology which studies *human* behavior. This concern with human behavior does not mean that it neglects the insights gained by the study of animal behavior. On the contrary, the contributions of animal psychology are integrated within anthropological psychology insofar as they shed light on certain aspects of human behavior which are similar to those of the behavior of animals. Anthropological psychology thus integrates the insights and data of the various empirical, clinical, and theoretical psychologies within a theory of man that is linked to one or the other implicit image of man such as the positivistic, rationalistic, behavioristic, or existential image. We find the counterpart of anthropological psychology in other fields of learning related to man, such as the anthropological physiology developed by Frederick Buytendijk, and the anthropological medicine developed by V. von Weisacker.

Humanistic and anthropological psychology are both interested in man. The interest of anthropological psychology is primarily academic, scientific-theoretical, while that of a humanistic psychology—in the tradition of the great humanisms—is primarily the improvement of the human condition by means of concrete psychological research. Anthropological psychology can be relevant to humanistic psychology insofar as its integrative comprehensive knowledge of the psychology of man can be used by the humanistic psychologist for the promotion of his humanistic aims; it may even suggest to him certain types of research to be done in order to close the gaps in our theoretical knowledge which prevent us from fostering the humanization of man in certain areas of his psychological development.

We are now ready to formulate a few tentative definitions which may elucidate our discussion.

Psychology: The science of behavior. (The meaning of the term "behavior" in this definition will differ according to the implicit view of man that at a certain moment of the history of humanization dominates culture and science. From an existential viewpoint, for example, behavior that is the object of psychology is always intentional and purposive.)

Existential Psychology: A temporary movement towards fundamental reconstruction of scientific psychology by means of the assimilation of the psychologically relevant insights implicit in the pre-philosophical contemporary view of man that is called existential.

Humanistic Psychology: A lasting movement concerned with the improvement of conditions of the humanization of man by means of psychological research in the light of one or the other view of man.

Existential Humanistic Psychology: A humanistic psychology that operates in the light of the existential image of man.

Anthropological Psychology: A scientific-theoretical movement within psychology that integrates empirical, clinical, and theoretical psychologies within an open theory of personality that serves as a comprehensive frame of reference for all the significant theories and data in the field.

Existential Anthropological Psychology: An anthropological psychology that roots its comprehensive frame of reference in the existential image of man.

BIBLIOGRAPHY

Allport, Gordon W. "The Psychology of Participation," *Psychological Review,* 53, 1945, 117-132.

Becoming. New Haven: Yale University, 1955.

Personality and Social Encounter. Boston: Beacon Press, 1960.

Pattern and Growth in Personality. New York: Holt, Rinehart and Winston, 1961.

Angyall, A. *Foundations for a Science of Personality.* New York: Commonwealth Fund, 1941.

"A Theoretical Model for Personality Studies," *J. Pers.,* 20, 1951, 131-142.

Argyle, Michael. *The Scientific Study of Social Behavior.* London: Methuen and Company, Ltd., 1957.

Arnold, Magda. *Emotion and Personality.* 2 vols. New York: Basic Books, Inc., 1961.

Arnold, Magda and Gasson, J. *The Human Person.* New York: Ronald Press, 1954.

Barnett, H. G. *Innovation: The Basis of Cultural Change.* New York: McGraw-Hill Book Co., Inc., 1965.

Barral, Mary Rose. *Merleau-Ponty: The Role of the Body Subject in Interpersonal Relations.* Pittsburgh: Duquesne University Press, 1965.

Bergmann, Gustav and Spence, Kenneth W. "Operationism and Theory Construction," *Psychological Theory.* Melvin H. Marx, ed. New York: The Macmillan Company, 1951.

Bergson, Henri. *The Creative Mind,* trans. Mabelle L. Anderson. New York: The Philosophical Library, Inc., 1946.

Bertalanffy, Ludwig von. *Problems of Life*. New York: Harper and Brothers, 1952.

Bevan, William. *Scientific Woozle Hunters? An Opinion in Outline*. Kopenhagen: Einar Munksgaards Forlag, 1953.

Binswanger, L. *Grundformen und Erkenntnis menschlichen Daseins*. Zurich: Max Niehans, 1942.

Trans. Jacob Needleman, *Being-in-the-World*. New York: Basic Books Inc., 1963.

Boas, George. *Dominant Themes of Modern Philosophy*. New York: The Ronald Press Company, 1957.

Boelen, Bernard J. "Philosophical Orientation," (pamphlet). Pittsburgh: Duquesne University, 1958.

Boring, Edwin G. "A History of Introspection," *Psychological Bulletin*, 50, 1953, 169-189.

A History of Experimental Psychology. Second Edition. New York: Charles Scribner's Sons, 1958.

Brentano, F. *Psychologie vom empirischen Standpunkte*. Leipzig: Duncker and Humblot, 1847.

Brown, Clarence W. and Ghiselli, Edwin E. *Scientific Method in Psychology*. New York: McGraw-Hill Book Co., Inc., 1955.

Buber, Martin. *I and Thou*, trans. Ronald Gregor Smith. New York: Charles Schribner's and Sons, 1958.

Buytendijk, F.J.J. "The Phenomenological Approach to the Problem of Feelings and Emotions," *Feeling and Emotions*. The Mooseheart Symposium in cooperation with the University of Chicago. New York, Toronto, London: McGraw-Hill Book Co., Inc., 1950.

De Vrouw. Haar Verschijning, Natuur en Bestaan. Utrecht, Holland: Spectrum, 1951.

Phénoménologie de la rencontre. Paris: Desclée de Brouwer, 1952.

La Femme. Bruges: Editions Desclee de Brouwer, 1954.

Cohen, Morris R. and Nagel, Ernest. *An Introduction to Logic and Scientific Method*. New York: Harcourt, Brace and Co., 1934.

David, Henry P., and von Bracken, Helmut. *Perspectives in Personality Theory.* New York: Basic Books, Inc., 1957.

Descartes, R. *Discourse on Method,* trans. Laurence J. Lafleur. New York: The Liberal Arts Press, 1956.

Meditations, trans. Laurence J. Lafleur. New York: The Liberal Arts Press, 1951.

Oeuvres de Descartes. Leopold Cert (ed.). Paris: Charles Adam & Paul Tanner, 1897.

De Waelhens, A. *Une philosophie de l'ambiguité. L'Existentialisme de Maurice Merleau-Ponty.* Louvain: Publs. Universitaires de Louvain, 1957.

Dollard, J. and Miller, N.E. *Personality and Psychotherapy: An Analysis in Terms of Learning, and Culture.* New York: The McGraw-Hill Book Co., Inc., 1950.

Dondeyne, Albert. *Contemporary European Thought and Christian Faith,* trans. Ernan McMullin and John Burnheim. Pittsburgh: Duquesne University Press, 1958.

Farber, Leslie H. "Despair and the Life of Suicide," *Review of Existential Psych. & Psychiatry,* Vol. II, (Feb., 1962), 125.

Farber, M. *The Foundations of Phenomenology.* Cambridge, Massachusetts: Harvard University Press, 1943.

"The Function of Phenomenological Analysis." *Phil. and Phenom. Res.* I (1941), 431-441.

Phenomenology as a Method and as a Philosophical Discipline. Buffalo, New York: University of Buffalo Press, 1928.

Feigl, Herbert. "Philosophical Embarrassments of Psychology," *The American Psychologist,* XIV (March, 1959), 115-128.

Fingarette, H. *The Self in Transformation,* Harper Torchbooks (New York, 1965).

Frankl, Viktor E. *The Doctor and the Soul: An Introduction to Logotherapy,* trans. Richard and Clara Winston. New York: Alfred A. Knopf, 1955.

From Death-Camp to Existentialism: A Psychiatrist's Path to a New Therapy, trans. Ilse Lasch. Boston: Beacon Press, 1959.

Frings, M. S. *Max Scheler.* Pittsburgh: Duquesne University Press, 1965.

Gatch, Vera Mildred and Maurice Kahn Temerlin, "The Belief in Psychic Determinism and Behavior of Psychotherapist," *Review of Existential Psychology and Psychiatry,* V (Winter, 1965).

Gendlin, E. T. "Need for a New Type of Concept," *Review of Existential Psychology and Psychiatry,* II, 37.

Goldstein, Kurt. *Human Nature in the Light of Psychopathology.* Cambridge: Harvard University Press, 1947.
The Organism. Boston: Beacon Press, 1963.

Gruhle, Hans W. *Verstehende Psychologie. Erlebnislehre.* Stuttgart: Georg Thieme Verlag, 1956.

Guillaume, P. *Psychologie.* Paris: Presses Universitaires de France, 1943.

Gurwitsch, Aron. *Field of Consciousness.* Pittsburgh: Duquesne University Press, 1964.

Gusdorf, E. G. *Speaking.* Chicago: Northwestern University Press, 1965.

Hall, Calvin S. and Gardner Lindzey. *Theories of Personality.* New York; John Wiley & Sons, Inc., 1957.

Harlow, Harry F. "The Nature of Love," *The American Psychologist,* XIII (Dec., 1958), 673-685.

Hebb, Donald O. *The Organization Of Behavior.* New York: John Wiley & Sons, Inc., 1949.

Hebb, Donald O. and Thompson, W.R. "The Social Significance of Animal Studies," *Handbook of Social Psychology.* Vol. I. Gardner Linzey, ed. Cambridge, Mass.: Addison-Wesley Publishing Co., Inc., 1954.

Hebb, Donald O. *A Textbook of Psychology.* Philadelphia: W.B. Saunders Co., 1958.

Heidegger, Martin. *Essays in Metaphysics,* trans. Kurt F. Leidecker. New York: Wisdom Library, a Division of Philosophical Library, Inc., 1960.

Existence and Being. Introduction by Werner Brock. Chicago: Henry Regnery Company, 1949.

An Introduction to Metaphysics, trans. Ralph Manheim. New Haven: Yale University Press, 1959.

The Question of Being, trans. William Kluback and Jean Wilde. New York: Twayne Publishers, Inc., 1958.

Being and Time. New York: Harper Bros., 1962.

Hengstenberg, Hans-Eduard, *Philosophische Anthropologie.* W. Kohl-Hammer Verlag (Stuttgart, 1957.).

Hilgard, Ernest P. *Theories of Learning.* New York: Appleton-Century-Crofts, Inc., 1956.

Holland, James G. and B.F. Skinner, *The Analysis of Behavior.* New York: McGraw-Hill Book Company, Inc., 1961.

Halton, Gerald and Roller, Duane. *Foundations of Modern Physical Science.* Reading, Mass.: Addison-Wesley Publishing Co., Inc., 1958.

Husserl, Edmund. *Cartesian Meditations,* trans. Dorion Cairns. The Hague. Netherlands: Martinus Nijhof, 1960.

Logische Untersuchungen: Zur Phänomenologie und Theorie der Erkenntniss. Halle: Niemeyer, 1901.

James, William. *The Principles of Psychology.* New York: Holt, 1890.

Jaspers, Karl. *Existenzerhellung.* Berlin: J. Springer, 1932.

Man in the Modern Age, trans. by Eden and Cedar Paul. New York: Doubleday Anchor Books, Doubleday & Company, Inc., 1957.

Jessor, Richard. "Phenomenological Personality Theories and the Data Language of Psychology," *Psychological Review,* 63 (1956), 173-180.

"The Problem of Reductionism in Psychology," *Psychological Review,* LXV (June, 1958), 170-178.

Kaplan, Bernard "Radical Metaphor, Aesthetic and the Origin of Language," *Review of Existential Psychology and Psychiatry,* II, No. 1.

Bibliography

Kelly, George A. *The Psychology of Personal Constructs*. New York: W.W. Norton & Co., 1955.

Kemeny, John G. *A Philosopher Looks at Science*. Princeton: Van Nostrand, 1959.

Kimble, Gregory A. "Psychology as a Science," *The Scientific Monthly*, LXXVII (September, 1953), 156-160.

Principles of General Psychology. New York: The Ronald Press Co., 1956.

Koch, Sigmund. "Clark L. Hull," *Modern Learning Theory*. William K. Estes and others, eds. New York: Appleton-Century-Crofts, Inc., 1954.

Psychology :A Study of a Science. 3 vols. New York: McGraw-Hill Book Co., Inc., 1959.

Kockelmans J. *Phenomenology and Physical Science*. Pittsburgh: Duquesne University Press, 1966.

Köhler, Wolfgang. *Gestalt Psychology*. New York: Liveright, 1929.

Gestalt Psychology. New York: The New American Library (Mentor Books), 1959.

Kuenzli, Alfred E. (ed.). *The Phenomenological Problem*. New York: Harper & Bros., 1959.

Kwant, Remy C. "De ambiguïteit van het feit," *Gawein* Nijmegen (Holland), III, 1, 1954, 9 - 23.

Encounter, trans. Robert C. Adolfs. Pittsburgh: Duquesne University Press, 1960.

The Phenomenological Philosophy of Merleau-Ponty. Pittsburgh: Duquesne University Press, 1964.

Phenomenology of Language. Pittsburgh: Duquesne University Press, 1965.

Phenomenology of Social Existence. Pittsburgh: Duquesne University Press, 1965.

Laing, R. D. *The Divided Self*. Chicago: Quadrangle Books, Inc., 1960.

Landsman, T. "Four Phenomenologies," *Journal of Individual Psychology*, 14 (No. 1, 1958), 29-37.

Lanteri-Laura, Georges. *La Psychiatrie Phénoménologique.* Paris: Presses Universitaires de France, 1963.

Lauer, Quentin J. *The Triumph of Subjectivity.* New York: Fordham University Press, 1958.

Luijpen, William A. *De psychologie van de verveling.* Amsterdam: H.J. Paris, 1951.

Existential Phenomenology, trans. Henry J. Koren. Pittsburgh: Duquesne University Press, 1960.

Phenomenology and Metaphysics. Pittsburgh: Duquesne University Press, 1965.

MacDougall, William and John B. Watson. *The Battle of Behaviorism - An Exposition and an Exposure.* New York: W.W. Norton & Company, Inc., 1929.

MacLeod, R. B. "The Place of Phenomenological Analysis in Social Psychological Theory." In J. H. Rohre and Sherif (eds.), *Social Psychology at the Crossroads.* New York: Harper, 1951, 215-241.

"The Phenomenological Approach to Social Psychology," *Psychological Review,* 54 (1947), 193-210.

Mahony, M. J. *Cartesianism.* New York: Fordham University Press, 1925.

Mandler, George and William Kessen. *The Language of Psychology.* New York: John Wiley & Sons, Inc., 1959.

Marcel, Gabriel. *Being and Having.* London: Dacre Press, 1949.

The Mystery of Being. 2 vols. Trans. René Hague. Chicago: Henry Regnery Company, 1950.

Man Against Mass Society, trans. G. S. Fraser. Chicago: Henry Regnery Company, 1950.

The Philosophy of Existence. London: Harvill Press, 1954.

Marx, M. H. (ed.). *Psychology Theory.* New York: The MacMillan Company, 1951.

Maslow, A. H. "A Theory of Motivation," *Psychological Review,* 50, (1943), 370-396.

Motivation and Personality. New York: Harper & Brothers, 1954.

May, Rollo and others (eds.). *Existence: A New Dimension In Psychiatry and Psychology.* New York: Basic Books Inc., 1958.

May, Rollo. *Existential Psychology.* New York: Random House, 1961.

"Toward the Ontological Basis of Psychotherapy," *Existential Inquiries,* I (September, 1959), 5-7.

Mendel, W. M. "Expansion of a Shrunken World," *Review of Existential Psychology and Psychiatry,* I (Winter, 1961), 27-32.

Merleau-Ponty, M. *Phenomenology of Perception.* New York: Humanities Press, 1962. Gallimard, 1945.

The Structure of Behavior. Boston: Beacon Press, 1963.

"What is Phenomenology," *Cross Currents,* 6 (Winter, 1955), 59-70.

Milner, Ester. "Differing Observational Perspectives as a Barrier to Communications Among Behavioral Scientists," *Review of Existential Psychology and Psychiatry,* II (Fall, 1962), 249-258.

Morgan, Clifford L. *Introduction to Psychology.* New York: Mc-Graw-Hill Book Company, Inc., 1961.

Mounier, Emmanuel. *Traité du Caractère.* Paris: Éditions du Seuil, 1947.

Moustakas, Clark E. (ed.) *The Self. Explorations in Personal Growth.* New York: Harper and Brothers, 1956.

Murphy, Gardner. *Historical Introduction to Modern Psychology.* New York: Harcourt, Brace & Company, 1949.

Nédoncelle, Maurice. *La réciprocité des consciences. Essai sur la nature de la personne.* Aubiers: Éditions Montaigne, 1942.

Nuttin, J. *Psychoanalysis and Personality.* New York: Sheed and Ward, 1953.

Osgood, Charles E. *Method and Theory in Experimental Psychology.* New York: Oxford University Press, 1956.

Perls, Frederick, Ralph Hefferline and Paul Goodman. *Gestalt Therapy.* New York: Julian Press, 1958.

Pieper, Josef. *Leisure, The Basis of Culture,* trans. Alexander Dru. New York: Pantheon Books, Inc., 1952.

Postman, Leo and Edward C. Tolman. "Brunswik's Probabilistic Functionalism," *Psychology: A Study of Science.* Vol. I, Sigmund Koch, ed. New York: McGraw-Hill Book Company, Inc., 1959.

Pratt, Carroll C. *The Meaning of Music.* New York: McGraw-Hill, 1931.

Rather, L. J. "Existential Experience in Whitehead and Heidegger," *Review of Existential Psychology and Psychiatry,* I (Spring, 1961).

Reymert, Martin L., (ed.) *Feeling and Emotions.* The Mooseheart Symposium in cooperation with the University of Chicago. New York, Toronto, London: McGraw-Hill Book Company, Inc., 1950.

Rogers, Carl. *Counseling and Psychotherapy.* New York: Houghton-Mifflin Co., 1942.

Psychotherapy and Personality Change. Chicago: University of Chicago Press, 1954.

"Some Observations on the Organization of Personality," *American Psychologist,* 2 (1947), 358-368.

"The Loneliness of Contemporary Man," *Review of Existential Psychology and Psychiatry.* I (Spring, 1961), 94-101.

Rogers, Carl R. and B. F. Skinner. "Some Issues Concerning the Control of Human Behavior," *Science,* 124 (1956), 1057-1066.

Sartre, Jean P. *The Emotions: Outline of a Theory,* trans. by Bernard Frechtman. New York: Philosophical Library, 1948.

Schachtel, Ernest. *Metamorphosis.* New York: Basic Books, Inc., 1959.

Scheler, M. *Man's Place in Nature.* Boston: Beacon Press, 1961. *Wesen und Formen der Sympathie Phänomenologie und Theorie der Sympathiegefühle.* Frankfurt-Main: G. Schulte-Bulmke, 1948.

Bibliography

Severin, Frank T. *Humanistic Viewpoints in Psychology*. Mc-Graw-Hill Book Co., (New York, 1965).

Skinner, Burrkus F. "Are Theories of Learning Necessary," *Psychological Review*, LVII (March, 1950), 193-216.

Science and Human Behavior. New York: The Macmillan Co., 1953.

Smith, Brewster. "The Phenomenological Approach in Personality: Some Critical Remarks," *The Journal of Abnormal and Social Psychology*, 45 (1950), 516-522.

Snygg, D. and A. W. Combs. *Individual Behavior*. New York: Harper, 1949.

"The Need for a Phenomenological System of Psychology," *Psychological Review*, 48 (1941), 404-424.

"The Phenomenological Approach in the Problem of 'Unconscious' Behavior: A Reply to Doctor Smith," *The Journal of Abnormal and Social Psychology*, 45 (1950), 523-528.

Sonneman, Ulrich. *Existence and Therapy*. New York: Grune & Straton, 1954.

Spranger, E. *Lebensformen Geisteswissenschaftliche Psychologie und Ethik der Persönlichkeit*. Halle, (Saale): Max Niemeyer Verlag, 1930.

Spiegelberg, H. *The Phenomenological Movement*. 2 vols. The Hague, Netherlands: Martinus Nijhoff, 1960.

Stevens, S. S. "Psychology and the Science of Science," *Psychological Theory*. Melvin H. Marx, ed. New York: The Macmillan Co., 1957.

Strasser, S. *Das Gemüt. Grundgedanken zu einer Phanomenologischen Philosophie und Theorie des Menslichen Gefühlslebens*. Utrecht: Het Spectrum, Freiburg: Verlag Herder, 1956.

The Soul in Metaphysical and Empirical Psychology, trans. Henry J. Koren. Pittsburgh: Duquesne University Press, 1957.

"Phenomenological Trends in European Psychology," *Phil. and Phenom. Research*, XVIII, (September, 1957).

Phenomenology and the Human Sciences, Pittsburgh: Duquesne University Press, 1964.

"Phenomenologies and Psychologies," *Review of Existential Psychology and Psychiatry*, V, No. 1, (Winter, 1965).

Straus, Erwin W., ed. *Phenomenology: Pure and Applied*. Pittsburgh: Duquesne University Press, 1964.

Sullivan, J. W. N. *The Limitations of Science*. New York: The New American Library, (Mentor Books), 1933.

Tolman, Edward C. "Behaviorism and Purpose," *Behavior and Psychological Man*. Los Angeles: University of California Press, 1961.

"Operationalism, Behaviorism and Current Trends in Psychology," *Behavior and Psychological Man*. Los Angeles: University of California Press, 1961.

Tauber, Edward S. and Maurice R. Green. *Prelogical Experience*. New York: Basic Books, Inc., 1959.

van der Berg, J. H. and Linschoten, J. *Persoon en Wereld*. Utrecht: Erven J. Bijleveld, 1953.

The Phenomenological Approach to Psychiatry. An Introduction to Recent Phenomenological Psychopathology. Springfield, Illinois: Charles C. Thomas, 1955.

van der Berg, J. H. and Buytendijk, F. J. J. (ed.) *Scientific Contributions to Phenomenological Psychology and Psychopathology*. Springfield, Illinois: Charles C. Thomas, 1955.

Van Breemen, P. "De mens en de Moderne natuurwetenschap," *Streven* (Brussels) 3, 1956, 212-220.

"De Natuurwetenschap zelfgenoegzaam?", *Streven* (Brussels), 3, 1957, 635-644.

van Croonenburg, E. J. *Gateway to Reality* (An Introduction to Philosophy), Pittsburgh, Duquesne University Press, 1964.

van de Hulst, H. C., and van Peursen, C. A. *Phaenomenologie en natuurwetenschap*. Utrecht: Erven J. Byleveld, 1953.

van Laer, Henry, *Philosophico-Scientific Problems*. Pittsburgh: Duquesne University Press, 1964.

The Philosophy of Science. (Part I, Science in General). Pittsburgh: Duquesne University Press, 1964.

Bibliography

The Philosophy of Science. (Part II, A Study of the Division and Nature of Various Groups of Sciences). Pittsburgh: Duquesne University Press, 1964.

van Kaam, Adrian. "The Addictive Personality," *Humanitas,* Vol. 1, No. 2 (Fall, 1965).

van Kaam, Adrian and L. V. Pacoe. "Anthropological Psychology and Behavioristic Experimentation," in *Festschrift Dr. Straus,* eds. Griffith, R.M., and von Baeyer, W., Berlin, Heidelberg, New York: Springer-Verlag, 1966.

van Kaam, Adrian. "Assumptions in Psychology," *Journal of Individual Psychology,* Vol. 14 (1958), 22-28.

"Clinical Implications of Heidegger's Concepts of Will, Decision, and Responsibility," *Review of Existential Psychology and Psychiatry.*

"Commentary on 'Freedom and Responsibility Examined'," *Behavioral Science and Guidance, Proposals, and Perspectives,* eds. Lloyd-Jones and E. M. Westervelt. New York: Teachers College, Columbia University Press, 1963.

"Counseling and Existential Psychology," *Harvard Educational Review* (Fall, 1962). This article was later published in *Guidance—An Examination,* New York: Harcourt, Brace & World, 1965.

"Differential Psychology," *The New Catholic Encyclopedia,* Washington, D.C.: The Catholic University of America, 1966.

"The Existential Approach to Human Potentialities," *Explorations in Human Potentialities,* ed. Herbert A. Otto. Springfield, Illinois: Charles C. Thomas, 1966.

"Existential Psychology," *The New Catholic Encyclopedia,* Washington, D.C.: The Catholic University of America, 1966.

"Existential and Humanistic Psychology," *Review of Existential Psychology and Psychiatry,* (Fall, 1965).

"Existential Psychology as a Theory of Personality," *Review of Existential Psychology and Psychiatry,* (Winter, 1963).

"Die existentielle Psychologie als eine Theorie der Gesamtpersönlichkeit," *Jahrbuch für Psychologie und medizinische Anthropologie,* 12. Jahrgang Heft 4.

"The Fantasy of Romantic Love," *Modern Myths and Popular Fancies*, Pittsburgh: Duquesne University Press, 1961.

"The Field of Religion and Personality or Theoretical Religious Anthropology," *Insight*, Vol. 4, No. 1. (Summer, 1965).

"Freud and Anthropological Psychology," *The Justice*, (Brandeis University), (May, 1959).

"The Goals of Psychotherapy from the Existential Point of View," *The Goals of Psychotherapy*, ed. Alvin R. Mahrer. New York: Appelton-Century-Crofts, 1966.

"Humanistic Psychology and Culture," *Journal of Humanistic Psychology*, Vol. 1 (Spring, 1961), 94-100.

"The Impact of Existential Phenomenology on the Psychological Literature of Western Europe," *Review of Existential Psychology and Psychiatry*, Vol. I (1961), 63-92.

"Francis Libermann," *The New Catholic Encyclopedia*, Washington, D.C.: The Catholic University of America, 1966.

A Light to the Gentiles. Milwaukee: Bruce Publishing Co., 1962.

"Motivation and Contemporary Anxiety," *Humanitas*, Vol I, No. 1 (Spring, 1965).

"The Nurse in the Patient's World," *The American Journal of Nursing*, Vol. 59, (1959), 1708-1710.

Personality Fulfillment in Spiritual Life. Denville, New Jersey: Dimension Books, Inc., 1966.

"Phenomenal Analysis: Exemplified by a Study of the Experience of 'Really Feeling Understood'," *Journal of Individual Psychology*, Vol. 15 (1959), 66-72.

"A Psychology of the Catholic Intellectual," in *The Christian Intellectual*, (Samuel Hazo, ed.). Pittsburgh, Pennsylvania: Duquesne University Press, 1963.

"A Psychology of Falling-Away-From-The-Faith," *Insight*, Vol. 2, No. 2 (Fall, 1963), 3-17.

"Religion and Existential Will," *Insight*, Vol. 1, No. 1 (Summer, 1962).

"Religious Counseling of Seminarians," *Seminary Education in a Time of Change*, eds. James Michael Lee and Louis J. Putz. Notre Dame, Indiana: Fides Publishers, Inc., 1965.

"Review of *The Divided Self* by R. D. Laing." *Review of Existential Psychology and Psychiatry* (Winter, 1962), 85-88.

Religion and Personality. New Jersey: Prentice-Hall, Inc., 1965.

"Sex and Existence," *Review of Existential Psychology and Psychiatry*, (Spring, 1963.)

"Sex and Personality," *The Lamp*, Vol. 63, No. 7 (July, 1965.)

"Structures and Systems of Personality," *The New Catholic Encyclopedia*, Washington, D.C.: The Catholic University of America, 1966.

The Third Force in European Psychology. Greenville, Delaware: Psychosynthesis Research Foundation, 1960. (Greek translation, Athens, Greece, 1962.)

The Vocational Director and Counseling. Derby, New York: St. Paul Publications, 1962.

van Melsen, A. G. *The Philosophy of Nature*. Pittsburgh: Duquesne University Press, 1952.

Science and Technology. Pittsburgh: Duquesne University Press, 1961.

From Atomos to Atom (The History of the Concept "Atom.") Pittsburgh: Duquesne University Press, 1952.

Verplanck, William S. "Burrhus F. Skinner," *Modern Learning Theory*. William K. Estes and others, eds. New York: Appleton-Century-Crofts, Inc., 1954.

Waelhens, Alphonse de. *Existence et Signification*. Paris: Beatrice-Nauwelaerts, 1958.

Watson, John B. *Behaviorism*. New York: W. W. Norton & Company, Inc., 1924.

Wertheimer, Max. *Productive Thinking*. Enlarged edition. New York: Harper & Bros., 1959.

Wolman, Benjamin. *Contemporary Theories and Systems in Psychology*. New York: Harper & Bros., 1960.

Woodworth, Robert S. *Contemporary Schools of Psychology.* Revised edition. New York: The Ronald Press Company, 1948.

Woodworth, Robert and Harold Schlosberg. *Experimental Psychology.* Revised edition. New York: Henry Holt and Company, 1954.

Wright, William Kelley. *A History of Modern Philosophy.* New York: The Macmillan Company, 1941.

UNPUBLISHED MATERIALS

Barton, Anthony. "The Experience of Estrangement." Unpublished Master's Thesis. University of Chicago, 1960.

Greiner, Dorothy. "Anthropological Psychology and Physics." Unpublished Master's Thesis. Duquesne University. Pittsburgh, Pennsylvania, 1962.

"A Foundational-Theoretical Approach Toward a Comprehensive Psychology of Human Emotion." Unpublished Doctoral Dissertation. Duquesne University. Pittsburgh, Pennsylvania, 1964.

Kraft, W.F. "Anthropological Psychology and Phenomenology." Unpublished Master's Thesis. Duquesne University. Pittsburgh, Pennsylvania, 1962.

"An Existential Anthropological Psychology of the Self." Unpublished Doctoral Dissertation. Duquesne University. Pittsburgh, Pennsylvania, 1965.

Linschoten, J. "Das Experiment in der phaenomenologischen Psychologie." (Paper read in Bonn, Germany, 1955.)

Pacoe, Larry V. "Anthropological Psychology and Behavioristic Animal Experimentation." Unpublished Master's Thesis. Duquesne University. Pittsburgh, Pennsylvania, 1963.

Reeves, Jeanne C. "An Introduction to the Methodology of Anthropological Psychology." Unpublished Master's Thesis. Duquesne University. Pittsburgh, Pennsylvania, 1962.

Bibliography

Rogers, Carl. "A Theory of Therapy, Personality and Interpersonal Relationships, as Developed in the Client-Centered Framework." Unpublished Paper. Chicago: University of Chicago, 1956.

Smith, David. "Anthropological Psychology and Ontology." Unpublished Master's Thesis. Duquesne University. Pittsburgh, Pennsylvania, 1960.

van Kaam, Adrian, "The Experience of Really Feeling Understood by a Person." Unpublished Doctoral Dissertation. Western Reserve University. Cleveland, Ohio, 1958.

van Kaam, Adrian. "Counseling and Psychotherapy from the Existential Viewpoint." (To be published in 1967).

van Kaam, Adrian and Healy, Kathleen. *The Demon and the Dove: Personality Development Through Literature* (To be published in 1967).

van Kaam, Adrian. *Personality Fulfillment in Religious Life.* (To be published in 1967 by Dimension Books, Denville, New Jersey).

INDEX

Index

Index